# Early Reviews of Angel's Truck Stop

*Angel's Truck Stop, A Woman's Love, Laughter and Loss during the Vietnam War* is an eye-opening account of an era many Americans did not/do not understand and that many choose to forget. Angelica Pilato pulls no punches - the stories make you laugh and cry - and you are left with a somber appreciation of what is asked of our servicemen and women. You'll be compelled to read it in one sitting, but take your time - absorb what she shares.
—Barb Randall, *Lake Oswego Review, West Linn Tidings*

Wonderfully written, very conversational. Angel courageously reveals her innermost thoughts about her hard times as well as her joys and triumphs.
—Mary Freider, Willamette View

A fantastic read. I didn't want it to end.
—Anne Marie Flora Lowe

Angel has done all the pilots of the 432nd Tactical Reconnaissance Wing proud with her telling of the Wing's fighting spirit and zeal to "Kill MiGs."
—Fred Olmsted

An honest and courageous portrayal of a woman's life in the military during the turbulent 1960's.
—Sarah Stephens, Ph.D.

The author deals with high-echelon egos and gung-ho fighter pilots and has readers feeling empathy with the men and women she introduces in her wartime memoir.
—Janet Goetze, writing in *The Oregonian*

Angel is a very talented storyteller. Those of us at Udorn spent 90% of our time on the flight line, flying, or at "Angel's Truck Stop." It was a great "Stop" because Angel had a Fighter Pilot's attitude and knew what made us tick. Thanks again from all of us for the memories.
—Joe Kittinger, Colonel, USAF, (ret)

In spite of her youth, idealism, relative inexperience and gender, Angel figured out how to get things accomplished in a man's military world.
—Robin Guariglia, Portland, Oregon

# Angel's Truck Stop

Rocky
to a woman trail
blazer in her own right.
Enjoy the read.

Angel

# Angel's Truck Stop

*A Woman's Love, Laughter, and Loss*
*during the Vietnam War*

Lieutenant Colonel Angel Pilato, USAF (Ret)

Cover and photo section design: AH HA Creative
Interior design and production: Another Jones Graphics

For information about permission to
reproduce selections for this book, or contact the author, e-mail:
angelpilato@gmail.com
www.angels-truckstop.com

Library of Congress Catalog Card Number: 2011910100
Publication date 2011

Pilato, Angelica
Angel's Truck Stop:
A Woman's Love, Laughter, and Loss during the Vietnam War

Angel Pilato – 2nd ed

ISBN: 978-0-9832108-1-8

Printed CreateSpace in the USA

Cover photo: Taken on Feb. 22, 1972. Captain Angel Pilato perched
on the Triple Nickel Squadron's Jeep. Fighter pilots parked it in the
o-club lobby to celebrate shooting down a MiG-21.

*To all the Airmen (Men and Women)*
*who served and to those who never made it home.*

# Contents

# Author's Note

THIS BOOK IS A personal and intimate narrative of how I, as an Air Force woman officer, experienced the Vietnam conflict during my five and a half years on active duty. The majority of the book focuses on my last year, 1971 to 1972, while I was at Udorn Air Base in Thailand. That year in Southeast Asia (SEA) became a life-changing event that would be forever etched in my brain. I have attempted to convey my experience and emotions as they were then, but I'm sure the passing of time has skewed my perspective.

For many years after I left the Air Force, I amused my friends with after-dinner war stories. Often they would tell me, "Angel, you should write a book. You're so funny." I flirted with the idea, but writing a book is totally different. It requires time, commitment, and confidence, and I was short on all three. However, in 1989, I decided to lay my fears aside and start the book. I began writing in notebooks, on legal pads, at night, and on the weekends. I wrote every spare minute I had. To my surprise, the stories that consumed me were not the funny ones, but those that brought me to tears. What surfaced were all the feelings of sadness and loss that I had convincingly sugarcoated with humor.

Then reality set in, along with many concerns. *Why did I think I could write a book? Did I really want anyone to know who I was back then? Besides, who'd want to read it?* Those haunting questions made me put the book away until 2006 when, out of the blue, a friend said, "Angelica, I think you ought to finish your book." I had recently read about a Native American tradition that a woman must not begin to weave a blanket unless she knows she is going to live long enough to finish it. She believes that if she dies without finishing her work, she will leave part of her spirit behind. These prompts stimulated me to complete what I had started.

I got up early every morning to write before I went to work and kept a log of my progress in a spiral notebook. By late 2009, I had something that began to resemble a book. Then finally, after thousands of hours and many rewrites and edits, in 2011, it was ready.

Many of the names in the book are real. I wanted to acknowledge some of the brave and heroic men who put their lives on the line and were never recognized for their efforts. Some names have been changed to protect the innocent as well as the guilty. Some of the language is crude, and not politically correct, but it represents the emotions of the era and the environment as it was. Many people advised me to omit accounts they thought were "too intimate." They were worried about what people would think of me. I contemplated the implications at great length. In the end, after much angst and soul-searching, I chose to be authentic. I am not the same person I was 40 years ago, but like any life-changing event, it shaped who I am today.

Many humorous incidents are included, because amidst all the mayhem it was my sense of humor that helped me keep my sanity. In completing this book, I feel my spirit has been set free so I can live again, feel again, and love again. Thank you for letting me share my story with you.

Footnotes:

Every effort has been made to verify that the web links cited in the footnotes at the end of the chapters are still valid. If the reader would like to view all the links mentioned in the footnotes go to www.angels-truckstop.com, click on the Resource Tab, find the chapter, and click on the desired link.

Appendices, Epilogue, and In Their Own Words:

In the second edition two appendices were added, one for the MiG killers and one for the POWs, MIAs, and KIAs that occurred during the time I was there—September 1, 1971 to September 1, 1972. Unfortunately, every KIA/MIA during this 10-year war could not be included. For that, one must go to the Vietnam Wall for a list of the 58,267 names etched in Black Granite. The wall includes names from 1957, the start of our involvement in Vietnam, to 1975, the official end of the war. http://www.virtualwall.org/aboutWal.htm

Epilogue and In Their Own Words sections at the end of the book contain updates and information that I think you will find interesting.

# Acknowledgments

THERE ARE MANY PEOPLE responsible for helping me successfully complete this book. I am deeply grateful to each and every person mentioned here, and to all those who offered kind and encouraging words along the way.

**Typists: Judy Flora** was the first person to transcribe some of my memories from cassette tapes when I started this book in the early eighties. In 1989, **Susan Dixon** typed several documents from my handwritten notes and printed them on a dot matrix printer. In 1993, **Ceil Tilney** helped some more, and in 2006, **Julie Piper Finley** retyped many documents that had not been saved on the computer. Thankfully, I still had the hard copies.

**Editors and Proof Readers:** The first individuals to read the initial draft of book were friends, all English majors: **Julie Piper Finley, Ellen Nichols,** and **Jane Stayer.** They gave suggestions for organizing the chapters and were horrified over my use, or rather misuse, of the semicolon and the word "however." The major editor for the manuscript, **Erin Barone,** helped bring my "C" writing up to an "A," suggested the title, and along with **Gail Anderson,** nailed down the subtitle. **Bennett Johnson** and **Jane Stayer** edited for continuity. **Linda Richey, Linda Holliman,** and **Julie Piper Finley** proofread and found still more opportunities for corrections. **Jody Grant** utilized her excellent editing skills and eagle eye to put the finishing touches on the final manuscript.

**Graphics and Website: Aubree Holliman,** principal of AH HA Creative, designed the awesome book cover, bookmark, and Facebook page. **Mark Kretschmer** designed the website and worked on the photos. **Anita Jones,** of Another Jones Graphics, formatted the manuscript. **CreateSpace** printed the book, and **Stevens Printing** printed the bookmarks and postcards.

**Reference and Technical Support: Archie DiFante,** Archivist at the Air Force History Center at Maxwell Air Force Base in Alabama provided countless documents, books, and historical information. The **Multnomah County Library's** reference line is on my speed dial and provided accurate fact checks that were invaluable. **Carter Boggs** and **Chuck McGregor** helped with aviation accuracies. **General McPeak** corrected the chain of command graphic.

**Moral Support:** In addition to those mentioned, I also want to acknowledge my many friends and family who have cheered me on to completion. **Ellen Nichols** spent hours brainstorming topics I wanted included in the book and continued to nudge me to finish. **Lorelei Stevens** questioned the compatibility of the first subtitle, which led to a subtitle that said it all. **Gail Anderson, Jolene Anderson, Katherine Carella, Diane Conner, Sharon Dougherty, Paula Krawczak, Judy Rossner, Helene Tallman, Agnes Tubbs, Helen Tuggy,** and **Sarah Stephens** kept telling me "you can do it." A special thanks goes to **Carter Boggs,** whose continual encouragement and patience sustained me when I felt I'd never finish.

A big thanks goes to all the men and the few women of the **432nd Tactical Fighter Reconnaissance Wing** from Udorn Air Base, Thailand, because without them there wouldn't have been a story to tell.

For the Second Edition:

I want to thank all of you who read the first book and contributed facts, corrections, and insights that have enriched the book. Special thanks goes to Colonel Roger Locher, Lieutenant Colonel Patty Locher, Captain Marty Cavato, and Lieutenant Colonel Sherwood "Woody" Cox who responded to numerous e-mails with valuable updates.

Also, there was one photo that misidentified three aviators. Thanks to the above who circulated the photo to dozens of their squadron buddies, we were able to identify two out of the three. Thanks to all who responded: Major John Mesenbourg, General Dan Cherry, Captain Fred "Broadway" Olmsted, Colonel Greg "Baby Beef" Crane, Colonel Joe Kittinger, and Colonel Marie Gutierrez.

Thanks to Aubree Holliman for her patience and the many hours she spent in revising the formatting. Thanks to Laramie Holliman for reedits and to others who noted corrections, Leslie Brunker, Katherine and Angelo Carella, Joe Holliman, and Ellen Nichols.

# Introduction

FROM 1964 TO 1975 the United States was involved in a war against communism in Vietnam. The U.S. feared that if Vietnam fell to the communists, it would lead to "falling dominos" in Indochina. I joined the Air Force in 1967 and became part of this war until 1972. I spent the last year in the war zone at Udorn Air Base in Thailand with the 432<sup>nd</sup> Tactical Reconnaissance Wing. I didn't carry a gun, fly a fighter jet, commandeer a tank, or serve in a MASH unit. I was what the fighter jocks called a "support puke," which put me at the bottom of the military food chain. My job was to run the officers' club, which provided for the morale and recreation of the officers.

I didn't know anything about Vietnam, where it was, its people, or its history. If I had, I might have known that the French colonized Vietnam, fought to control it, and occupied it for almost a century. Ho Chi Minh, which means "one who enlightens" (a name he chose for himself) intensely wanted Vietnam to be free of the French. In 1919, after World War I, while Ho Chi Minh was living in Paris, he tried to petition President Woodrow Wilson at the Versailles Peace conference for the self-determination in Vietnam. Ho Chi Minh saw the struggle to free Vietnam from the French as similar to America's fight for their independence. The United States continually ignored requests to support the nationalization of Vietnam. Ho Chi Minh went to Moscow, became a communist, returned covertly to Vietnam, and formed the Vietminh (League for the Independence of Vietnam).

In 1941, during World War II, the OSS (later the CIA) helped train the Vietminh in their effort to successfully oust the Japanese and the French. However, in 1945 the allied forces split Vietnam into the North and South. The British were tasked with disarming the Japanese in the South, and the Chinese were to do the same in the North. Ho Chi Minh declared Vietnam's independence to a cheering crowd and started his speech with, "We hold the truth that all men are created equal, that they are endowed by their Creator with certain unalienable rights, among them life, liberty, and the pursuit of happiness."

The Chinese returned the North to the Vietminh. However, the British soon returned authority of the South to the French, which the U.S. backed in exchange for France's commitment of troops and funds to the newly formed NATO. Betrayed by the Americans, Ho Chi Minh sought Soviet assistance to help free Vietnam from French exploitation. In 1954, after seven years, the Vietnamese defeated the French, who lost 50,000 troops and had 100,000 injured. Meanwhile, Ho Chi Minh's nationalist rebels were infiltrating the South and gaining support from the peasants. Finally, an accord was reached. Vietnam was separated at the 17th parallel pending a nationwide election to determine who would lead the Vietnamese people.

Backed by the U.S., Ngo Dinh Diem ascended to power in the South. Diem, a Catholic in a Buddhist county, was an anti-Communist and rejected the nationwide election because it was known that Ho Chi Minh would win. Eisenhower reaffirmed support of Diem's oppressive regime and began to send aid and military "advisors" to train the South Vietnam military against the infiltration of the Vietminh, elements of which joined the Viet Cong.[1]

Kennedy continued to support Diem with aid and increased the number of military advisors from 700 to 12,000. When Kennedy was asked if he thought getting involved with the Vietnamese struggle would end in a quagmire like the French, his response was, "But we're not the French." This was the first denial of the resolve of the Vietnamese to eliminate outside interference. In 1963, Diem's generals and the people turned against him. In protest, a Buddhist monk set himself on fire. The generals devised a plot against Diem, and the U.S. turned a blind eye. A coup ensued; Diem surrendered, and was murdered the next day.

President Johnson took office after Kennedy's assassination and continued to escalate his fight against communism. He, along with other policymakers, assumed that the Vietnamese shared the same idea of Western democratic freedom. The U.S. tried to impose that philosophy on the Vietnamese rather than support their idea of nationalism. With this concept in mind and a fervor to defeat communism, Johnson deployed the Navy destroyer USS *Maddox* to the Gulf of Tonkin. The North saw the U.S. as another "white" oppressive force and stepped up its attacks in the South. On August 2, 1964, patrol boats attacked the *Maddox* and an air strike systematically destroyed the patrol boats. Shortly afterwards, intelligence reports stated that the North was going to torpedo the *Maddox*.

In response to the attack of August 2$^{nd}$ and the suspected torpedo attack of August 4$^{th}$, the President ordered the Seventh Fleet carrier forces to launch retaliatory strikes against North Vietnam. On August 5$^{th}$, aircraft from carriers USS *Ticonderoga* and USS *Constellation* destroyed an oil storage facility at Vinh and damaged or sank about 30 enemy vessels. Of greater significance, on August 7$^{th}$ the U.S. Congress overwhelmingly passed the so-called "Tonkin Gulf Resolution," which enabled Johnson to employ military force as he saw fit against the Vietnamese communists. In the first months of 1965, the President ordered major U.S. ground, air, and naval forces deployed to South Vietnam. Thus began a new phase in America's long, costly Vietnam War. Much later, an investigation determined that torpedoes were never launched towards the *Maddox*. The bombing of North Vietnam continued with the hopes that it would bring the North Vietnamese to their knees.

In 1966, France called for America to withdraw from Vietnam and pushed for a settlement. Ho Chi Minh said there could be no talks unless the bombing in North Vietnam stopped. It didn't stop, and it didn't bring them to their knees. It just furthered their resolve to expel the American foreigners whom they saw as replacing the French as occupiers.

Oblivious to most of these events, I volunteered for the Air Force. By 1967, U.S. troop strength in Vietnam had reached well over 500,000. All I knew was I wanted to travel, do something patriotic, and help defeat the "commies." I was going to be part of the United States military, and after all, we were the good guys.

[1] Viet Cong, or the People's Liberation Armed Forces, was formed by the North Vietnamese communists and infiltrated South Vietnam with the main purpose of overthrowing the Diem regime and unifying Vietnam into one independent Communist country. They used guerilla warfare to fight against French and American occupation.

Summary compiled from: *Vietnam: A History*, Stanley Karnow, New York, Viking Press, 1983; *The March of Folly: From Troy to Vietnam*, Barbara W. Tuchman, Ballantine Books, 1985; and the U.S. Navy Historical Center home page at http://www.history.navy.mil/.

# Map of Thailand Air Bases

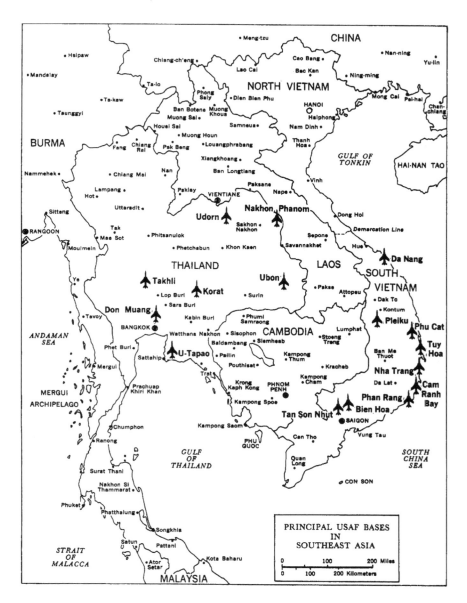

PRINCIPAL USAF BASES
IN
SOUTHEAST ASIA

# Military Chain of Command

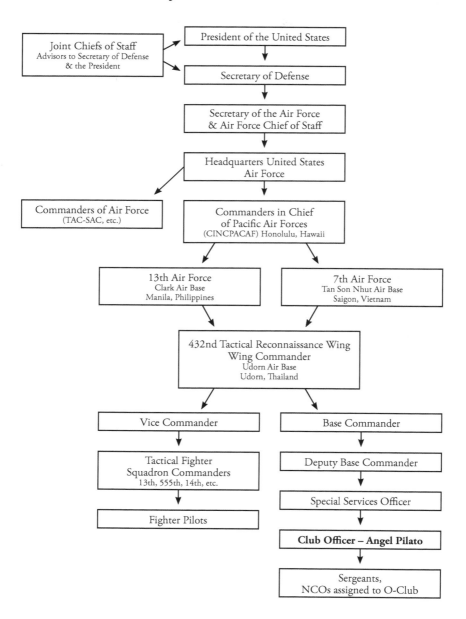

Joint Chiefs of Staff
Advisors to Secretary of Defense
& the President

President of the United States

Secretary of Defense

Secretary of the Air Force
& Air Force Chief of Staff

Headquarters United States
Air Force

Commanders of Air Force
(TAC-SAC, etc.)

Commanders in Chief
of Pacific Air Forces
(CINCPACAF) Honolulu, Hawaii

13th Air Force
Clark Air Base
Manila, Philippines

7th Air Force
Tan Son Nhut Air Base
Saigon, Vietnam

432nd Tactical Reconnaissance Wing
Wing Commander
Udorn Air Base
Udorn, Thailand

Vice Commander

Base Commander

Tactical Fighter
Squadron Commanders
13th, 555th, 14th, etc.

Deputy Base Commander

Special Services Officer

Fighter Pilots

**Club Officer – Angel Pilato**

Sergeants,
NCOs assigned to O-Club

*"History is indeed little more than the register of the crimes, follies and misfortunes of mankind."*

—Edward Gibbson, British historian (1737 – 1794)
From *The History of the Decline and Fall of the Roman Empire*

SECTION ONE

# I Do So Solemly Swear

*Ask not what your country can do for you—*
*ask what you can do for your country.*

—John F. Kennedy, 35th President of the United States, (1917 - 1963)

# The New Recruit

*"I, ANGELICA PILATO, DO solemnly swear that I will support and defend the Constitution of the United States…"*

It was March 17, 1967 in Detroit, Michigan. There I stood, right hand raised, surrounded by the American flag, the Air Force insignia, and photos of President Johnson and Secretary of Defense McNamara, repeating the oath of induction into the United States Air Force. My recruiter, Sergeant Keith Gaston, looked on while my mother, her huge grin illuminating the recruiting office, fought to hold back tears.

At 25 years old, my decision to join the Air Force was based on core beliefs formed from an accumulation of experiences, stored knowledge, and every action I'd ever taken until then. Besides, it was 20 degrees outside, and my car was buried under eight feet of snow. I'd broken off my wedding engagement, wanted to travel, and do something exciting. The fact that the Air Force recruiter was good looking and Officer Training School (OTS) was at Lackland Air Force Base in San Antonio, Texas, where it was 70 degrees, didn't hurt either. At the time, it all made sense.

When I was growing up, Mom emphasized patriotism. She told me about the sacrifices people made during WWII and how the entire country pulled together to win the war. They saved their tin cans and had to ration sugar, gas, and nylon stockings. They bought war bonds and prayed that everyone would come home safely. Mom saved the hundreds of letters that she'd written to my uncles during their stints in the military. All the envelopes were posted with those purple "Win the War" stamps, which quickly found their way into my childhood stamp collection.

I was raised a strict Catholic, afraid that anything I might think, say, or do would send me straight to hell. I feared God, the priests, and the nuns with their scary black habits and their dangling rosary beads. I was convinced that they and my parents knew every move I made and were determined to keep me from sin.

It was hard trying to figure out how to be good enough to stay in a state of grace. Nevertheless, I tried. I said my rosary, did my Friday Stations of the Cross, gave up candy during Lent, gave all my pennies to build the Immaculate Conception Basilica in Washington, D.C., and tried my best to keep from having impure thoughts.

Sister Denise, my dogmatic, eighth grade teacher, frequently used our classroom to expound on her viewpoints about democracy and communism. I think she was president of Senator Joe McCarthy's fan club and praised him for standing up to communism and all the foes of American idealism. "God bless Joe McCarthy," she would say. "His courage saved this country from a fate worse than Satan himself." So, I blessed Joe McCarthy, too. The nuns couldn't be wrong. After priests, nuns were the second closest thing to God. I knew I didn't have a shot at ever being a priest.

We began each school day with the Sign of the Cross, morning prayers, and the Pledge of Allegiance to the Flag. Sister Denise reminded us that Congress added the "under God" part through the concerted efforts of the Knights of Columbus. So, we blessed the Knights of Columbus, who sounded very impressive, but I couldn't be one of them either. Everything appeared to be so black or white, right or wrong. I knew what I was supposed to do, but mostly I knew what not to do. As a Catholic, I accepted most teachings on pure faith, especially those things that couldn't be explained, like turning water into wine, multiplying the loaves and fishes, and the concept of Mary as a virgin. The good priests said, "You must have faith, Angelica. It's important to guard your faith at all times my child, because if you don't, God could take your faith away in the blink of an eye."

The 1950s was an era of idealism and wide-eyed optimism. As a teenager, I was immersed in those wonderfully pure, cosmetically clean Mouseketeer years. Everything was good. God, country, motherhood, and apple pie were the ideals preached and praised. America could do no wrong and we all liked Ike. Everyone trusted that the government would always act in our best interest, just like the Catholic Church. My faith in God and country was unparalleled.

I was in college in 1960 when John Kennedy was elected as our first Catholic president. Even my mom and dad, who were Republicans, voted for Kennedy. Their rationale was, if an Irish Catholic can become president then someday one of our Italian-American boys could, too.

Kennedy mesmerized us with his charismatic smile and his patriotic speeches. We fell in love with him and had high hopes. Then he was assassinated. We were all in shock and it left me in a quandary. I tried to figure out what I could do to make it right, to bring things back to normal again, and to stop hurting. I wanted to believe in something. I wanted to believe that I could make a difference.

*"...against all enemies, foreign and domestic; that I will bear true faith and allegiance to the same..."*

While studying at Rochester Institute of Technology (RIT), I took a class in American foreign policy taught by a retired Army colonel. I decided to do my term paper on the U.S. policy toward Cuba. It was after the Cuban Missile Crisis and Cuba was in the forefront of the news.

I decided to attend a meeting some peace activists were having at a local church because I thought they might give me some information I could use in my paper. I was shocked to hear the speaker advocating nonviolence and ways to defy the government by refusing to support defense efforts, not paying taxes, or by not serving in the military. I wasn't going to sit there and listen to that. I stood up and said something that sounded like I was channeling Sister Denise, "I don't want violence any more than you do, but we must protect ourselves against the evils of communism. If we lay down our arms there's no guarantee that the Russians will do the same. Our country is a democracy," I continued, "and it deserves the support of its people. It's because we are a democracy that you have the right to speak at this meeting tonight."

Unbeknownst to me, a news reporter was in the audience. He came over and asked my name and the whole encounter ended up in the Rochester *Democrat and Chronicle.* He characterized me as a local hero who had stood up to those misguided peace marchers.

My mother was absolutely frantic. "Angelica, I want to know why you can't keep your big mouth shut!" she scolded. "Those people are gonna find out where we live and come over and retaliate against you for speaking out against them!"

"Mother, they aren't gonna do that," I countered. "They're peace marchers. They're nonviolent. Besides, what did you want me to do? Just sit there and not say anything when they were speaking out against the country?"

"Well, did you have to be the one to put in your two cents?" she retorted. "Wasn't there anyone else there that could've spoken up? Your friend Diane was there. Why did it have to be you?"

The next day my mother got a call from Mr. Al Davis, Vice President of Public Affairs at RIT. "Mrs. Pilato," he said, "I called to tell you how pleased and proud RIT is about how Angel presented her views publicly in defense of our great democracy. It certainly put her and RIT in a favorable light in the community. I'm sure you and Mr. Pilato are as delighted as we are with the courageous position she took."

"Well, ah…ah…yes, we are," she said in a sheepish tone. "I must say we were a little surprised to read about it in the paper. Angelica has always liked expressing her opinions."

"It certainly reflects well on her character and upbringing," said Mr. Davis, "you have a fine daughter, Mrs. Pilato. Please pass on my congratulations to Angel."

"Of course…yes…I will," my mother said, stumbling over her words. "Thank you for calling."

I graduated from RIT, got engaged, and my fiancé and I were accepted into the Peace Corps. We decided to delay going on assignment until we both finished our master's degrees. I went to Michigan State University and enrolled in a master's in food management, which I thought would be a good career to combine with having children. Also, I'd have a degree to fall back on in case something happened to my husband. But, things didn't quite work out as planned. Five weeks before the wedding, I broke off the engagement. Marriage scared me and I didn't believe in divorce. If it didn't work out, I might be trapped for life.

In1967, East Lansing, Michigan had one of the worst winter snowstorms ever. I walked three miles to work every day and dealt with unruly college students who couldn't understand why we had to ration food. Then it hit me. What was I doing here? Why finish my master's degree now? If I wasn't getting married, I could do it later. Three things I knew I wanted for sure: to utilize my degree in food management, to travel, and to do something worthwhile. My thoughts turned toward the military. After all, there was a war on, and they might need someone like me.

I narrowed my search down to the Navy and the Air Force. I couldn't see myself in the Army or the Marines. They were too rough and stogy. Besides, I didn't like their uniforms. The Navy's idea of jobs for women was limited to personnel or office administration. Women weren't allowed to serve on ships and were only stationed on the East or West coasts. They also wanted me to be able to swim, which seemed incongruous considering they didn't allow women on ships. My conversations with the Navy recruiter ended when I found out their Officer Training School was in Rhode Island, where it was snowing.

The day I walked into the Air Force recruiting office a man in a tailored blue uniform stood up from behind his desk, put out his cigarette, and greeted me with a warm smile. "Hi!" he said. "Welcome to the Air Force Recruiting Office. My name is Sergeant Keith Gaskin." He shook my hand and offered me a seat next to his desk. "How are you today?"

"Just fine, how are you?" I said and returned his smile. I liked him right away. Gaskin's uniform accentuated his tall, lean physique. His dark hair with its receding hairline put him at about 35 years old and his hazel brown eyes held a gleam of mischief.

"What can I do for you today?" he asked.

"Well, I wanna get out of here and I was thinking that I might join the military," I explained. "I was wondering what the Air Force had for a girl like me. I've already talked with the Navy, and they don't have any jobs I want. They don't even let women on ships!"

"That's the Navy for ya," he affirmed. "Our Air Force has lots of jobs for the ladies. What kind of job are you looking for?"

"I have a B.S. in food management and I want to keep working in that field," I replied. "I spent all that time in school and I don't wanna waste it."

"That's no problem. The Air Force can get you into any career field you're qualified for," he assured me. "We like to match up our recruits with their skills."

"You do?" I said, my interest growing.

"We sure do. Tell me a little bit about yourself," he said, taking a few notes on a pad of paper. Like a skilled fisherman he cast his line into the water as he trolled for a fish. After a few screening questions he asked, "What do you think? Would you like to fill out an application?"

As he pulled out an application, he saw the concerned look on my face and said, "It's only a preliminary questionnaire. There's no obligation. It's just to see if you meet the entrance requirements," as he slowly let out a little more fishing line.

"OK. I guess I can do that," I said. "Is the Air Force gonna make me learn how to swim?" He assured me that wasn't a requirement.

"That's good," I said with a relieved look. "I'm terrified of the water. My mom didn't think us three girls needed to know how to swim—only my brother learned." Then I said, "The reason I asked was because I heard Mickey King, that Olympic swimmer from the University of Michigan, was joining the Air Force. And I was just wondering does the Air Force only want girls like her?" I said, rolling my eyes, half kidding, half not, and looking for a little reassurance.

"We're real proud to have Mickey King," he replied. "But all of our Air Force ladies are outstanding."

When I finished filling out the application, he took time to review it and said, "It looks like you've been involved in lots of extra curricular activities while you were in college. You were president of your sorority, student council representative, chairman of the spring weekend, on the student advisory board to the President, and you kept a 3.0 GPA. Hmmm. That's impressive!"

"I also worked a part time job to help pay for college," I stated proudly.

"Yes, I see that. I don't think we'll have any trouble processing your application."

"This is just a preliminary application, right?"

"Right. If you decide to apply, I think it'd go smoothly. By the way, this weekend I'm driving some new recruits up to Wurtsmith Air Force Base in Oscoda to have them see the real Air Force in action. Would you like to come along?"

"Wow! You mean it?" I said, not realizing that this whole process was going a little too fast.

"Sure. You can see the entire base, the officers' quarters, and those incredible B-52 bombers."

"You mean like the ones in *Strategic Air Command* with Jimmy Stewart and June Allyson?" I asked, wide-eyed.

"That's right. Those are the ones," he said. He'd hooked his fish and was starting to reel it in.

When we got to the base we received the grand tour. A pilot in his flight suit showed us around. I was dwarfed and awed by those humongous B-52s. Everyone welcomed us with warm smiles, hardy handshakes, and glowing reports of their experiences in the Air Force. We went to lunch at the officers' club, and it was there that I made my decision. If I joined the Air Force, I wanted to run an officers' club. It would be the perfect job for me.

"Say, Sergeant Gaskin, do you think the Air Force would let a woman run one of their officers' clubs?" I asked.

"I don't see why not. The Air Force lets its gals do just about everything," he reassured me.

"That's great! OK. I'll sign up under one condition—that you request my career field be a club officer."

"You got it!" was his swift reply, as he expertly put his net in the water and scooped up his prize catch.

The application process seemed endless—a series of tests, physicals, and photos taken of me from every angle. It became a waiting game to see whether or not I'd get accepted. I started to lose enthusiasm. They must have found something wrong with me. Maybe they didn't like the pictures; my grade point average wasn't high enough; or maybe they questioned why I hadn't finished my master's degree. There must be some reason why I hadn't heard from them.

Sergeant Gaskin reassured me, "There's no problem, Angel. Things move slowly in the Air Force. It's always hurry up and wait."

I'd been trying to get my mother to come to Michigan from Rochester, New York for a visit. She never went anywhere and was afraid of flying. After much coaxing, I convinced her to come out by train, and I'd pick her up in Detroit. She knew I was worried about not getting accepted into the Air Force. In fact, I'm sure she thought I wouldn't be accepted. Italian mothers always think the worst, and I was glad she would be with me when I got the bad news. For once in my life, I'd have her all to myself, without having to compete with three other siblings for her attention.

Two days after she arrived, Sergeant Gaskin called and said, "Hi, Angel! I just wanted to congratulate you. You've been accepted into OTS." I screamed into the phone, "God, I can't believe it! Finally! Wow!" I held the receiver out and shouted, "Mom, I got accepted! Can you believe it? I got in!"

She smiled, blessed herself and folded her hands in prayerful thanksgiving. I quieted down just long enough for the sergeant to say, "And guess what, Angel? You got what you wanted. You're gonna be an open mess secretary."

"Does that mean club manager in Air Force lingo?"

"Yes, it sure does. You're gonna be a club officer and run an Air Force officers' club."

"Do you really mean it? Hooray! I'm so happy!"

What I didn't realize was that the Air Force could have assigned me to any job it wanted, "for the good of the mission." I just figured the recruiter had pulled some strings. Then he popped the big news.

"Angel, there's just one thing. The Air Force wants you to report to OTS on Sunday."

"What? Wait a minute. What day is it?"

My mom called out, "Wednesday."

"And they want me there on Sunday?" I said. "I can't possibly do that. I have to give my boss more than three days notice!"

My mother raised her eyebrows, grimaced, and put her hand on her cheek.

"Couldn't I just go to the next class?" I questioned.

"No. Each class has its quota and you don't wanna miss out on this class," replied Gaskin. He wasn't going to let his fish jump back into the water.

"Well, I guess if my boss lets me go, I can be ready."

Sergeant Gaskin said, "Don't worry. I'll come with you tomorrow to talk to your boss."

"OK, I'll see you tomorrow," I said and hung up the phone.

Mom was smiling, "Oh, Angelica! Maybe, coming out here was a good omen."

"Yes, Mom. You definitely brought me good luck," I said, giving her a big hug.

The next morning Sergeant Gaskin and I went in to talk to my boss, Miss Mishler.

"Good Morning, Miss Mishler," he said with a warm, confident smile as he shook her hand. "As you know, there's a war on and we need gals like Angel to help us win it. I'd like to ask your permission, on behalf of the United States Air Force, to let Angel leave her position early to go to Officer Training School."

She hesitated for a moment, and then said, "I understand. We'll work something out." She couldn't say no. She'd do what was best for her country.

During the next few days, while I frantically prepared to leave for San Antonio, I kept asking Sergeant Gaskin exactly what I should expect while at OTS.

"You don't have anything to worry about Angel. There'll be lots of studying, marching, and some lawn parties. Nothing you can't handle."

"Are you sure about that?"

"Ya, no problem," he said, smiling.

I figured I could handle the work, and those lawn parties sounded like fun. I imagined they'd be like Sunday afternoon Bar-B-Ques or afternoon teas.

Mother was visibly nervous about the fact that I had to be ready to leave by Sunday. Sergeant Gaskin reassured her. "Mrs. Pilato, don't worry. Your daughter will be in good hands. The Air Force and the United States really need her." I left my car and furniture with my roommate Marge, packed a few essentials, and was ready to go.

On Friday morning Sergeant Gaskin drove my mom and me down to Detroit so I could fill out more paperwork and get sworn in.

*"…that I take this obligation freely, without any mental reservation or the purpose of evasion and that I will well and faithfully discharge the duties of the office which I am about to enter. SO HELP ME GOD."*

My mother was convinced the Air Force was going to take good care of her daughter. I was going with her blessing. I'd make her proud.

# The New Recruit

Angel's Swearing in at Detroit Recruiting Office

The new recruit with Sergeant Gaskin,
a happy mom, and Captain Kyle

# Officer Training School Graduates

Officers Training School
May 1967 – the OTS women graduates

Proud dad and the new
Lieutenant Pilato

*We gotta get out of this place*
*If it's the last thing we ever do*
*We gotta get out of this place*
*Cause girl, there's a better life for me and you*

—Barry Mann, American Songwriter (1939 - )
Cynthia Weil, American Songwriter (1940 - )

## Officer Training School

I ARRIVED IN SAN Antonio about 11 p.m., excited and apprehensive. Outside the airport terminal was a Blue Bird bus waiting to take me to Lackland Air Force Base. The bus dropped me off in front of a concrete building and I walked up the stairs, suitcase in hand. A menacing looking, cigar-chewing sergeant offered no pleasantries and greeted me in a gruff voice, "Let me see your orders."

I quickly handed him the manila envelope Sergeant Gaskin had given me. He looked it over, mispronounced my name, and ignored my attempt to correct him. He handed me a nine-digit number and growled, "This is your service number. Memorize it, and don't forget it. Got it?" I was given a set of sheets, two towels, a pillow, and a duffle bag and told where to find building number 2909—my barracks.

As I turned to leave, I said, "Thank you." But he just ignored me and went back to chewing his cigar with the oral fixation of a child weaned too soon. I figured he was serious about memorizing my service number so I started repeating it to myself, "FV3208330…FV3208330…FV3208330."

When I entered building 2909, I was greeted by a pixie-like strawberry blonde woman in uniform who wasn't much friendlier. "What's your name?"

"Angel Pilato," I said.

"Where are you from? Let me see your orders," she directed.

"Rochester, New York" I said, handing her my orders.

"Your orders say you enlisted out of Detroit, Michigan."

"Well you see, I was going to school and working at Michigan State University, but I was born and raised in Rochester."

"OK, OT Pilato. I'm OT O'Neill. I'll be the upper classman in charge of getting your class of trainees shaped up. Your room is down the hall, the third one on the left. Get some sleep tonight, what's left of it. You'll be getting up at 0600 hours tomorrow morning to get fitted for your uniforms."

"OK. By the way, what does the OT mean?" I asked.

"It means Officer Trainee," she replied in a condescending voice. I went to my room, made the bed, and fell soundly asleep.

Morning came with OT O'Neill's shrill voice announcing, "All right everyone get up, get dressed, and fall out into the hallway by 0630." Eleven of us, one by one, formed up in single file, wondering what was next.

OT O'Neill barked, "All right ladies, listen up." She quickly began listing our schedule for the day. "We're going to march over to the chow hall, eat breakfast, and then come back here where a Blue Bird bus will take you to get your Air Force uniforms. When you're through, you'll come back here, where you'll be shown how to wear your uniforms correctly, and then you'll go to lunch. After lunch, you'll put your room in order and be assigned a duty that you'll be responsible for while you're here at OTS. Also, you'll be given a tour of the base and pick up the books you'll need for your Air Force classes. Dinner is at 1700 hours and lights are out at midnight—no exceptions. All right, are you ready to go?"

"Yes," we all replied in a rather hit and miss fashion.

"That's 'Yes, ma'am.' Say it together. Got it?" she snapped.

"Yes, ma'am!" we replied in unison. Our first orientation was complete.

Captain Miller was my FTO (Flight Training Officer). Out of 11 women in a class of more than 600 students, he had three in his flight of 14. He was thirtyish, tall, with a dark brown crew cut that matched his eyes. His sandy colored uniform fit his form perfectly. His gig line, the alignment of an officer's uniform shirt, belt buckle, and pant zipper, was always in place. You could see your reflection in his corfam shoes. Miller's demeanor was pleasant and unassuming.

"The mission of OTS," he announced at our first class, "is to produce world class officers who are prepared to lead airmen and who embody the Air Force Core Values: integrity first, service before self, and excellence in all we do. Each officer trainee is expected to adopt this code of standard and live up to it. In the Air Force we uphold the motto 'To Fly, Fight and Win.'"

Our studies focused on leadership skills, military tactics and history, communication skills, and Air Force policies and procedures. We also studied Air Force commands, the mission, and military aircraft. Tests were given on each section. A passing grade was 70. If you failed, you had one chance at a make-up test. If you flunked too many make-up tests, you flunked out of OTS. After failing the section on the SAC (Strategic Air Command), I was asked to report to Captain Miller's office.

"You see OT Pilato, it's like football," said Captain Miller. "There's an offensive team and a defensive team. SAC plays defense while TAC, the Tactical Air Command, plays offense."

"Yes, sir. Defense," I responded, with a pathetic look on my face.

"Do you know the difference between offense and defense?" he asked.

"No, sir. I can't say that I do. I just know that in football, if they get a touchdown, that's six points, and if the guy kicks the ball over the goal post after the touchdown that's another point. And, whoever gets the most points wins."

He shook his head in disbelief, and I heard the flight-training officer in the adjacent cubicle chuckle.

"Well, ah, I guess you're not gonna be my Air Force summa cum laude graduate," he said.

"No, sir. I'm so sorry, sir. Do you think I'll ever get it, sir?" I grimaced.

"Sure you will," he said in an encouraging tone. "Where was I? OK, let's look at it this way. SAC flies these huge B-52 bombers and has all these missile silos. When other nations assess the odds of coming up against all this firepower, we call it 'a show of force.' It's a deterrent to the enemy. SAC is an example of defense—you see? They're the second line of attack. We're not gonna use them unless we have to."

"Now, on the other hand," he continued, "There's TAC. They are the first line of attack. When there's a war on, all our fighter jets go in and attack the targets and knock them out. That's offense."

"Yes, sir...ya...I think I get it," I said. "Ya...thank you, sir. I really appreciate all your help. I'll do better on the make-up test, sir." I returned to the barracks to study. I was determined not to fumble the ball the second time around. My lack of interest in military strategies and war tactics had me wondering if I'd make it through OTS. I wondered what all this had to do with running an officers' club? They didn't let women fly planes, so why did I need to know about offense and defense?

My anxiety increased one night while I was on CQ (Charge of Quarters) duty and saw a report addressed to Captain Miller in the outgoing mail basket. The subject line read, "Progress Report for OT Pilato." Curious, I couldn't help but read on. It stated, "OT Pilato has not visibly demonstrated any leadership skills." Under my breath I said, "What?"

I knew after Captain Miller read this report, I'd be back in his office for another consultation, and sure enough I was. When I arrived at his office he said, "OT Pilato, come on in and sit down."

"Yes, sir." I saluted and sat down.

"Do you have any idea why I've called you in here today?"

"Not exactly, sir." I hesitated, and then with a hangdog look I said, "Would it be because of my progress report. The one I read, unintentionally of course, while I was on CQ duty the other night? Would that be it, sir?"

"Yes, OT Pilato. That's it." He looked slightly surprised that I had clearly read a report addressed to him, but he didn't pursue it. "It appears that you were very active in college, which seems to imply that you have some leadership skills. I think you'd make a good, solid Air Force officer, but you've got to turn this perception around. Here's what I want you to do. The next time one of the upperclassmen gets your group together and asks for a volunteer, I don't care what it is, I want you to volunteer for it. Got it?"

"Yes, sir, I'll do that sir," I promised.

I left there more determined than ever to get through OTS, no matter how many demerits I racked up or how tired I was. No, I wasn't going to let them kick me out, or SIE (Self-Initiated Elimination) either. If I failed, I'd be so embarrassed and so would my mother. I started volunteering for any task I could, from picking up the mail to creating a farewell skit for the upperclassmen. No matter what it was, I was sure to be the first one to say, "I can do that." The next report sent to Captain Miller read, "OT Pilato has shown marked improvement in the area of leadership." It was reassuring, but it didn't do anything to relieve my sleep deprivation. I was still plagued by nightmares of having to go through OTS all over again.

My spirits were buoyed by the announcement of our first lawn party. Finally, time to relax and have some fun. We formed-up outside, dressed in our fatigues, and I thought, *where's the Bar-B-Que going to be?* But, this wasn't any Bar-B-Que. The Air Force's definition of a lawn party was policing the grounds for trash and cigarette butts. A lawn party was what the OTs with the most demerits ended up doing on Saturday afternoons. Needless to say, the base was always inspection perfect.

As a woman, I was required to take additional classes designed to prepare me to be the perfect Air Force representative. The Pentagon set up a separate office designated to oversee the orientation of the Women in the Air Force (WAF). The Director was Colonel Jeanne Holm, a dynamic WAF, who was an enlisted person during WWII and had worked her way up to a full colonel.

At OTS, Captain Diane Ordez was the instructor assigned to deliver these special classes. Ordez was polished, professional, and the perfect example of military bearing. Her uniform looked like she never sat down in it. Her black hair, sprinkled with silver, was perfectly coiffed. Her makeup was a flawless blend of natural colors with a touch of blush that accented her disarming smile. Her hourglass figure held her posture erect, yet her walk was graceful and confident. She was warm, had a wry wit, and was a breath of fresh air in our otherwise staid environment.

Ordez's classes resembled the curriculum of a finishing school. Now, I realized why my Air Force application required all those pictures of me from every angle. It seemed they wanted to upgrade the image of female recruits from girls "ordered by the pound" to something more like the women depicted on recruiting posters. Never mind that the poster girls were actually professional models.

We were taught military protocol, etiquette, and how a WAF should conduct herself in formal and informal situations. We learned what we affectionately called the "Ordez pose," shoulders back, head straight, right heel perpendicular to your left foot, and an Air Force smile on your lips.

We spent one afternoon with a cosmetic rep from *Max Factor* who showed us how to apply makeup correctly. "Ladies, you spread the dark blue eye shadow evenly on the lower eyelid, with the lighter colors blended in on the upper lid," she coached. We practiced putting on our makeup while giggling like high school teenagers. Captain Ordez told us, "Ladies, now that you know how to put on your makeup properly, you'll need to wear it every day."

Captain Ordez also gave us tips that weren't part of the curriculum such as how to tell if a man was married. "Ladies, if a guy at the officers' club bar tries to pick you up, check his left ring finger to see if there's a suntan mark."

I was unaccustomed to primping. My all-girls Catholic high school didn't encourage it and neither did my mother. The only time I ever wore makeup was if I was lucky enough to go to a prom. I certainly didn't see any need for it now. Besides, who had the time to mess with makeup? I decided to ignore the makeup directive. Anyway, I figured they couldn't be serious. To my chagrin, I was confronted one morning by an upperclassman. "OT Pilato, why aren't you wearing makeup?"

My thoughtless reply was, "I didn't have time, ma'am," which promptly earned me a demerit. So, for the first time in my life, I started wearing make up every day.[1]

Demerits were something I became familiar with during my time at OTS. I collected them like Halloween candy. I earned demerits for leaving finger smudges on the brass plates I was required to polish, flunking sections of the Air Force tests, marching out of step, having wrinkles in my uniform, and laughing and chewing gum in ranks, to name a few. If you racked up more than 12 demerits, you were restricted to the barracks and chow hall. Needless to say, I never saw San Antonio the entire time I was at OTS.

My naïve antics may have kept me on the base, but they did bring some comic relief to my classmates who voted me "Miss Morale." They made me wear a pair of red, white, and blue striped epaulettes on my uniform. When real officers noticed them, they'd stop me and inquire, "Why are you out of uniform?" Or, "What are those God-awful things on your shoulders?" When I told them, it usually got a grin accompanied by, "OK! I see. On your way."

As we prepared for our final exams and the end of OTS, we eagerly awaited our first-ever dining-in. A dining-in is a celebration meant to develop camaraderie and esprit de corps among the officers. At every dining-in, one person is designated as Mr. Vice, whose role was to facilitate the flow of events for the evening. He opened the lounge at the appropriate time, sounded the dinner chimes, and served as emcee. He prepared appropriate toasts, sayings, and witticisms (all in good taste) that related to the people and organizations in attendance. As Miss Morale, I was at the top of the list for nomination as Mr. Vice. Talking was one of my strong points, but Mr. Vice had always been a Mister, and no amount of protesting by the women was going to change that. There wasn't going to be any exception to the rule.[2]

During the last couple of weeks at OTS, we received our assignments. All the OTS graduates filled out a form that was called the Dream Sheet, indicating where we'd like to be assigned. I checked off all the U.S. bases in warm climates, indicating in the comment section that I would go anywhere as long as it was sunny and no snow. When I learned I was going to be stationed at the Headquarters of the Strategic Air Command at Offutt Air Force Base in Omaha, Nebraska, I wondered if anyone had actually read my Dream Sheet.

Graduation day, May 27, 1967, was a wonderfully warm, sunny Texas day. Eight out of the eleven women in our class were graduating, and all three of Captain Miller's girls had made it. Our flight met in our classroom for the last time. During the past ten weeks, we had all become fast friends, and the room was filled with a mixture of excitement and sadness. Captain Miller greeted us with smiles, administered the oath of office, and pinned on our second lieutenant gold bars.

I saluted him and said, "Thank you so much, sir, for all you did to get me through OTS. I couldn't have done it without you, sir."

He saluted back and said, "Good luck, Lieutenant Pilato." Hearing the title Lieutenant attached to my name for the first time was thrilling.

My dad flew in from Rochester and sat in the bleachers, waiting to catch a glimpse of his little girl in a sea of newly commissioned officers. We marched onto the parade field in perfect unison while the band played John Philip Souza's *The Washington Post March*. We stood at parade rest as the Base Commander gave us some "Go Air Force" speech. Then, at the exact moment we threw our hats up into the air in celebration, four low-flying fighter jets roared overhead, kicked in their afterburners, rolled their wings from left to right, and flew off. It was exhilarating and rocked me to my toes.

We exited the parade grounds while the band played our class theme song, *We Gotta Get Out of This Place*. And we were out of there.

[1] In 1976 the Air Force disbanded the special office for women in the Air Force, and makeup was no longer a directive! The gals were totally on their own.

[2] I am happy to report that the title of Mr. Vice was changed to Mister Vice and Madam Vice. Later it was completely de-sexed to the title of Vice President of the Mess, which ended the tradition that only men could Emcee for dining-ins. Reference Air Force Pamphlet 34-1202.

*Because I am a woman, I must make unusual efforts to succeed. If I fail, no one will say, 'She doesn't have what it takes.' They will say, 'Women don't have what it takes.'*

—Clare Boothe Luce, American diplomat, playwright (1903 - 1987)

## No Woman Is Going to Run My Officers' Club

IN JUNE 1967, I arrived at Offutt Air Force Base at 0800 hours dressed in my newly tailored Air Force blues ready to begin my assignment. I entered Major Bill Henderson's office, gave him a snappy salute and said, "Lieutenant Pilato reporting for duty, sir."

He seemed a little startled and gave me a wimpy salute back. "So, you're gonna be my assistant. Personnel said they were sending me a second lieutenant," he said, rolling his eyes. "They didn't tell me it was a girl." He glanced over at the man standing next to his desk who seemed to be suppressing a grin.

"Yes, sir, here are my orders," I replied.

He gave them a cursory look and said, "Lieutenant Palatti, have you been to Open Mess School yet?"

"No, sir, I just drove here straight from OTS."

Major Henderson had a reddish complexion, a chin with a slight jowl, and thinning strands of hair he kept flinging off his forehead like he was waving off a fly. He spoke with a Southern drawl that seemed to inhibit his ability to pronounce my name correctly, even after I repeated it for him. I surmised he was in his forties. He had a scattered look about him.

"Lieutenant Palatti," he said, "this is Senior Master Sergeant Dan Ferguson. He's the NCO assigned to the club." A Senior Master Sergeant was one stripe short of a Chief Master Sergeant, which was the highest rank for a noncommissioned officer (NCO). I figured he must know his stuff. The major stood up, put his hand on Sergeant Ferguson's shoulder, and said, "Dan here, he's my right hand man."

"Good to meet you Sergeant," I said and extended my hand.

"Likewise Lieutenant," Sergeant Ferguson said with a wide grin that drew attention to a missing top molar. He gave me a firm handshake and I noticed his huge hand had a couple of fingers that were only stumps. He wore a suit and tie, as civilian clothes were allowed for any NCO assigned to an officers' club. He was tall, had a solid build, and looked a little like Mr. Clean with a G.I. crew cut.

Henderson interjected, "Sergeant Ferguson, you'll need to find out when the next open mess training starts at the Quartermaster School and get Lieutenant Palatti signed up for it right away."

"Yes, sir. I'll get right on it, sir," he replied.

"Lieutenant Palatti, do you have a first name?" Major Henderson inquired.

"Yes, sir. It's Angel."

"Angel! Oh, brother, that ought to go over well."

"It's a nickname, sir. You can call me Angelica, if you prefer."

"No, Angel will work. Sergeant Ferguson, show Angel here around the club."

"Yes, sir, happy to oblige," Ferguson said flippantly.

As Henderson exited his office, he said, "Angel, I'll see you later for happy hour."

"Happy hour, sir?" I thought, *happy hour? It's only 0830 in the morning!*

"Yes, it starts at 1630 in the main bar."

"Yes, sir. What did you want me to do until then, sir?"

"Sergeant Ferguson will figure something out for you to do. Isn't that right, Sergeant?"

"Yes, sir. She'll be in good hands," responded Ferguson with a smirk.

Both Ferguson and Henderson seemed to be in a quandary over how they were going to utilize me, and my days consisted of aimlessly waiting for them to find something productive for me to do. My orders for Open Mess School were issued, but I wasn't going until October.

In the meantime, I got acquainted with the other junior officers who came into the club to eat or go to happy hour. The happy hour crowd was always packed with an over abundance of "bird colonels." A bird colonel was a nickname for a full colonel who wore an eagle on his epaulette to indicate his rank. Lieutenant colonels were designated by a silver oak leaf cluster and were one rank below a full colonel. They were nicknamed "telephone colonels" because, when a "Colonel Jones" answered the phone, you couldn't distinguish whether it was a lieutenant colonel, or a full colonel. Needless to say, the junior officers felt a little inhibited hanging out at the bar with all those colonels.

One night on my way to eat dinner at the club, I met my first fighter pilot, Captain David Reed, who asked me to join him for dinner. Captain Reed was an F-100 Air National Guard pilot who'd landed at Offutt because his aircraft needed repair. He'd left the active duty military to pursue his medical degree and stayed in the Air Guard because he loved flying. The next day he brought me out to the flight line to show me his fighter jet and told me, "It's too bad your first assignment was SAC Headquarters because 'SAC sucks.' That's what we fighter pilots say about it." That was the first time I heard that expression, but it wouldn't be the last.

"You've gotta get an assignment to a real Air Force base," he continued. "A fighter base, where you'll have more fun. There'll be more junior officers and real pilots—fighter pilots. All these old fogies here will bore you to death." Captain Reed had a spark and an enthusiasm I found exciting. I remembered the thrill of those fighter jets zooming overhead during graduation ceremony. And he was right about SAC being stodgy.

October finally arrived, and I headed to Open Mess School in Ft. Lee, Virginia. I was the only female in a class of forty. I learned everything about running an officers' club. I learned rules and regulations, club accounting, bar management, inventory controls, budgeting, menu planning, the role of the club advisory council, and how to do ice carvings. Every military club was required to make a profit, with three percent year-to-date being the ideal. Officers and NCOs had separate clubs and paid dues to belong. All military personnel were "encouraged" by the commander to become members. The club's advisory board, the number of club members, its location, and the financial condition of the club determined the amount of dues paid by the members. The club buildings, utilities, and maintenance were paid with appropriated funds, but everything else was supported through membership dues and club activities. Prices at the clubs were usually much lower than off-base, and people enjoyed having their special events there. A member could charge his meals and activities on his club card and would receive a statement at the end of the month. The NCO clubs had more members than the officers' clubs. Their dues were lower and they usually operated in the black. On the other hand, the officers' clubs were smaller and struggled to make a profit.

With new ideas and enthusiasm, I arrived back at Offutt raring to go, but nothing had changed. The major still hadn't decided what he wanted me to do. I continued to ask him how I could help, and eventually he found a desk for me in the catering office with the civilian catering manager.

The manager realized I wanted to be productive, and soon she began letting me schedule parties on my own. I played a key role in assisting the Protocol Office with an annual reception for the Governor of Nebraska and local dignitaries that was given by the SAC commander who was a four-star general. All of the generals' wives directed many of the details for the event such as the menu, flowers, and the invitation design. It was a real learning experience. Those women knew what they wanted, and I had to deliver.

As for Sergeant Ferguson taking good care of me? It wasn't long before I found out what that meant! He tried everything he could to get me to sleep with him. I kept saying no, which to him seemed to mean, "Try again." I wasn't the least bit interested in him, not only because the military had a no fraternization policy which prohibited officers and NCOs from dating, but because he was married. Besides, I didn't find him the least bit attractive.

In 1967, no policies existed against sexual harassment or hostile work environments. The unwritten policy was simply, "If you can't stand the heat, get out of the kitchen." Although I tried to ignore him and roll with it, my interactions with Dan became strained.

One day, a project officer came into the catering office and asked for Sergeant Ferguson. "There seems to be a discrepancy with the open bar inventory from the party we had last weekend, and I'd like to talk with him about it," he said.

When he arrived, I said, "Sergeant Ferguson, the major has a question concerning the bar inventory from his party last weekend."

The major chimed in, "Yes, Dan, I just don't think our group drank that much liquor. The bill seems a little excessive."

"Well, sir, I'm not sure what happened, but I'll check it out for you A-S-A-P," responded Ferguson, and left the office.

Moments later he returned and said, "By gosh, sir, you're absolutely right. There was a mistake, and I'm terribly sorry about that, sir. It seems as though your inventory got mixed up with another party. I really don't know how the bartender made that mistake, but I'll take care of it right away for you, sir." He quickly adjusted some numbers on the major's bill, apologized profusely, and thanked him for bringing it to his attention.

After the major left, I questioned Ferguson further. "Dan, what was that all about? We didn't have any other party last weekend."

"Well, Lieutenant, you know we're gonna have an employee party, and we needed some booze for it. Just how d'ya think we were gonna get it?"

"What?" I snapped. "You inflated the bar inventory just to get some alcohol for the employee party? You can't do that, Dan. You can't cheat the members. If you wanted some liquor for the party, you could've asked Major Henderson or the Advisory Council. I'm sure they would've allowed you to use some liquor from our regular inventory."

His response was, "You know, Lieutenant, just because you went to Open Mess School, you're still a brown bar."

I knew what that meant. A brown bar is what they called second lieutenants. Although a second lieutenant's bars were gold, the reference to brown meant a second lieutenant didn't know shit.

"Well Dan, it still looks like stealing to me," I retorted.

"Lieutenant, let me tell you something. You're never going to make it in this business. You're just too damn honest," he fired back.

Unfortunately that wasn't the end of my interactions with Sergeant Ferguson. Sergeants assigned to the clubs were allowed to earn up to 100 hours a month in overtime pay. This was a small compensation they received for all the extra hours they worked. I began to notice that Ferguson would habitually punch in on the time clock, then he'd leave, go over to the NCO club to drink or play golf. Later, he'd return to the o-club to punch out. When I confronted him about this, he blew me off and continued to abuse the privilege. Determined not to let him get away with it, I took his time card in to the bookkeeper and told her to dock his pay.

She looked at me like I was crazy and said, "OK, Lieutenant, if you say so."

When Ferguson found out, he went ballistic. I heard his orders to the bookkeeper. "Leave that time card the way it was, and tell Lieutenant Pilato to keep her WOP[1] Lieutenant hands off my time card." The bookkeeper promptly reversed the timecard.

It was futile for me to tell Major Henderson. He was a passed over major, who knew he'd never make lieutenant colonel and spent most of his time in the bar. He never gave me any real authority, and as long as the club was making money, he didn't care what Ferguson did.

However the Chief of Staff to the four-star general of SAC, a sweet, fatherly colonel, had befriended me. Periodically, he'd check-in to see how things were going, and it was during one of these check-ins when I decided to tell him everything that had transpired at club. I laid it all out in black and white. After our conversation, the president of the Officers' Club Advisory Council came to me and asked what was going on. I told him everything and thought, *Great! They're finally going to straighten this whole mess out and put a stop to all this cheating and stealing.*

It probably wasn't a coincidence, but not long after these conversations took place I received orders for a new assignment. I was going to run my very own officers' club at Morón Air Base in sunny Seville, Spain. I was so excited. I could hardly believe I was getting my own club and was going to someplace warm. I thought, *finally, someone read my Dream Sheet!*

Spain was just like I had imagined it—beautiful, warm, and sunny. My sponsor, an officer appointed to welcome me, got me settled in, and she and her boyfriend gave me a tour of downtown Seville and the local sights. My first taste of sangria went down as easy as grape juice and went even quicker to my head. I tried fried calamari and found it delicious, but I didn't know it was squid until after I'd eaten it. I saw a bidet for the first time and thought it must be something used to wash your feet.

All the fun was stifled when the Personnel Officer informed me that I was not going to be the club officer. I was being reassigned to work in keypunch.

"Keypunch! Why's that? My orders say that I'm supposed to run the officers' club," I said.

She responded with, "Well, there's been a change, and that's what the Base Commander wants."

"What's his reason? Can I talk with him?" I asked in a puzzled tone.

"That wouldn't be advisable," she instructed.

"Who's going to run the o-club?" I asked.

"Captain Allen, from accounting," was her bland response.

"Accounting! Has he ever run a club? Does he have any food management background?" I was hoping to find some reason, other than that he was a man, that made him more qualified than I was to run the club. However, her answer to all my questions was simply, "no."

I was slated for a three-year tour at Morón Air Base, and I didn't want to rock the boat, so I dutifully went to keypunch. I felt like I'd been unjustly sent to detention. Keypunch was the most boring job imaginable. It involved punching holes in cards coded with specific information, then running them through a sorting machine. The only interesting piece of information I discovered was that 11 other people on base had the same O negative blood type. I thought, *I'm not going to last three years doing this, even with sangria.*

One night, about a month after my arrival, I came face-to-face with the Base Commander at the officers' club. I walked over to him and introduced myself. "Good evening, sir. I'm Lieutenant Pilato, newly assigned here from Offutt Air Force Base." Before he had a chance to respond, I said, "Sir, I just wanted to ask you why you didn't want me to run the officers' club?"

He looked at me like I'd just asked him to take his clothes off. "Because, I'm not going to have any woman run my officers' club—it's as simple as that!"

"Well, sir, I think this might have been the first mistake you've ever made," I challenged.

Startled by my bold response, he blurted out, "Maybe so, but it's still my decision!"

Although I felt better speaking my mind, it made no impact. It was 1969, and in 1964 Congress had passed the Civil Rights Act with a Title VII amendment that "prohibited discrimination by employers on the basis of race, color, religion, sex, or national origin." I was clueless about my civil rights, and in the military, it was rank that had the rights.

Fortunately, that Base Commander's three-year tour was coming to end. When the new Base Commander arrived, I decided to pitch my case to him. Also, there was a new Vice Commander, who was from Offutt Air Force Base and knew me. They initially waffled, but when their wives found out what was going on, they got involved. Soon afterwards, I was assigned to my rightful position as manager of the o-club.

I wanted to prove I could do the job and worked like hell to get the small club with a few hundred members humming. After eight months of managing the club, a member of the Inspector General's (IG) Team from Wiesbaden Air Base, in Frankfurt, Germany came to inspect our club. He gave the club a glowing report and selected me to go to the Hotel Restaurant Management School at Cornell University for summer classes. Only four Air Force club personnel from the European command were selected. Cornell was only 90 miles from Rochester, which meant I could take a bus home to see Mom and Dad on the weekends. At Cornell, there were hospitality managers from all over the world. The courses involved every aspect of the commercial restaurant industry: menu planning, French cuisine, catering, the newest commercial equipment, and club design. I felt lucky to be at a school that was an educational leader in restaurant management and to interact and learn from other professionals.

While at Cornell, I received orders for a new assignment to Bitburg Air Base in Germany, which was a real fighter base. Although I was thrilled about it, my excitement was tempered by my preconceived prejudices about the Germans and their Nazi past. Still, it was a promotion to a larger club and a chance to see a new part of Europe.

I had no idea where Bitburg, Germany was. One of the international students from the Netherlands, Robert Posman, told me his hotel wasn't far from Bitburg, and he pointed it out to me on a map. It was on the far western border of Germany near Luxembourg and not far from Holland's southern border. Robert was bright and friendly and had come to Cornell to upgrade his skills. He planned to manage the Grand Hotel in Heerlan after his father retired.

I asked him, "If I come to Holland, will you show me the tulips?"

He responded with his charming Dutch accent, "Tulips! Is that all you Americans think we have in Holland?"

"Well, no, you've got those windmills, too, don't you?" I said, grinning.

He cracked a smile and said, "OK. Here's my number. When you get to Bitburg, call me."

"That sounds great. I'll look forward to seeing those tulips."

"OK, we'll see," he said.

When I got back to Spain, the movers packed up my belongings to ship to Germany, and I prepared to drive the entire 2,275 kilometers (1,365 miles) to Bitburg in my '67 Mustang. Maureen, a friend and the daughter of one of the officers, accompanied me. We drove from Seville, north to Madrid and San Sebastian on the northern coast of Spain, then on to Paris. I said good-bye to Maureen in Paris and completed the remainder of the trip alone through France and Luxembourg. During the entire week I was traveling, the American Armed Forces radio was broadcasting a public service announcement in a desperate attempt to reach me: "Lieutenant Pilato, please contact the Red Cross," but I never heard it.

[1] WOP is a slang insult for a person of Italian decent and stands for "Without Papers." As a point of clarification, all my ancestors had papers when they arrived in the U.S. in the early 1900s.

*However long the night, the dawn will break.*
—African Proverb

## Please Contact the Red Cross

ON A SATURDAY, JUST around dusk, I arrived at Bitburg Air Base. As I was waiting to check into the BOQ, I noticed a note under the glass desktop. It read, "Lieutenant Pilato, contact the Red Cross." I thought, *that's strange. Why do I have a note to contact the Red Cross? The only time the Red Cross is ever notified is if there's an emergency.*

I told the clerk, "I'm Lieutenant Pilato. I see this note's for me," as I pointed my finger at it.

He said, "Yes, ma'am. Good evening, ma'am. We've been waiting for you."

"The note says I'm supposed to call the Red Cross. What's happened? Can you tell me?"

"I really don't know. I'll call the Red Cross Representative for you, ma'am."

My stomach churned as I anticipated the worst. While I waited for the Red Cross Representative, I decided to busy myself by unloading my car. Two officers, who were checking into the BOQ, had overheard my conversation with the desk clerk and offered to help me. I got more anxious as I speculated what might have happened. No one at home was sick. Had there been an accident?

The two officers tried to reassure me, "It's probably nothing serious. Don't worry. Your parents are probably just concerned that they hadn't heard from you in awhile."

I hoped that's what it was, but I had sent them a postcard from every stop along the way. Maybe they just hadn't gotten them yet. Mail in Europe was slow. I thanked them for their help and waited alone in my room. After what seemed like an eternity, I heard a knock on the door. I took one look at the emotionless expression on the face of the man standing before me and knew the news wasn't going to be good.

"Lieutenant Pilato?" he asked.

"Yes. Come in. What's happened? Who is it?" My stomach tightened.

"It's your mother, Lieutenant."

"My mother! What's happened to her?"

"I'm sorry to have to tell you that she's passed away."

I burst into tears. "Passed away! Passed away! You mean she's dead? How could she be dead? I just left her 10 days ago."

He started to read from a telegram, "The message says that she died suddenly on September 1st."

I said, "I've gotta get back there. I've gotta get back there right away. I just knew something terrible would happen if I came to Europe. I have to get back there for the funeral. My family needs me." My tears were uncontrollable.

Then he read another telegram, "Every attempt was made to locate Lieutenant Pilato. We could not delay the funeral any longer. Mrs. Pilato was buried on Saturday, September 6th."

"What's today?"

"It's Saturday, Lieutenant."

"Oh my God! They buried her today! I'm too late. Why did it have to be her? She wasn't even sick. She was only 61." In between my sobs, I continued, "I can't believe she's dead and I'm too late." In an effort to gain some composure, I said, "Can you help me get a call through to the States? I need to talk with my family."

"Yes, I can. Let's go over to the officers' club, and I'll see if I can get a line out to the States."

He contacted the base operator and after several tries the call went through.

"Hello," it was Dad on the phone.

"Dad, it's Angelica." We both started crying.

"Angelica, where are you?"

"I'm in Germany, Dad. I just got here a few hours ago."

"We waited as long as we could, Doll, but they couldn't find you. Where were you?"

"Dad," my words were mixed with tears. "I was driving from Spain to Germany, and there wasn't any way for them to reach me."

"Your Uncle Sam tried all his veteran connections. He even called the Pentagon, but they couldn't find you."

"I'm so sorry, Dad. I can't believe Mom's gone. What happened to her? How did she die? She was OK when you visited me at Cornell a couple of weeks ago."

"Well, Angelica, she was having chest pains all weekend and she wasn't sleeping well. I kept telling her she needed to see a doctor, but she didn't think it was necessary. You know how your mother felt about going to a doctor."

His words were interspersed with tears. "Finally, I decided to call the doctor myself, and he told me to bring her right over. That was on Labor Day. When we got there, the doctor checked her out and put mother at ease. He said it was probably just a case of nerves. He prescribed some sleeping pills for her and said he'd get her an appointment with a cardiologist later in the week."

"I went off to the drug store," Dad continued, "to get the sleeping pills, and that's when it happened. She'd been resting on the couch. When your brother went in to check on her, she wasn't breathing. Charles was alone and didn't know what to do. He ran next door to Mrs. Hall's who rushed over and called the ambulance. By the time I got home, they had already taken her away. I never even had a chance to say good-bye."

"Oh, Dad, I'm so sorry. I loved her so much."

"I know, Angelica. She was a wonderful mother. I'm going to miss her, too."

It was so hard to hear my dad cry. He was always such a tough guy, but his tears engulfed both of us.

"Are you coming home, Doll?"

"I don't know, Dad. They've already held this assignment open for me because I was at Cornell. I don't know if I can. It's too late now."

"OK, Angelica. We'd like you to come home and be with us, but you know what's best. I'll see you soon, Doll."

"Dad, let me talk to Charles and Nancie." He turned the phone over to my sister. Charles was too distraught to talk. I have no recollection of what we said, but I know we were both crying. Exhausted, I ended the call and walked back to the BOQ alone.

On the way back, I saw Sid and Maria Ruffu walking towards me. They were friends of mine from Morón Air Base who'd arrived at Bitburg about three weeks before. I ran over to them and said, "Do you know what happened? My mom died."

Maria responded in a soothing voice, "Yes, Angel. We know. That's why we're here. We came over to see if you'd arrived yet." They came with me to my BOQ room.

Sid told me, "The Base Commander contacted me this week and asked if we knew you and did we know what route you were taking to get here. They called Torrejon Air Base in Madrid to see if they could reach you, but you had already left. They even broadcasted a message on Armed Forces Radio for you to contact the Red Cross."

"I never heard it. I couldn't get any radio reception driving through France." I started crying again and Marie hugged me. They stayed with me most of the night.

That Monday, I met with the Base Commander. He offered his sincere condolences and told me that if I needed to go home, I could take some emergency leave. But he added that the club had been without a manager for a month. I got the distinct impression that he didn't want me to leave, so I didn't. The Base Commander had a Catholic Mass said for my mother at the base chapel. He and his wife attended, along with Marie and Sid, and some people the Base Commander's wife had asked to attend. That was how I began my assignment at Bitburg.

*You love a lot of things if you live around them, but there isn't any woman and there isn't any horse, nor any before, nor any after, that is as lovely as a great airplane, and men who love them are faithful to them even though they leave them for others. A man has only one virginity to lose in fighters, and if it is a lovely plane he loses it to, there his heart will ever be.[1]*

—Ernest Hemingway, American writer (1899 - 1961)

## Fighter Pilots: Who Are Those Guys?

SINCE THE BEGINNING OF time, humans have marveled at birds in flight. They have watched in awe at their ability to be the predator, flee from danger, and travel great distances quickly. They have dreamed of surpassing the bird, conquering the skies, and having power over all that was above and below. Leonardo de Vinci's imaginative drawings formed the concept of man in flight. Over the centuries, many inventors combined their talents to create the airplane. From wire, wood, and propellers evolved the sleek fighter jet. It roars through the sky at velocities faster than the speed of sound, makes the atmosphere boom, and all earthly creatures shake with fear.

Anyone can learn how to fly an airplane. I can attest to that. But not everyone who flies an airplane can be a fighter pilot. Even some men who fly fighter jets are not fighter pilots. It takes a certain breed. Who are these airmen called fighter pilots? The only way I can portray them is through my experiences with them. The very core of who they are was what immediately attracted me, what I hopelessly tried to resist, and what ultimately ensnared me.

On the days that I was enthralled with them, they impressed me with their bravado. I saw them as confident, talented, and dashing, and I wished to be like them. But on the nights they trashed my officers' club bar with a drunken fracas, a *clong* sweep,[2] or a food fight in the dining room, I saw them as one step below a bunch of immature, out-of-control frat boys.

A fighter pilot is mesmerized with flying, like a cobra is entranced with the melody of a snake charmer's *pungi*.[3] Once he's under its melodic spell, he remains hopelessly hooked. Flying is his obsession and his drug of choice. Flying consumes his mind and permeates every fiber of his body. He lives to fly. Together, he and his aircraft are one precision machine. Ask a fighter pilot to choose between flying and sex and he would, without hesitation, choose flying. A fighter pilot once told me, "Angel, flying is better then sex. In fact, Angel, I can't believe they actually pay me to do this!"

Why do they fly? Love of country is somewhere on the list, but it's the love of flying that will always be number one.

The quintessential fighter pilot has been portrayed as a larger-than-life figure. He has the right stuff. He is an arrogant and brash top gun living in the danger zone. Fighter pilots believe they are indestructible. If a pilot happens to meet his destiny in the sky, the others explain it away as a bad break or a fluke. Their buddy's fate will not befall them. No, they will not end up in a spin, crash, and burn.

Their thinking can be classified as either delusional or optimistic. If they let those bad breaks take hold of their psyche, they might be doomed to meet the same fate. Instead, they go to the bar, have a few drinks, toast their fallen friend, and wake up the next day to fly another mission. Getting shot at is just a minor inconvenience they have to put up with in order to fly their magnificent jets.

In the face of constant danger, it is imperative for a fighter pilot to create physical and mental distractions to keep their nerves of steel intact. For example, they invented the bar room carrier landing. Put a couple of six-foot banquet tables together, soak them down with beer, and body surf across the top. This only becomes dicey when the trajectory of his head is aimed at a brick wall or the glass front of a booming jukebox. Yell "dead bug" in a bar room full of fighter pilots and everyone hits the floor on their back, puts their feet and hands up in the air to simulate a dead bug—last one down buys a round of drinks. They'll play endless dice games of HORSE, aces wild, and acey-ducey for another round of drinks.

A fighter pilot is a courageous and focused risk-taker, committed to the mission. Once he stops being consumed by the mission, he's toast. Decisiveness is a crucial element. When he has to make the decision to "pickle the bomb" on a target, his go/no go action is what determines his fate. There is no concern that his bomb might kill people. To him, it's a game of target practice. Those other guys are the bad guys. They'll get him, if he doesn't get them first.

Loving fighter pilots is like loving chocolate. While you're indulging and those serotonins are being released, it's so intoxicating. But if you continue to indulge, you become addicted. I loved fighter pilots as much as they loved flying. I was as addicted to them as they were to their jets. You can love them or leave them, but mostly they will love you and leave you.

[1] "Hemingway, London Fights the Robots," Collier's August 19, 1944 reprinted in *By-Line: Ernest Hemingway: Selected Articles and Dispatches of Four Decades,* edited by William White, Charles Scribner's Sons, New York, 1967, page 356. He was talking about the WWII P-51 Mustang.

[2] A *clong* sweep was what the guys called it when they gathered up a bunch of huge banana leaves, brought them into the bar and started swinging them from side to side, hitting everyone and everything in their path. *Clong* means river in Thai.

[3] A *Pungi* is the instrument played by the snake charmers in India. It is typically one to two feet in length. It consists of two reeds or bamboo tubes, attached to a larger cavity made of a gourd or coconut.

*I see my path, but I don't know where it leads. Not knowing is what inspires me to travel it.*

—Rosalia de Castro, Galician writer (1837 - 1885)

## Bitburg and Beyond

AFTER A FEW WEEKS at Bitburg, I met the Wing Commander. He greeted me with, "Good to meet you, Lieutenant! We're glad to have you here."

My startled reply was, "You are?"

"Yes, the European Command said you were a real professional."

"Thank you, sir. I'm glad to be here." I thought, *Wow! What a switch! Somebody's glad to have me assigned to his base!*

After awhile, no one thought it was odd to have a woman running the officers' club. I worked well with the commanders' and officers' wives, which was very important. Those women had a direct line to their husbands and believe me it was in my best interest to pay attention to what they wanted.

Bitburg was the real Air Force: F4 Phantom fighter jets roaring off the runway at all hours of the day and night, pilots three deep at the bar for Friday night happy hour, lots of young junior officers, weekend parties on and off-base, and road rallies with everyone showing off their Porsches. The American schoolteachers stationed there to teach the children of the military families made things interesting for the unmarried officers. It was a fun, close-knit group.

Something was always happening at Bitburg. If the junior officers weren't drinking at the club, they were having a party off-base, or getting into some kind of mischief. One stunt we pulled off involved a senior officer, Colonel Thompson, the Director of Maintenance (DOM).

The DOM had a reserved parking space right in front of the officers' club, along with the Wing Commander, the Vice Wing Commander, the Base Commander, and a space reserved for any junior officer. Those colonels were very protective of their reserved parking spaces. They'd put in their time and by God, they'd earned a reserved parking space.

One day, Colonel Thompson drove up to the club for lunch and found someone had parked a car in his space. He was so incensed that he pulled his car right up behind it, bumper to bumper, blocking it in completely. The car belonged to Marti, one of the schoolteachers. When I looked out my office window and saw what the colonel had done, I shook my head and thought, *that little prick.* He marched into the club with a disgruntled look on his face, sat down, and ordered lunch. He figured that the delinquent who had parked in his space would have to come beg him to get it out, and then he'd give him hell.

I thought there had to be some way to get Marti's car out of the colonel's space without using a crane. On the left, in a space reserved for a junior officer, was Captain George William's car. I knew it because it was a dumper of a car. I had Marti paged to my office, while I went into the dining room looking for George. When I spotted him, I went to his table, leaned over and said, "George, we have a situation. I need your help. Please come with me."

He sensed the urgency in my voice and followed me back to my office. "What's up, Angel?"

Marti stood in my office, looking out the window at the colonel's car parked tightly behind hers.

"Boy, am I in trouble now," she said. "How am I ever gonna get out of this?"

George found the whole thing rather amusing. "Don't sweat it Marti. We'll figure something out," he said.

I replied, "Yeah, but we have to work fast. Thompson will be done with his lunch in no time. George, what if you move your car? Do you think Marti can wiggle her way out?" Marti just stood there frozen.

George, being the navigator that he was, assessed the situation and said, "If I back my car out, she might be able to maneuver her car back and forth and angle her way out. It's going to take some work, but yeah, I think it's possible."

We quickly headed outside. George moved his car, and Marti, with our guidance, used every inch of space there was between the wall of the officers' club and her front bumper to get out. With no power steering it took a lot of hard back and forth wheel turning, but finally she angled her way out through George's space. With a sigh of relief she drove off smiling. George pulled his car back into his parking space and went back into the dining room to finish his lunch.

When Colonel Thompson came out of the club, he was flabbergasted. He saw an empty space in front of his car, and all the same cars still parked where they'd been when he came in. The look on his face was worth a million bucks. Colonel Thompson never found out how the car had gotten out of that space, and the junior officers had a great story to tell at the bar a dozen times over.

It wasn't all fun and games, though. Each year the entire base, from the flight line to the latrines, was subjected to an IG (Inspector General's) inspection by higher headquarters. These inspections were vital to a Wing Commander keeping his job and getting a promotion. We were never sure when the IG would hit the base, but we always needed to be ready.

One day, after passing an IG inspection with flying colors, we were celebrating at the o-club bar. Our Wing Commander had just found out that he was slated for his first star as brigadier general. I figured he was in a good mood, so I decided to ask him a question.

"Good evening, Colonel Robertson, congratulations on making BG," I said and shook his hand.

"Thank you, Angel," he said, with a slight smile.

"I have a question for you, sir."

"What is it?"

"Well, sir. Seeing that you passed the IG inspection with flying colors and you just made your first star, I figure the heat's off and that this might be a good time to ask you for a ride in the F-4. What d'ya think?" I said all in one breath and with an anticipatory, yet tentative, smile on my face.

"What? You want a ride in the F-4? Good grief," was his response.

"Yes, sir. You got it, a ride in the back seat of the F-4."

With a grin he said, "OK, Angel, I'll tell you what I'll do. If you really want a ride in the F-4, you have to get the club's year-to-date profit up to three percent."

"That's it? Three percent? You've got it!" I said firmly.

I'm sure he never thought I'd do it. The club had slot machines that helped supplement the bottom line, but it wasn't quite enough to put us at three percent. I decided to get creative. I was going to get that three percent come hell or high water. I cut a few expenses, raised prices just enough so the officers wouldn't scream, and planned some fun events that generated additional income.

Six months later, I sent the Wing Commander the o-club's financial statement with the three percent year-to-date profit circled in red, along with a note reminding him of our bet. He was a little reluctant, but he agreed to honor his wager. My reward caused some consternation on the base. One Squadron Commander said, "How come you get a ride in the F-4 when some of our crew chiefs can't?" He had a point, but it wasn't my problem.

A few weeks later, all the details were worked out. I'd be flying with the 22nd Tactical Fighter Squadron (TFS). I borrowed a flight suit from one of the pilots, and they put me through emergency ejection procedures, just in case. While I was preparing for my flight, I heard rumors that some of the guys were making bets on whether or not I'd throw up. I said to myself, *there's no way I'm going to barf, even if I have to swallow it before I land!* I didn't eat or drink anything but water the day before my ride.

I entered the squadron, stepped into my flight suit, and was fitted with a G-suit. Every pilot wears a G-suit that is plugged into the aircraft to counteract the effects of g-forces experienced during high acceleration or aerial maneuvers. When the g-forces become too high, the G-suit inflates and keeps the pilot's blood pressure from dropping, preventing him from losing consciousness. After I was fully geared up, the pilots surprised me with a flight helmet that had "Angel" painted in red on the front.

There would be two F-4s in the flight. I was going to fly in the back seat with Lieutenant Colonel Don Miller, Operations Officer for the 22nd Tactical Fighter Squadron. Major Chuck McGregor, with his GIB (guy in the back), would be the lead. McGregor briefed us on the route. It was a medium altitude flight to Bavaria, with the obligatory circles around Neuschwanstein Castle, and a return to one of the Military Operating Areas (MOA's) near Bitburg.

A half-hour before we were to climb into the aircraft, I said with a pitiful look on my face, "I'm sorry guys. I've gotta go to the bathroom." This brought a roar of laughter and one of the pilots in flight crew room said, "See! This is why women can't be pilots!"

"Damn it! I'm sorry I don't have one of those appendages," I snapped, pointing to the fly opening on my flight suit. "They just make these suits for you guys!" They removed my G-suit and one of the pilots watched the door of the men's room. I unzipped my flight suit all the way down the front, let it fall down around my ankles, relieved myself, zipped it up, and came back out.

Smiling, they strapped me back into my G-suit, and out we went to the aircraft. I climbed the ladder, got into the backseat, and an officer fastened me in. Then, he carefully placed a sick bag on the dash right in front of me and said, grinning from ear to ear, "Angel, I'm going to put this right up here, in easy reach, just in case you need it."

"Thanks, but I don't think I'll need it," I quickly responded. He was probably one of the ones betting I'd throw up.

The two F-4s taxied out to the runway. I took a deep breath. Then the brakes released. We accelerated to 165 mph for take off, which gave me a quite a jolt. Twenty-five seconds later we reached a speed of 350 mph[1] to join-up with the flight leader. While in the air, Miller let me take hold of the stick and do a couple of 360-degree aileron rolls. Wow! I was flying upside down. I could see why fighter pilots loved flying this mighty machine. What an adrenaline hit.

When we landed, a crowd was waiting. Some of them were part of a welcoming committee, while the others were there to see if they'd won their bet. As soon as the aircraft canopy lifted up and my helmet was unstrapped, I waved my empty sick bag over my head, and the crowd started cheering. A lot of the officers' wives were there; they'd bet I wouldn't throw up.

I disembarked from the aircraft and climbed down the ladder. Out of nowhere, I was doused with a huge bucket of water and soaked from head to toe. They'd given me a "splash down," usually reserved for pilots in SEA on their last fight before returning home. They popped open a bottle of champagne, and the crowd shouted, "Chug it! Chug it!" I started guzzling, and that's when I almost lost whatever was left in my stomach. I pulled the bottle away from my mouth as some of the champagne dripped down my chin. The crowd clapped, and Lieutenant Colonel Miller handed me a plaque imprinted with the 22nd Tactical Squadron's bumblebee insignia. It read "Captain Angel Pilato, First Flight in the F-4D Phantom II, 16 April 1971." To this day that ride was the thrill of a lifetime and the plaque is proudly displayed on my office wall.

Things were going well at Bitburg. After two years, I had made captain, which was pretty much automatic. The Base Commander signed an extension to my four-year commitment in the Air Force and wrote, "Angel can stay in the Air Force as long as she doesn't piss off any full colonels or any chief master sergeants."

My friendship with Robert Posman, the Dutchman I'd met at Cornell, was blossoming into something more intimate. I went to visit him at his beautiful hotel in Heerlen, Holland, and he'd come to see me on the base. He showed me the beautiful tulips at the Keukenhof Gardens, the windmills, and the nightlife in Amsterdam. His mother loved me. He was the perfect gentleman and always brought me flowers or chocolates when he visited. He called me a "smart American chick" and wasn't obsessed with my body. It was unusual after hanging around fighter pilots, who seemed to only see my body. I wasn't sure where our relationship was going. When I asked him he said, "Angel, we have an expression in Holland, 'hurry slowly.'"

Everything seemed to be at a standstill. I started feeling like there was more to do and more to see. Maybe it was time to move on. I'd seen a lot of Europe, and now I was itching to see another part of the world. I decided I'd volunteer for a tour in Southeast Asia. Many of the pilots stationed in Germany had served in SEA and flown missions over North Vietnam. One of the pilots was a MiG killer who'd shot down an enemy aircraft during an aerial dogfight. They talked about their time in Vietnam as mission driven and fraught with perils, but nevertheless thrilling. I wanted to go where the real action was, do some good, and help win the war. While I was there, I could travel to other parts of the world: Australia, New Zealand, Hong Kong, and who knows where else. I saw it as an adventure.

When I announced that I wanted to go to the war zone, I got a variety of reactions. Most people thought I was crazy and didn't understand why I'd want to leave Europe. I dismissed all their concerns and decided to put my papers in to go to SEA. I waited and waited with no response. I was unaware of it at the time but, with the exception of nurses, there was an unwritten ban on assigning women to SEA. I decided to pursue this with the Wing Executive Officer, Colonel Doug Wood. We were friends, and he always called me "sweetie." If anyone could find out why I hadn't gotten a response, he could.

"Angel, I know you think you'd like to go to SEA, but you won't like it over there. There's no need for you to go. You're doing just fine here at

Bitburg. Why do you wanna leave? Besides, we'd miss you," he said with a warm smile.

"Doug, you know I have the highest regard for you, but I think the whole thing smells like bullshit. I think they don't want a woman going to SEA and they probably don't want a woman running an officers' club in a war zone either. I can just bet that's what it is."

"Angel, for God's sake, there's no need to go down that road."

"Doug, let's not forget that recalcitrant Base Commander at Morón who sent me to keypunch because he didn't want any woman running *his* officers' club."

"Yes, Angel, I know. You've told me that story several times," he said, rolling his eyes. "Besides, that's old news."

"Colonel, if they don't send me to SEA, I wanna know why. There shouldn't be any trouble finding me an assignment. They rotate yearly and people are coming and going all the time. A club manager's slot ought to open up relatively often."

Then I added the cherry to the Manhattan, "Well, Doug, I guess I could always write a letter to my congressman and yell discrimination. In fact, I've got one started in my desk drawer."

"OK, OK, Angel. I guess you're really serious about going. There's no need to write your congressman. Angel, I wish you'd reconsider going to Vietnam. I think you'd be making a mistake. But if you really wanna go, I'll see what I can do."

The threat of letters to congressmen sent chills up any commander's spine. Complaints ranged from, "The food in the chow hall stinks," to "My sergeant has me working 16-hour shifts with no breaks, and I'm only getting two hours of sleep."

Some were easy fixes, but congressional inquiries were still taken seriously. They indicated that the commander had lost control of his troops. When a congressional inquiry hit the base, everyone, from the commander down to the lowliest airman, jumped through hoops to prepare a satisfactory response.

I'm not sure whether it was my idle threat to write my congressman, or whether Colonel Wood pulled some strings, but in a matter of weeks, I got my orders to go to Southeast Asia. I was going to Udorn Royal Thai Air Base with a week stopover in Hawaii for o-club training. I was elated.

When Robert found out I was leaving he said, "Angel. My God. What prompted this? Why are you going so far away? When will I see you again?"

"It's only for a year, Robert," I said, "and then I'll come back to see you."

Before I left, my friends and coworkers threw me a couple of farewell parties and gave me lots of advice. "Save some money while you're there and you'll have a bundle when you get back." "Be sure to eat at Nick's Hungarian restaurant in Bangkok." "Buy some gold, and there's loads of precious stones—jade, opals and sapphires—that you can get for real cheap."

One has to ask why I did this. Why did I volunteer for one of the most controversial wars in American history, one that had little or no support back home? Why did I want to leave a place where everything was going well, I was accepted, and someone seemed to love me?

After all these years, I guess I'd have to say it was because—things were going too well. I needed to create some chaos or excitement. At the time, it all made sense. I wanted to travel, be part of the action, and do what the guys were doing. So, I was off to Thailand.

---

[1] Aircraft use knots to indicate airspeed, but for understandability I used miles per hour (mph). 100 knots = 115 mph.

Captain Angel Pilato wins her ride
in the F-4, April 1971
Getting ready to pull some "Gs"

Captain Angel Pilato gets suited up

Angel gets ready to go

Angel gets a splash down surprise

Thanks for the champagne, the plaque
and the ride

*Be kind, for everyone you meet is fighting a hard battle.*
—Plato, Greek philosopher (428 BC - 348 BC)

## Born a Little Too Soon

---

IT HAD BEEN ALMOST two years since I'd been home for any length of time. It was the summer of 1971, and my agenda was packed with things I wanted to do before shipping out to Southeast Asia.

During my thirty-day leave, I planned to complete my requirements for my private pilot's license. I had started to learn to fly while stationed at Offutt AFB, continued to pursue it at Bitburg, and was determined to pass the flight exam and get my license. I figured as long as I was in the Air Force and around all those fly boys, I should learn to fly too. Major Hank Hall, a friend from Bitburg, made the arrangements with one of the Aero Club instructors at Langley AFB, Virginia. I spent a week getting checked out in a Cesena 150 and passed my pilot's test by landing on a grass strip in Elizabeth City, North Carolina. I kissed Hank good-bye and headed to Rochester, New York.

When I got home, I started making the rounds to see all of my family members, which was a requirement imposed on me by my dad. With 18 aunts and uncles and triple the number of cousins, I was busy. I tried to spend as much time as I could with my dad, brother, and sister.

Charles was home on summer vacation from the University of Buffalo Law School. He'd never been the same since Mom passed away. He'd been home alone when she died, and he was plagued with thoughts that he could have done something to save her. Even though there wasn't, he was inconsolable and still felt pangs of guilt.

We discussed what he planned on doing after he finished law school. "I'll probably come back to Rochester after school," he said. "I've got friends here, and after all, Dad is all alone." He sounded resigned to the fact that this was his only choice.

"Charlie, I hope the reason you're coming back here isn't to look after Dad. He's old enough to take care of himself. He's 61, for God's sake, and he's still going strong. You don't have to look after him. You have your own life to live. If you stay here, this place will swallow you up."

"So you think I ought to traipse all over the world like you, and leave Dad here to fend for himself?"

"No, you don't have to be thousands of miles away. A couple hundred would be better than being right here in town," I replied, ignoring his sarcasm.

"Angelica, you can't imagine what it's been like. You haven't been here. Since Mom died, Dad has been acting more indecisive and erratic than ever."

"Well, maybe he's always been that way, and Mom covered up for his wackiness," I quipped.

"You don't have to worry; I can take care of myself," he said and then changed topics. "There's a party tonight at my friend Scahill's house. Do you wanna tag along and hang out?"

"Sure, ought to be fun."

He briefed me on the way to the party. "It's probably best if you don't mention that you're in the Air Force. It's not that kind of a group, if you know what I mean."

"I get it. A bunch of your hippie friends, right?"

"Well, I guess that's what you'd call them, but they're still my friends."

"Don't worry, I won't embarrass you," I said, understanding full well that I was on the opposite side of the political argument.

My brother was part of the baby boomer generation. I was born during World War II. We were only six years apart in age, but it seemed to make a world of difference in our points of view. I volunteered to join the military and found it strange that people were protesting the war. After all, if the government said it was our duty to fight communism, then we should line up and do our part for our country.

Charles was adamantly opposed to the war. He marched on Washington, carried protest signs, and wondered how he'd get out of it if he were ever drafted. Unlike Dick Cheney, he didn't know any influential people who could get him a single deferment, let alone five. He was my only brother, and his antiwar protests forced me to confront the reality that if he were drafted, he might die. I was deeply conflicted. I didn't want him to die, but wouldn't dying for your country be a worthy cause? Our family would be presented with a triangle-folded flag, a Purple Heart, a silver star, and a citation from the President. The bugler would play taps and the guns would issue a twenty-one-gun salute. It would all be very touching, but he'd still be dead. I didn't want him dead no matter how noble the reason.

On the other hand, he could be a JAG officer (military lawyer) or any number of positions that would keep him far away from the front lines. He could get in, do his time, get out, and forget all this protesting. Most of all, he could stop embarrassing me. It was easy for me to give him advice. As a woman, I didn't have to worry about getting drafted. Besides, as a club officer, I was in charge of serving booze, not spraying bullets. There wasn't any deadly threat in that. Besides, my view of the war was that we were the good guys, and the good guys always won.

During the past four years, I'd been in the isolated environment of the military. Most of my time was spent overseas without any television to influence my view on the war. Years later, when anyone would ever ask me about where I was during the sixties, I'd always say, "I was out of town." This made it easy for me to ignore what was going on in the States: the anger, the antiwar protests, the 1970 National Guard shootings of four Kent State students. My brother was my only contact with a diverse opinion, which was difficult to reconcile.

The military's definition of people like my brother was that they were yellow bellies, hippie-dippies and, worse yet, traitors. To the career military, the peace symbol symbolized chicken feet. Needless to say, I never mentioned my brother in any of my conversations with my military friends, and I assumed he didn't talk about what I did with much pride either. A lot was left unsaid between us during those turbulent times.

When we arrived at the party, a crowd was gathered in a small living room and an even smaller kitchen. They all had a ragged, unkempt look about them in their tie-dye shirts and tattered jeans. My brother fit right in. His long, black, straggly hair was quite a change from the clean-cut, altar boy look my mom had adored.

He started to introduce me around. "I want you to meet my sister, Angelica. She's home visiting for week or so."

"Good to meet you," said his friend Scahill, who wore a Santana t-shirt, had a big mustache, and was taking drags off a funny looking cigarette.

"Hey, Charlie, I didn't know you had another sister. Where've you been keeping her?"

"We don't let her out much," joked Charles.

His friend laughed and turned to me and said, "Glad you're out tonight. Can I get you a beer or something?"

"No thanks, I don't drink beer," I replied.

"OK, then. We got some rotgut wine over here, or we can get you a toke off someone's joint. Just help yourself. No formalities here."

"Thanks, I will," I said with an uncomfortable smile. I tried to blend in, which was a little difficult considering my clean-pressed, white cotton slacks and red blouse. It was like wearing clothes in a nudist colony. Luckily, no one asked me where I worked.

Then, out of nowhere, a woman came up to me and said in a loud, angry voice, "Oh, I hear you are one of those military industrial complex assholes in the Air Force, bombing the Vietnamese and killing all those innocent people. I don't know why the hell we are over there in the first place. Our guys are getting killed over this fucked up war, and it's tearing this country apart. How the hell can you be a part of that?"

Startled by the attack, I tried to defend myself. "I'm not one of those people. I am only in charge of—"

She continued her assault. "My husband came home from Nam and he's been all fucked up ever since. He can't sleep nights. He has endless nightmares and cold sweats." Her voice reached a feverish pitch as she pointed an accusatory finger at me, like she'd discovered the villain who had caused her husband's hardship. The whole room went quiet as everyone turned their attention toward the two of us. Finally, Scahill intervened. "Patti, come on, knock it off. This is Charlie's sister. She's not one of those kind. Come on, man. This is a party."

I thought, *if I could just explain I was in charge of morale, not murder, she'd understand I wasn't a bad person. I hadn't joined the Air Force to kill people. All I wanted to do was travel and maybe do some good for the country.* But you can't reason with a drunk. I politely said, "I'm really sorry about your husband. I'm just doing what I can."

She stormed off, mumbling to herself, and looking for someone to back her up. My stomach was churning.

Scahill turned to me and said, "Jesus, I'm really sorry. She's been drinking and she gets that way sometimes. She's been a little erratic since her husband came home. I'm really sorry."

"It's OK," I said, trying to keep my composure. "It's not your fault." What I really wanted to say was, *"Have you all gone mad? Is there no one with any sense left? Why are you blaming me for this war? You're all a bunch of degenerates!"*

My brother turned to me and said, "Angelica, I think we've had enough partying for tonight. Let's go."

"You've got that right," was my hasty response. We couldn't have hit the door fast enough.

Still shaken from the confrontation, we drove home in silence. I realized this was my first real encounter with the other side.

My brother turned toward me. "Angelica, I'm sorry you had to be subjected to that. It's not your fault. You were just born a few years too soon, that's all."

Three years later, after I was out of the Air Force and home for one of my yearly visits, my brother took me to a baseball game with some of his friends. After the game a woman came up to me and said, "Are you Charlie's sister?"

"Yes, I am," I said. I didn't recognize her.

"I'm really sorry about how I acted that night at Scahill's party. I've thought about it a lot, and I feel guilty about how rude I was towards you. I hope you can forgive me."

Then it hit me. It was Patti. Startled by her apology, I just looked at her. The years had made me forget the discomfort of that evening. Only the blatant unresolved issues of the war still lingered.

"Sure. No sweat," I replied. "It's OK. Besides you were right."

Astonished by my response she said, "I was?

"Yeah!" I said, "The war was totally fucked."

"Thanks," she said, smiling, and walked away shaking her head. After all this time, she was finally free of her guilt. I was envious.

*Each friend represents a world in us, a world possibly not born until they arrive, and it is only by this meeting that a new world is born.*
—Anais Nin, French-Cuban writer (1903 - 1977)

# The Meeting

My WEEKLONG ORIENTATION IN Hawaii gave me my first inkling that operating an officers' club in SEA might be more involved than I imagined. Horror stories were rampant about stolen supplies, difficulties dealing with foreign personnel, and problems with inconsistent procurement. Even though classes occupied most of the day, I did find time to book passage on a small plane and do some island hopping. I relished the islands' balmy breezes, the colorful flowers, and lush greenery. One of nature's wonders came into view, as we flew over the large island with its steaming volcano and black sand beaches. The water was so blue that it was hard to tell where the ocean ended and the sky began. It was breathtaking and I could see why people called Hawaii paradise.

The Hickam officers' club was a beautiful facility with all the amenities an officer could ask for—a dream assignment that I could only hope to get one day. Every night I ate dinner at the club and then went to the bar to chat with whomever happened to be there. That was one of the things I enjoyed about the officers' clubs. You could arrive at any Air Force base in the world, go into the bar, have a drink, and feel at home. Often you would see someone you had been stationed with, or meet someone new and discover you had friends in common. Even if you didn't know anyone, you felt like you belonged.

One night, while sipping a gin and tonic, I caught a glimpse of a familiar face. Colonel Bill Sifford was stationed at Offutt Air Force Base while I was there and was aid to General Joseph Nazzaro, the Commander of the SAC. I hopped off the bar stool and gave him a hug. "Colonel Sifford, it's good to see you again. How's it goin'?"

"Great Angel! How the hell are ya?" he said, returning my hug.

"I'm wonderful. Enjoying Hawaii to the fullest. Can I buy you a drink?"

"Sure, if you let me buy you one."

"OK, it's a deal," I agreed, and signaled the bartender.

"I'd heard you were on your way to SEA," he said.

"Boy, news travels at Mach speed in the Air Force."

He smiled and said, "I've been looking for you."

"You have? What on earth for? I can't be in any trouble. I haven't been here that long," I said with a grin.

"I'm stationed at Ubon Air Base in Thailand, and Colonel Thompson is the Wing Commander there," he explained. "When he heard you were going to be the club officer at Udorn, he sent me here to get you to come to Ubon. He wants you to be his club officer."

"He does? Well, that's interesting." I responded, rather surprised. Colonel Thompson was the Director of Maintenance (DOM) while I was stationed at Bitburg. I didn't remember saying much to him, and I didn't think he ever noticed me, let alone had an opinion about how I did my job.

As Colonel Sifford and I continued to talk, I remembered the practical joke we'd played on Colonel Thompson when he boxed in the schoolteacher's car at the club. I couldn't help but smile as my thoughts strayed to how we managed to get Marti's car out.

I quickly redirected my attention and told Colonel Sifford, "Please tell Colonel Thompson that I'm flattered by his offer to run his officers' club at Ubon, but I think it's too late to switch assignments. I hope he'll understand. I'm glad he got a commander's assignment. They're waiting for me at Udorn, and I'm already late getting there."

Colonel Sifford seemed disappointed. "Well, you'll like Udorn, Angel. A good friend of mine, Colonel Tim McHale, is going to be the Vice Commander. In fact, I saw McHale here the other day. He's getting briefed on his SEA tour this week."

"Good people, that McHale," he continued. "He's the best. You'll like him." Almost on cue, an attractive couple walked in the door. "That's McHale and his wife," said Sifford. "I'll have him come over, so I can introduce you."

McHale was handsome and lean, with black curly hair, thick eyebrows, and a round face that showed his dimples when he smiled. He had a twinkle in his eye that exuded a warm, friendly quality. His wife was a pretty, petite blonde who appeared to be an Air Force issue wife—charming and totally devoted to her husband.

Sifford introduced us. "Colonel McHale, Mrs. McHale, this is Captain Pilato. Angel and I were stationed together at Offutt when she was a second lieutenant." I extended my hand to both of them and said, "Nice to meet you, Colonel and Mrs. McHale."

"Please call me Barb," she said, smiling, which I thought made her down-to-earth.

Colonel McHale shook my hand and said, "Good to meet you, Angel."

Colonel Sifford looked at McHale and said, "Angel is going to be your club officer at Udorn. She's a good troop and did a bang-up job for General Nazzaro at Offutt. She'll do a hell of a job for you, too."

McHale replied, "That's good to know. I look forward to working with you."

That's all he had to say to win me over. Immediately, I sensed that McHale was a cut above the other officers. Or maybe, it was just that I'd always been a sucker for those Irish boys.

It started in first grade with Thomas O'Grady and it didn't stop there. In college there was Jack O'Sullivan and then Bill Maloney. My father became very concerned that I might get hooked up with one of those Irish boys. He knew I wouldn't listen to anything he said, so he asked my Uncle Sam, one of the attorneys in our family, to talk to me.

They confronted me together. "Sam, I don't know what's gotten into her. She'll only date these boys with an 'O' at the beginning of their name," explained my father. "God forbid that she might date somebody with the 'o' at the *end* of his name!"

My Uncle Sam looked at me. "Angelica dear, why don't you listen to your father and find a nice Italian boy to go out with?"

"Because there aren't any!" I said. "If I find one, I'll let you know." I ignored their concerns. Irish boys were fun and full of malarkey. Their attention was a feel-good drug that was just what this awkward Italian girl needed.

At the bar, conversation was flowing as fast as the alcohol. Sifford, McHale, and I bought each other another round of drinks, but it was getting late and my eyelids were drooping. Finally, I finished off my gin and tonic and said, "Gentlemen and Barb, I hate to break up this party, but I've gotta call it a night. I've got class in the morning. Bill, it was so good to see you again. Please tell Colonel Thompson 'hello' and wish him all the best—you, too." I gave him a good-bye hug. "Barb, enjoy your stay in Hawaii."

I looked at Colonel McHale, shook his hand, and said, "Nice meeting you, sir. I'll see you when we get to Udorn."

He looked at me with his intense blue eyes and said, "I'm looking forward to it too, Angel." Our eyes lingered a little too long before I looked away and withdrew my hand. I knew at that instant that he could be trouble.

*We don't receive wisdom; we must discover it for ourselves after a journey that no one can take for us or spare us.*

—Marcel Proust, French writer (1871 - 1922)

## The New Boss is a Woman

As THE AIRCRAFT DOOR swung open, a blast of Thailand heat filled the plane. I pulled my dark blue Air Force beret over my brunette hair pinned up in a French twist, gathered up my regulation 66 pounds of baggage, and readied myself for my new assignment.

The bright sun reflected off the white concrete with such intensity that even my dark sunglasses couldn't keep me from squinting. I had a panoramic view of the base, which appeared to extend over a vast area of flat land. The familiar sound of fighter jets taking off from the adjacent runway broke through the relative silence. The sign on the operations building read, "Welcome to Udorn Royal Air Base, Home of the 432nd Tactical Reconnaissance Wing."

I proceeded down the boarding stairs and walked towards the ops building where a group of Americans and Thais were waiting for me. One of the American guys came up and greeted me with a friendly smile. He was about an inch taller than I was in my Air Force black heels and looked to be in his late 20s.

"Welcome to Udorn. You must be Captain Pilato," he said as he put a fragrant floral lei around my neck and shook my hand.

"Yes, I am. But everyone calls me Angel," I said beaming.

"I'm Captain John Hightower, the outgoing club officer. We figured you must be her because you were the only gal that got off the aircraft."

"Thank you for the beautiful flowers. They smell like jasmine." The u-shaped lei had a thick neck ribbon that was strung with white pikake flowers. Some yellow-trumpeted plumeria hung at each end. The exotic aroma filled my nose.

Hightower started the introductions. "This is your boss, Major Bob Anastasio. He's in charge of Special Services."

"Good to meet you, sir," I said as I extended my hand. He was in his civilian clothes so I didn't salute.

"Welcome! Glad you're going to be with us for the next year, Angel," he said, grinning. "They ought to have a lot of fun with that name."

"They usually do," I retorted.

Hightower continued his introductions. "This is Captain Lee Paulson, base finance." Paulson was dressed in short-sleeved, olive-green combat fatigues and was the only other person in uniform besides me. He wore black combat boots, and his thick, gray-framed, G.I. issue glasses covered his face. He didn't have a hat on, and at about six feet tall, he stood above everyone in the crowd.

"And this is Pip. She's the officers' club secretary."

"*Sawadee kah!* Good to meet you, ma'am," she said as she put another flower lei around my neck.

"Thank you, Pip. Good to meet you, too," I said and shook her hand. She was about five feet tall. Her long, jet-black hair flowed down past her shoulders. Her turquoise, short-sleeved dress stopped about three inches above her knees.

"This is Dang, the daytime head waitress," said Hightower, "and Nit and Nat, two of your dining room waitresses."

"*Sawadee kah,* Kapton," they said in unison, with their hands in a prayer position and bowing ever so slightly.

I turned to Hightower and said, "What does *sawadee* mean?"

"*Sawadee* is the Thai greeting for hello and good-bye. If you're greeting a girl you say *sawadee kah;* if you're greeting a guy you say *sawadee krup.*"

"OK, I get it," and repeated, "*Sawadee kah, sawadee krup.*"

Then Hightower started introducing me to some of the Thai men in the group. "This is Pren, your head cashier—Khun Ack (Mister Ack), club maintenance—Supon, head cook—Jaturun, head bartender—and Tallman, the accountant. You can see why we call him Tallman." He stood taller than any of the Thais there, and he was even taller than Hightower.

One of the Thai women started handing out champagne glasses. Then a cork popped off a bottle of *Cold Duck* making a firecracker sound as it flew into the air. Everyone was smiling and laughing as Hightower quickly tried to capture the foaming pink bubbles with my glass. When everyone's glass was filled, Hightower offered a toast, "Here's to Captain Pilato. May her year here be a fun-filled one."

"Does everyone who arrives here get this red carpet treatment?" I asked.

"Around here, in our own small way, we try to do things with style," Hightower said, grinning.

"Wow, this is great," I said, "I think I'm going to like it here."

After all the introductions, the *sawadees,* the hand shaking, and champagne sipping, Hightower and I got into the small blue Ford pick-up truck and headed over to the officers' club.

"This is the officers' club pick-up," he said. "It's convenient for getting around the base and running into town. It's been a real lifesaver. Can you drive a stick shift?"

"Oh yeah, my dad taught me when I was 16, but it wasn't pretty. He took me out in his truck on a four-lane highway and kept yelling, 'ease up on the clutch!' After stalling out in traffic a few times, he gave up. All I can say is thank heavens for Driver's Ed."

"Well, at least that's one thing you won't have to learn here," he said, laughing.

"You know, Angel, all the Thai employees were anxious to meet you. They kept asking me, 'what does she look like?' I imagine they were quite surprised to see how attractive you were," he said in a flirty tone.

"Oh, how funny that they were concerned about what I looked like," I replied.

"Pip even got all spiffed up for your arrival," he continued. "She put on makeup and wore her hair down. She usually wears it up. She's a real good secretary, educated in the States at Berkeley. She'll be your translator when you need her. The rest of the staff is leery of her. They see her as Chinese, even though she was born in Thailand. The Thais aren't too fond of the Chinese, as they run most of the businesses. On top of that, they see her as part of management and not one of them."

"Hmm, that's good to know."

"That's not all they are concerned about. They've never had a woman officer for a boss."

"They'll get used to it." I said in a determined tone. "I have to get the job done just like anyone else. It seems I have to prove myself everywhere I go, even though I've got a degree in food management, lots of experience, and this is my third club assignment."

"Well, this place will be a challenge, that's for sure, but you can handle it," he said in a reassuring tone.

I nodded. "I do believe I'm the first woman assigned to SEA as a club officer."

"I wouldn't be surprised," he said. "If that's the case, we ought to get you an article in the *Stars and Stripes* newspaper and get you some press."

"I don't think that's necessary," I said reluctantly.

"I'll get the base photographer to come over to take your picture, and I'll send it in. Hey, it never hurts to have some good publicity," he persisted.

"Well, we'll see."

After he parked the truck, I got my first look at the officers' club. It was a dreary, liver-colored, nearly windowless, rectangular building. Rickety wooden steps led up to the front swinging doors, which were covered with squadron insignias ranging from stenciled paw prints to stick-on squadron patches from a multitude of units.

"There are no locks on these doors," I commented with a perplexed look.

"No need for locks," replied Hightower. "We're open 24 hours a day, seven days a week."

"I guess that's a good enough reason," I said.

Hightower proceeded to tell me everything I needed to know about running the club. "This is the dining room. The rug needs to be replaced," he said, pointing to the dirty, badly frayed carpeting. "It's been ordered but tied up in customs in a Hong Kong warehouse for six months."

"How come?" I asked.

"Seems we can't get a military plane in there to get it out—not a priority."

We walked through the dining room and through a swinging door. "Here's the kitchen." He said, "I'm afraid this is as good as it gets."

I looked around the crowded space. Equipment was jammed everywhere, supplies were piled to the ceiling, and a rusted-out steam table unit sat in one corner. I wondered how they could ever get any meals out of this place.

"I sent the cooks to Bangkok to give them some additional training on how to cook American-style food. That was interesting," Hightower said, rolling his eyes. "They do the best they can. After all, it's pretty hard to mess up steak and potatoes!"

We went outside to the back of the officers' club. Hightower pointed to the storage units. "Our freezers hold about $10,000 worth of inventory. We've got 'em on 24 hour watch."

"How often do the freezers break down?" I asked.

"This hot weather overworks the generators a lot, and we're constantly monitoring them," he said, pointing to the temperature log affixed to the freezer door. "Civil Engineers are on duty 24/7, too. When we call 'em, they're usually pretty good about getting right over here. And a case of cold beer doesn't hurt either."

Hightower walked past the freezers. "These are the liquor lockers, bolted and guarded at all times. A shipment of booze comes up from Bangkok once a week. We pay extra to have a Thai guard ride shotgun on the delivery truck. We started doing that after a couple of the clubs at other bases had their shipments hijacked."

"Shotgun? Hijacked? My God this sounds like the Wild West," I said.

"Pretty close. Liquor sells at a great price on the black market here in Thailand."

We went back inside and passed through the dining room where a Thai waitress was counting the silverware. John pointed to her and said, "The waitresses have to sign in and out for their silverware every day." He noticed my puzzled look and said, "They were stealing it left and right. If we didn't have them do this, the U.S. government would be supplying half of Thailand with silverware."

We went outside to the yard adjacent to the club. It was a huge grassy area surrounded by a brown wooden fence that was falling down in places. One small tree was growing in the middle of the yard.

Hightower explained, "This is where the Wing Commander, Colonel Gabriel, thinks we should build a patio for Bar-B-Ques and *sawadee* parties. Well, I never got around to it," he said, rolling his eyes.

"I gather you don't think a patio is such a good idea," I said.

"As I said, I never got around to it."

On our way back into the bar area, I stopped to read a sign posted at the entrance. It read "$1.95 All-You-Can-Eat Steamship Round of Beef Buffet

Lunch." There was no indication of what I was about to see next.

"This is our 'Topless Tuesday Buffet,'" Hightower said matter-of-factly as he led me through the door.

"I see," I said, as I found myself eye to eye with a topless go-go dancer, and tried not to show my embarrassment. A surge of heat flashed through my body making my skin flush. A young, small-framed Thai girl danced on top of a small, raised platform. Her long, charcoal black hair fell down the sides of her face and over her shoulders. Her eyes were outlined with heavy black eyeliner, and her ruby lips matched the color of her skimpy red g-string. Her black stiletto heels kept beat to the music of Three Dog Night's *Joy to the World* blaring from the jukebox. The lights in the bar were low, with only a red spotlight illuminating her breasts and the steamship round of beef. My eyes moved away quickly, feeling as though I had been caught in the act myself.

"Do you wanna eat lunch in here?" Hightower said with a subtle smirk.

"No, I'm not in the mood for beef today."

Even though the bar lights were low, I was sure he had caught my discomfort. I knew my body language must have been screaming *get me out of here*. Although we were in the bar for only a few minutes, it seemed like it took an eternity to reach the exit.

As we were leaving the bar, Hightower called my attention to one of the bar waitresses who was serving a beer to one of the pilots. She was very attractive and wore a skimpy mini skirt. She seemed totally blasé about being in the same room with a topless go-go dancer.

"That's Lot," he said. "She's Colonel Conrad's *tealock*. Don't try to do anything to her, or he'll be on your tail."

"*Tealock?* What does that mean?"

"He's sleeping with her. A *tealock* means 'sweetheart' or 'lover' in Thai. For us, it's someone you mess around with—someone who helps you get through the year. There aren't a lot of round-eyes around here, and the Thai gals are the next best thing. In fact you'll probably wanna get yourself a *tealock* while you're here. You might think about Colonel Gabriel, as your *tealock*. He's a good guy."

"What?" I said with a shocked look on my face. "Good Lord, I haven't even met the Wing Commander yet, and you've already got me sleeping with him?"

"It was only a suggestion. I've had a *tealock* while I was here."

"Who is it?" I asked.

"Dang, the head daytime waitress. She was at the airport today. She was the prettiest one there."

"One of your employees?" I said with a judgmental look.

"We were pretty discrete about it, but after all, we're in Thailand, not Stateside."

"I see," I replied, attempting not to appear like I was drowning in a flood of information.

As we walked through the lobby to the main dining room, Hightower stopped and pointed to a plaque on the wall. "This is our Honor Roll plaque. Anytime someone gets shot down, we add a brass name plate with the guy's name, rank, the date he was shot down, and whether or not he's KIA or MIA. Pip knows where to get them made," he said in a detached tone, like it was just another mundane part of his job. It struck me that all a guy got for losing his life was a small bronze name plate on a plaque in the lobby of an officers' club, outside a bar with a topless go-go dancer.

We sat down to lunch, and the waitress hurried over to take the boss' order. Our conversation continued. "We've got about 850 club members, and only about three dozen of them are American women. Most of them are nurses, a few teachers from the Air America compound, some civilian secretaries, and the rest are support officers. It's going to be interesting having a woman running the officers' club."

"Oh, why's that?" I said, trying to be nonchalant and not wanting to show I was annoyed.

"The guys are worried you'll try to change things," Hightower replied.

"What things?" I wondered why he was bringing this up.

"They're afraid you'll cut out all their fun stuff. You know how these fighter jocks like their amusement, and they want a place to let off steam. After all, there's a war on. They just don't want anyone messing things up."

"They needn't worry," I retorted. "I won't plant any flowers in the urinals."

Before I ever set foot on the base, rumors had spread that a woman was replacing Captain Hightower, the *wunderkind* club officer. I found out later that the Base Commander had extended Hightower's tour and tried to get me reassigned to another base. Maybe that was why Colonel Sifford had met me in Hawaii and asked me to come to Ubon. These guys probably thought I'd be a prudish, stiff-faced, unreasonable moralist who was ugly to boot. They were conjuring up tales that I'd make the bar waitresses wear long skirts, put a stop to the topless go-go girls, or cringe at them saying the "F" word.

Hightower laughed, "Well, the Air Force sure is changing. It hasn't been the same since they lifted the ban on women officers being allowed in the o-club stag bars."

"Yeah, who knows what they'll do next? They'll be letting women in the Academies and allowing them to fly airplanes," I said sarcastically.

Hightower replied, "Don't know if we'll see it in our time."[1] Then quickly added, "Frankly, I think women should be allowed to do any job they're qualified for."

Hightower had put me to the test on the very first day. At that moment, I decided exactly how I'd handle this assignment. I wasn't going to play into any of their preconceived notions of how a woman might run an officers' club. I knew I could run the club as well as any guy, and I sure as hell was no prude. All those repressive rules I'd learned in my 13 years of Catholic education were not going to stand in my way. No, that was not part of my life any more. I'd broken away from all of that guilt and trauma. I was free to do as I pleased without anyone or anything tugging at my conscience. After all, a stripper was just a stripper. It was no big deal. Besides, my job was to be in charge of morale, not morals.

---

[1] In 1975, a congressional mandate called for the integration of women into the U.S. Air Force Academy. In 1976, women entered pilot training. All the fuss about women flying seemed strange because during World War II the WASP (Women's Air Service Pilots) flew every plane in the Army Air Corps' inventory but weren't allowed to fly combat missions until 1993.

*There are no exceptions to the rule that everybody likes to be an exception to the rule.*

—Charles Osgood, American news broadcaster, journalist (1933 - )

## Phantom Roommates

AFTER MY BRIEF TOUR of the officers' club, I headed over to the BOQ to get my room assignment. The sergeant on duty asked for my orders and opened up a logbook. "Please sign in, ma'am."

I wrote, "Angelica Pilato, Captain USAF, 432nd Combat Support Group, 10 Sept 71."

"Your room is 309 in the BOQ building right next to us," he said. He handed me my room key, a set of white G.I. sheets, a pillowcase, and two small towels.

I walked over to the BOQ, lugging my overstuffed suitcase up three flights of stairs until I found room 309 on the corner of the building. I unlocked the door, took one look and thought, *is this where I'm going to have to live for the next year?*

The 11 by 13-foot room was crammed with two unmade twin beds, a refrigerator, a small G.I. veneer desk, and a dark green vinyl reading chair. The drab beige drapes were torn and falling down. The wax bean yellow walls were marred and dingy. There was no air conditioning, just a ceiling fan. Cut into the wall was a narrow three-foot opening for a closet with enough room to hang a few sets of uniform blouses and skirts. Underneath that space were three built-in drawers.

Next to the closet was a door that led to the bathroom. It was a standard latrine with a shower, two sinks, and one toilet. The door on the opposite side led to another BOQ room, which housed two male officers who'd be sharing the bathroom with me. For the entire year, I was at Udorn I never knew or saw who shared the adjoining BOQ room. Occasionally, I'd hear the sounds of someone slipping in and out, and sometimes I'd have to put down the toilet seat. Just to be safe, I always put my ear up to the door, knocked, and waited a second before going in. If there was a peek-hole, they never saw much because I was always sure to quickly wrap myself in a towel after getting out of the shower.

Since this sorry-looking room was going to be mine for the next year, I immediately set out to spruce it up. I asked the billeting office if they could initiate a work order to civil engineering to paint the room. I don't know why I even bothered to ask. A work order for painting a BOQ room wasn't going to be a top priority in a war zone.

I decided to take matters into my own hands and hired two of my Thai employees from the officers' club to paint the walls with white paint that I procured off-base. It looked as though the project was proceeding well until I spotted a monstrous looking creature scurrying across the ceiling.

I shouted at Khun Ack, "What is that thing?"

"It gecko, Kapton," was his casual response.

"Well, it has to go. Get that thing out of my room," I insisted.

"It good luck, Kapton," he said with a smile and continued painting.

"Oh really! I don't think so," I replied. I imagined waking up one night and finding this thing had fallen off the ceiling onto my head. The gecko had to go.

Khun Ack gave me a strange look and said, "No can do, Kapton, bad luck to take out. Good luck to have in house."

Then I repeated more emphatically, "I don't care if it is bad luck, you guys get it out of here." They both kept insisting, "No, Kapton. No can do, bad luck to take out."

My painting crew was ignoring me. I finally realized, if I wanted that thing gone, I'd have to get rid of it myself. But it had already disappeared. Then it occurred to me; maybe I shouldn't tempt the hand of fate and invite bad luck in a war zone.

That geckos are good luck was my first lesson in Thai culture. I understood that while I was in Thailand I was going to have to learn to honor the culture even if it meant living in peaceful coexistence with geckos. Occasionally, while I lay quietly in bed, my gecko would come out of hiding. I became fascinated with how its tiny toe pads appeared to stick to the surface, yet it glided rapidly and effortlessly on the ceiling. Nature had given these little creatures something unique that allowed them to walk upside down without falling, which was a relief to me.

With the painting completed and the gecko issue resolved, I bought some colorful material and commissioned an Indian seamstress to make some new drapes. I moved the two twin beds together and found a turquoise chintz bedspread. I hung some Thai temple rubbings on the walls and purchased an air conditioner from a sergeant who was rotating back to the States. The room was now my own. I could come and go when I wanted, entertain a lover without fear of being interrupted, and have a refuge when things got chaotic.

There remained one minor detail. What if they decided to assign another female officer to my room? That was always a possibility, even though there were only a couple of dozen of us on base. I decided to devise a little scheme that I thought would work perfectly. The billeting office was open 24 hours a day with people always checking in and out. Hopefully, with the large amount of turnover in personnel, troops on different shifts didn't talk to each other too much.

One night I decided to carry out my plan. I went to the billeting office, walked in, and said, "Evening, Airman." I was wearing my navy blue raincoat with my captain's bars on the shoulders, but my nametag was covered. I carried an overstuffed canvas bag and set my black leather purse on the counter.

"Evenin', ma'am, what can I do for ya?" replied the airman.

"I'd like to check in, please."

"Sure enough, ma'am," he said as he looked through his listings for an available room. "Let's see what we got here."

"Ah, there's no need to look," I interrupted, "I already know what room I want—room 309 with Captain Pilato. I roomed with her in OTS."

"Sure enough, ma'am. That'll work. Where are your orders?"

"Just a minute, I've got 'em here someplace." I searched through my purse. Then I got down on the floor, opened up the canvass bag and started pulling things out: bikini panties, slips, bras, and tampons started falling onto the floor. Appearing frustrated, I said, "Gosh, I must've left them on the desk at my duty station when I reported in today."

The airman watched with a slight look of embarrassment. "No problem, Capt'n, that won't be necessary. You can bring them in tomorrow. I'll take care of it. Just sign your name here," he said as he opened up the logbook.

I signed in as Sally S. McCoy, Captain USAF, 432nd Intelligence Wing, 1 Oct 71. I thought, *it would be fun to be an Intel Officer.*

I started picking up everything off the floor and throwing it quickly back into my bag. A couple of the other airmen in the office were grinning. They looked like they wanted to help me but seemed embarrassed about picking up my underwear.

I hurried back to my room smiling all the way. Now the room was all mine!

"Sally" dutifully paid her housing fee every month for the next five months until the Wing Commander announced that an additional fighter squadron from Homestead Air Force Base in Florida was arriving to supplement air strikes over North Vietnam. That meant they'd need more housing space. Still, I figured I was safe. After all, I had a roommate.

Unfortunately, the billeting office decided to do an unannounced inspection of all the officers' quarters. When they got to room 309, they found two twin beds merged together. Suspicious, they started poking around and discovered the uniforms in the closets only had one name on them—Pilato. The inspectors checked the billeting roster and saw that two officers were assigned to room 309, but where were Captain McCoy's uniforms?

It didn't take them long to realize that Captain McCoy was a phantom. Immediately, they turned the twin beds into bunk beds and assigned another female officer to my room. Captain Anna Mercedez from Montana turned out to be a lot like the gecko. She was quiet, kept to herself, and I didn't see her much. We tossed a coin for the lower bunk and she won. My days of comfort and privacy were over.

*Any change, even a change for the better, is always accompanied by drawbacks and discomforts.*

—Arnold Bennett, British writer (1867 - 1931)

## Orientation at Udorn Continues

WITH THE SHORT TIME Hightower had left, we continued my orientation. We took off in the club pickup, left the base, and headed to downtown Udorn. It was a confusing place to navigate. There were few street signs, and the ones that were in Thai script were undecipherable to an uneducated foreigner. Our truck stirred up the dust from the dirt streets as we dodged potholes and men pedaling *samlors,* the Thai equivalent of a pedicab or rickshaw.

Vendors lined the streets selling their wares. Many of their signs were in English to accommodate a lucrative American market from the air base. The women wore long wrap-around skirts with sleeveless blouses and plastic flip-flops. They stood over large woks sputtering with grease and made batches of fried rice, crispy spring rolls, and a host of other stir-fried dishes. Hightower urged me to try some, but they'd warned us in Hawaii not to eat the food from street vendors. So I decided against it.

He pointed out the road where all the jewelry shops were, and we decided to stop at Pat's Souvenir Shop next to the Udorn Hotel. Gold chains, bracelets, and Buddha amulets were in abundance, along with jade in all shades and shapes. Princess rings made from opals, rubies, and sapphires were only $25, which was dirt cheap by American standards. John took me to another jewelry shop and pointed out a four-seasons bracelet. It was18-karat gold and beautifully designed with eight panels, each intricately carved with Chinese symbols and flowers that represented the four seasons. It was called a *tealock* bracelet.

"Why's it called a *tealock* bracelet?" I asked.

"Angel, it's called a *tealock* bracelet because lots of G.I.s give their Thai girlfriends one when they leave. You know, it's sort of a thank you for taking care of them while they were here."

"I see." I said, " What do they do with it after their lover is gone?"

"It's worth a lot of money to a Thai, and they can sell it and get *maak maak baht,* "[1] he said, rubbing his fingers and thumb together.

We continued to explore the bustling little town. We watched women weaving all types of wicker furniture and baskets, and skilled craftsmen carving teak that had been logged by elephants in Thailand's northern jungles. They feverishly chiseled ornate tri-paneled screens, heavy furniture, and carved elephants in every size imaginable. Elephants made of multi-colored ceramic were also plentiful. The elephant, Thailand's national symbol, has been revered for centuries. Thai kings rode into battle on top of their howdahs[2] armed for battle to fight the Burmese. Now, tourists paid to ride on one.

John pointed out the Buddha statues and paintings that appeared in every shop. He said, "Thailand is predominantly Buddhist.[3] I think you ought to get yourself a Buddha, so you'll have good Karma while you're here."

"Karma, what's that?" I inquired.

"The Thais believe that, if you do good works in this life, when you're reincarnated, your next life will be a better one," he explained.

"That's good to know. So, I'm gonna have to come back and do it all over again?" I mused.

Hightower showed me the Thai version of a beauty shop. "If you want your hair done, this is it. You can get a manicure and pedicure, too." It was an open-air shop with one sink in the back for shampooing hair. They used a small basin for a pedicure and then tossed the water out into the street.

At night we made the rounds of the local bars that were dark, cave-like places blaring loud rock music. They were crowded with Thai women sizing up the young airmen to see if they could score a *tealock* that would deliver some cash. Hightower pointed out the Yellow Bird massage parlor, a spot frequented by officers and airmen. The price varied with the services rendered.

One Sunday afternoon Hightower, his *tealock* Dang, and I ventured out to see the countryside. We got as far as the Laotian border, about 60 miles north of the base. Vientiane, the capital, was a stone's throw across the Mekong River, which flowed through a large portion of the Eastern border of Thailand. That was as far as we dared to go, as Laos was off limits.

As we looked across the border, Hightower said, "Air America is flying covert missions over there."

"I thought we weren't supposed to be there," I said with a puzzled look.

"Right," he quipped. "Air America's entire compound is on the other side of the base—their planes use our runway. Some of pilots brought their families with them. They've got a school for the kids and even a small o-club."

"I see. I guess that's why they call them covert."

On the way back we saw some local farmers tending to their water buffalo. A couple of kids were riding them bareback across the river. Carved teak bells hung around the water buffalos' necks to help the kids find them if they strayed too far. Hightower decided to stop and talk to them.

"*Sawadee,*" we called out. They looked at us and returned the friendly greeting. Hightower turned to Dang and said, "Ask them if we can buy the teak bells."

Dang laughed and said, "John, they think you *bâa bâa bor, falong.*"[4]

"No, they won't. Tell them I'm going to pay them and ask them how much."

With a smile she obliged and began a lengthy conversation with the Thai farmers. They laughed and smiled. I was sure she was right; they probably thought the Americans were crazy. Why would we want the bells when we had no water buffalo?

Dang explained that we wanted a souvenir. They had no concept of what a souvenir was. She must have done some fancy talking because they finally agreed on a price of 10 *baht,* or 50 cents, for each set of bells. The farmer removed the teak bells from the water buffalo and handed them to Dang. We smiled, gave them the *baht* and a slight bow as we said, "*Sawadee.*"

Hightower handed me the bells and said, "Here's your first souvenir from Thailand."

"Great, I love them. I'll hang them in my BOQ room. They'll add a little charm to my décor."

Hightower was very helpful and it was fun having someone show me around. He even got the base photographer to come over and take my picture to send to the *Stars and Stripes* newspaper. They printed a short story with a headline that read, "It's a WAF! Club Officer First in SEA." The article ended with a quote from me: "I know it will be a challenging assignment. The club has a fine staff, and I'm looking forward to working with them just like I did in Spain and Germany." Just how challenging remained to be seen.

One afternoon, preoccupied with learning the ropes of my new assignment, I ran into Colonel Tim McHale who had recently arrived from Hawaii.

A smile lit up my face as I saluted him. "Hi, Colonel McHale. I see you made it here all right. Welcome to Udorn!"

"Thanks, Angel," he said, returning the salute and the smile.

"My framed pictures of my F-4 ride are on their way here from Germany. I can't wait to show them to you," I said enthusiastically.

"I'm looking forward to seeing them. You were very lucky to get a ride in that F-4, not many non-pilots have done that." I was surprised that he'd remembered my first name and appeared to recall our conversation in Hawaii.

Colonel McHale had an impressive military record. He was a West Point graduate, a "ring banger" as the pilots affectionately called them, and had made colonel "below-the-zone," which meant he was promoted ahead of his peers. His claim to fame was that he'd been selected to fly the first operational flight of the SR-71 Blackbird, the Air Force's most advanced, supersonic, reconnaissance jet. He'd probably flown every aircraft in the Air Force's inventory and why I thought he'd be remotely interested in seeing my F-4 pictures never crossed my mind.

"Yeah, I'll say, that ride was the thrill of a lifetime. By the way Colonel McHale, I understand you're going to be the chair of my advisory council. That's great!"

"Yes, I asked for that assignment," he said, smiling.

"Well, I guess I got lucky again," I flirted. "Gotta go, Colonel. See ya. I'm looking forward to having you here," I called out as I hurried off.

Later, when I got back to the club, Hightower told me that he'd met McHale. He thought he'd be a good Vice Commander to compliment Gabriel's style. Hightower said, "I heard McHale is an outstanding leader and the troops really liked him. I think he's on his way to being a star candidate for general. Then he added, "You know, Angel, I think he'd make a good *tealock* for you."

"For Christ sake John! Why are you so intent on getting me a *tealock*? Is that all you think about is sex?" After I said it, I realized he's a guy, what else would he think about?

"I just want you to have a good time while you're here. It's going to be a long year if you don't have someone to occupy your time." I began to think that maybe his advice was more realistic than perverse.

Hightower's departure came quickly. A few of us went to the airport to see him off. His *tealock* Dang and some other employees were there on the tarmac to wish him farewell. I watched Dang crying and hugging Hightower. I heard her say, "John, I go to States with you. Please, John, I love you."

He pulled away from her, leaving her to be consoled by the other Thai women who were there. He walked towards me with a somber look on his face and said, "I knew this wasn't going to be easy."

"John, how can you leave her like this?" I asked.

"Angel, I've gotta go. This'd never work back in the States. These kinds of things never do. She'll get over me. I told Colonel Gabriel she'd make a good *tealock* for him. He'll treat her right."

"What! You're passing her off to the Wing Commander?" I said, shaking my head. "John, all I can say is, you're a real cad."

He didn't respond, but I noticed his eyes were getting a little watery. He went back to Dang, gave her one final hug and handed her a small box. In it was a *tealock* bracelet, his thank you for her year of service. He grabbed his bag and took off up the boarding stairs, leaving Dang in tears. He never looked back.

This was the first of many good-byes I would witness at Udorn. I realized that Dang had given herself to Hightower with the hopes of going to the States. After he left, all she could say was, "John—he number ten," which meant he was no good. Her feelings of sorrow and sense of disappointment bridged our cultures. I vowed this would never happen to me.

[1] A *baht* was worth about five cents at the time.

[2] A *howdah* is a seat, usually fitted with a canopy and railing, placed on the back of an elephant. It was used most often to carry wealthy people or for hunting or warfare.

[3] Buddhism is practiced by 94% of the Thai population, but the law protects religious freedom. Muslims comprise about 5% and animists, Christians, Confucians, Hindus, Jews, Sikhs, and Taoists make of the rest of the population.

[4] *Falong* is a Thai term to indicate an American. Loosely translated it means a fair-skinned person.

# Welcome to Udorn September 1971

Captain John Hightower, Captain Angel Pilato, Major Bob Anastasio and Khun Ack

Thai staff welcoming "New Boss Lady" with *Cold Duck*

## It's a WAF!
## Club Officer First in SEA

Capt. Pilato

"The men are a little apprehensive about a woman club officer, but they don't know that is my trade," quipped Capt. Angelica Pilato. The captain recently took over as secretary of the Udorn Officers' Open Mess, the first Woman in the Air Force (WAF) to hold a Club Officer's position in Southeast Asia.

The captain was graduated from Rochester, N.Y. Institute of Technology with a bachelor of science degree in institutional management. She also worked as a food services supervisor at Michigan State University.

Besides being the first woman club officer in SEA, Captain Pilato is a licensed civilian pilot with over 150 hours in the air.

"I know it will be a challenging assignment. The club has a fine staff and I am looking forward to working with the Thais just as I did the Spanish and Germans."

Captain Angel Pilato
First Air Force woman Club Officer

# Udorn Air Force Base, Thailand

Welcome to Udorn – main gate entrance

Fighter squadron hootches

432nd Tactical Reconnaissance Wing
Commander's Office

SECTION TWO

# Reality Sets In

*Bachelors know more about women than married men. If they didn't,*
*they'd be married, too.*

—H. L. Mencken, American journalist, satirist (1880 - 1956)

# The Rules for Sex and Marriage in the Military

IN THE MILITARY, RULES and regulations govern everything from setting up an office filing system to repairing a jet engine. They're organized a little bit like the Bible—book, chapter, and verse. For example, Air Force Regulation (AFR) number 200-2 deals with how the Air Force should respond to a threat from UFOs. The purpose and scope of regulation AFR 200-2 is defined in Para 1.a., and on it goes. There isn't much thinking involved—simply pick a topic, find the number, and follow the reg.

The military also has many unwritten rules that are either handed down through oral tradition or picked up through osmosis. For those unfamiliar with the military, I've decided to disclose the unwritten rules for sex and marriage. My years of managing officers' clubs and hours of field observation make me uniquely qualified to summarize these rules. This may be the first time they've ever been seen in print.

In keeping with the Air Force documentation system, I've assigned names and numbers to the rules. It's worth noting that not all military men follow these rules, only the ones I associated with. That's why I can consider myself somewhat of an authority on the subject.

## AFR 69-4
### Rules for Sex and Marriage in the Military
### Para 1. Rules for sexual behavior for military married men

*a. Do not cheat on your wife.* Note that this rule is suspended when on TDY (temporary duty away from base), or PCS (a permanent change of station to a remote location—usually a war zone), and when unaccompanied by your wife or family.

(1) TDY can also be defined as "temporarily single while out of town." For example, when on TDY if a woman asks, "Are you married?" An appropriate response might be, "I'm separated from my wife." This is not entirely false, since technically you have been separated from her ever since you left your base.

(2) PCS can also be defined as "permanently convinced of being single while away from home and unaccompanied."

*Historical note:* In the late seventeen hundreds Vice Admiral Horatio Nelson of the Royal British Navy was reputed as saying, "When East of Gibraltar, men, everyone's single!"

***b. Do not blab.*** On TDY or PCS it is imperative to take an omerta, or code of silence. If an officer cheats on his wife, do not tell. The correct mindset is: If you can get away with it, then "good on ya."

*Note:* Even though everyone is supposed to keep a secret, everyone likes to gossip, which often puts this rule in jeopardy.

## Para 2. Rules for sexual behavior for career military married men

The key word here is career. These rules must be followed if a man has any intention of making the military a career.

***a. Do not cheat on your wife.*** This is a hard and fast rule unless you are TDY or PCS and unaccompanied. If so, refer back to Para. 1.a.

***b. Be discreet.*** Discretion is the better part of valor. Encounters must be kept private. In the event of a public encounter, be cordial and exchange pleasantries, but keep it brief. Getting caught is likely to result in a transfer to a remote location like Thule, Greenland. Sordid affairs and high-ranking promotions are incompatible.

***c. No touching of body parts.*** This includes pats on the butt, pecks on the cheek, or prolonged eye contact. Public flirting is out of the question. This requires immense self-control but must be taken seriously, or it may result in undue embarrassment and raise something more than a red flag.

A polite handshake is acceptable. A handshake with an undetected glide of the forefinger across the palm of the hand is acceptable and useful when communicating the desire to do the "wild thing."

Never leave the officers' club with her. This is a direct violation of Para 2.b.

*d. Tell no one.* Control your urge to brag. This can best be accomplished by controlling the amount of alcohol consumed. Blurting out, "Suzie, yeah, she's really got great tits," while enjoying time off with your drinking buddies at the bar will severely limit your promotion opportunities.

*e. Select a woman who understands the rules.* This is imperative. Women who understand the rules are: military single women, women married to military men, and some single women. However, most single women want to get married and like to blab. The most acceptable single woman is one with no connection to the military, but finding one requires a lot of time and effort.

*f. Maintain appearances.* Maintaining the appearance of a loyal family man is paramount to becoming a candidate for promotion.

## Para 3. Rules for sexual behavior for single, non-career military men

*a. There are no rules.* However, there are a few helpful guidelines: It is considered poor judgment to sleep with any of the military wives on base. It is OK to sleep with military wives while on TDY or non-military wives from on or off-base. There is NO limit to the number of single women that a single man can sleep with—women are suckers for a man in uniform. In the name of discretion, it may be in your best interest to select one woman on base, one off-base, and perhaps another while on TDY. Brag all you like. It makes the married men envious, and it enhances your stature to be known as a guy that "gets more ass than a toilet seat."

## Para 4. Rules for marriage for single career military men

*a. Get married.* Marriage gives the appearance of a stable, solid, all-American officer.

*b. Marry the right woman.* The right woman is one who understands that her husband's career comes before hers. She must know how to deal with the military brass and their wives (who wear their husbands' rank on their shoulders), to entertain guests with grace and flare, to dress conservatively but with a certain amount of style, to speak diplomatically, to smile a lot, and if possible, to be blonde. She must know how to play bridge or be willing to learn. The right woman is an essential part of the total promotion package.

*c. Stay married.* Divorce is out of the question.

As a military woman I understood these rules, but I also had to decide how to get through the year. So, I figured I'd create a few rules of my own. The old rules that restricted women sexually had been thrown out during the sixties. Free love reigned. Why couldn't a woman sleep with whomever she wanted? The guys could.

I was overseas and far enough away from any watchful eyes. Besides, I was single and not career military. If I chose a *tealock* who was married, I'd have to protect myself from the ultimate disappointment—the day when he returned home to his wife. I decided one of my rules would be to just have some fun— no need to fall hopelessly in love. Maybe I'd even have several *tealocks*. After all, why be monogamous? The guys weren't.

If an Air Force pilot's unwritten motto was the three "Fs"—to Fly, Fight, and Fuck, then my three "Fs" would be—Find 'em, Fuck 'em, and Forget 'em!

*Everything is determined, the beginning as well as the end, by forces over which we have no control…we all dance to a mysterious tune, intoned in the distance by an invisible piper.*

—Albert Einstein, German-American, scientist (1879 - 1955)

# Just a Matter of Time

WITH HIGHTOWER GONE, I soon got into the swing of running a 24/7 o-club. With officers coming and going, a squadron *sawadee* party was always in the works to celebrate their hails and farewells. There was a monthly newsletter to write, entertainment (including go-go dancers) to be booked, inventories to be watched, and the popcorn machine in the bar that had to be kept running and full. Most people were surprised when I introduced myself as the new club officer, but they didn't seem too bothered by it as long as I didn't make any changes that would affect their fun.

I saw him one evening while I was making my rounds. He was standing at the bar having a drink with some of the Squadron Commanders. I walked right up and greeted him with a smile. "Evening, Colonel McHale." I barely acknowledged the other officers that were with him. If they said anything, I didn't hear it.

"Hi, Angel, can I buy you a drink?"

"Yes, sir. Thanks, I'll have a gin'n tonic," I said.

We chatted over our drinks for a while, and then I said, "It's getting late. I've gotta get going."

"I was just about to leave," he replied. "I'll walk you back to the BOQ." He finished his drink and put his glass down on the bar.

"Thank you, sir, but that won't be necessary. It isn't that far."

"I'm going right past your BOQ to get to my hootch. It's on my way," he insisted, as he picked up his flight cap.

"OK then, I guess that settles it," I replied. I didn't really have a choice. In the military you don't set boundaries; they're set for you by rank.

As we were leaving, I overheard Colonel Joe Kittinger, the Triple Nickel Squadron Commander, mumble something under his breath. The Triple Nickel was what they called the 555th Tactical Fighter Squadron (TFS).

McHale ignored it, but I shot him an annoyed look and said, "He's just walking me to the BOQ!"

When we reached my building, I said, "Thanks for walking me to my Q, Colonel. I enjoyed talking with you tonight, and thanks for the drink. Good night, Colonel McHale."

As I turned away and started to walk up the stairs he said, "Wait a minute. Where's your room? I'll walk you to your door."

"You don't have to do that, sir. It's way up on the third floor," I said, pointing up to my room. I knew what walking me to my door meant.

"It's no trouble, Angel. I want to," he said with a determined voice.

I knew he wasn't going to take no for an answer. As we walked up the stairs, I filled the moments with idle chatter. "You can recognize my room from all the rest. It's the one with the turquoise curtains. I had them made when I got here. I paid my Thai employees to paint it, bought an air conditioner, and it looks pretty good now."

"I'm sure it looks much better," he replied.

When we got to the door, I knew what was coming. It was as predictable as thunder following lightning. "Are you gonna invite me in?" he said. "I'd like to see what you've done with your room."

"No, sir…Not tonight. I think it's best not to," I said.

"Why not?" he asked.

"Well, sir, if you come in, I know it's going to lead to nothing but trouble," I replied and continued to shake my head no.

"Trouble! Is that what you call it? Let's sit down here and talk about this." He sat down on the top step. I could've said goodnight and walked inside, but I didn't. I sat down on the narrow steps right next to him, with only a sliver of space between us.

"Look, sir—it's like this," I began.

"Please call me Tim," he said.

"OK…right…thanks. Look, Tim, as I was saying, it's like this. If you come into my room, we both know what's going to happen. And I don't wanna get anything started with you. It's not that I don't find you very attractive. I've always had a thing for you Irish boys. But you're married, and I really don't wanna get involved with a married man. Surely, you can understand that."

"OK, Angel," he acquiesced. "Maybe it won't be tonight, but you and I both know it's only a matter of time before we go to bed with each other."

"Oh, you think so?" I said as I thought, *am I that transparent?*

Then he leaned over, put his hand on my face and kissed me gently on the lips. I didn't move. I welcomed it. Then, realizing what had happened, I jumped up and said, "Good night, Tim," and opened the door to my room.

A knowing smile came over his face. Our little dance had begun. I did my best to deflect his subtle overtures, but while my words stated one thing, every other part of me was screaming, *Take me, you fool!*

He knew it. I knew it. It was just a matter of time. Having a Vice Commander for a *tealock* was exciting, even flattering, but I knew it would have to be kept top secret. Keeping my emotions in check wasn't going to be easy and resisting his advances was going to be a bigger challenge.

*Once I make up my mind, I'm full of indecision.*
—Oscar Levant, American musician, writer, and actor (1906 - 1972)

# A *Tealock* or Two

ONE AFTERNOON AT THE o-club I heard my secretary, Pip, laughing and chatting with someone in the outer office. A few moments later, she interrupted me and announced, "Kapton, Major Mendellson is here to book a *sawadee* party." I looked up and saw him standing at the top of the stairs.

The first thing I noticed about him was his smile, which made his eyes twinkle. It wasn't the typical mischievous fighter pilot look, but rather a pleasant, personable one. His wavy, salt and pepper hair gave him the distinguished appearance of a seasoned professional. Pip seemed delighted to see him, and she appeared to be charmed by his warm, friendly demeanor.

She introduced us. "Captain Pilato, this is Major Mendellson. He is the Operations Officer from the 13ᵗʰ Squadron."

I held out my hand and smiled. "Nice to meet you, Major. I'm Angel."

He looked straight at me and said, "Call me Pete, call sign—Mouse." That was it. No pretense and no cracks about by name being Angel. I liked him immediately.

"Come on in and sit down, Pete," I said and pointed to a chair. "I'm not going to ask you how you got your call sign."

"Probably best not to," he grinned.

I pulled out a party requisition form and asked, "So, when's your party?"

"Next Wednesday. A couple of guys are leaving and a couple are rotating in."

"OK," I said as I wrote down the details. "How many will be there?"

"About 40-45," he said.

"What time do you wanna start the bar and what time for dinner?"

"Let's see. Start the bar at 1830, and make dinner at 1930. That's about right."

"What would you like to have as the entrée? We've got prime rib and then there's always prime rib. How does that sound?" I quipped.

"OK," he said with chuckle, "I think we'll go with the prime rib." He appeared to get a kick out of my humor, which was another point in his favor.

I proceeded to fill in the blanks, "You'll probably want a baked potato with sour cream, chives and bacon bits, rolls with butter, a green salad with assorted dressings, and French cut green beans au gratin." In the military we had our ways of making even frozen green beans with canned mushroom soup and cheddar cheese sound gourmet.

"Yeah, that'll work," he replied with a pleasant look.

"Do you want a head table?" I asked.

"Yeah, we'll need one of those."

"How many at the head table?" I queried.

He paused briefly, and then said, "Let's make it six."

I said, "You can always change it later, if you want. What would you like for dessert? I can make you a tasty *Kahlua* or *Crème de Menthe* parfait. What d'ya think?

"Perfect idea. Let's make it the *Kahlua.*"

Then he said, "I'll leave all the details in your hands. I know it'll go off without a hitch. Thanks for making it easy for me."

"Hey, no problem. Happy to oblige, Major. I mean, Pete."

As he started to leave my office, he turned around and almost timidly asked, "Would you like to come to the party?"

Surprised, I said, "Will you be taking me?"

"Yes, of course," he said with just a touch of fighter-pilot confidence.

"Then I'd love to," I said. I was elated about being invited to a fighter squadron party. This was a switch from how the fighter squadrons had treated me in Germany. I had only been invited to one party there, and my invitation was rescinded because others were concerned that I really wasn't part of the squadron. That tactless gesture cost them extra for that party.

"What time can I pick you up and where?" he asked.

"You can pick me up right here in my office just before the party."

"Great, I'll look forward to it," he replied, still smiling.

"Me, too. I'll see ya then, if not before," I said and returned his smile.

I was looking forward to going to my first fighter squadron party as an attendee. My thoughts turned to, *what would I wear?* For *sawadee* parties, every squadron donned flight suits specially made in the colors that designated their squadron. The 13th Tactical Fighter Squadron wore black, the 14th Tactical Reconnaissance Squadron wore maroon, the Triple Nickel wore dark green, and the Combat Support Group, which was my squadron, wore white. I decided that the traditional flight suit with long pants needed an update, so I instructed the Indian tailor to make mine with hot pants instead.

A squadron is like a fraternity. It has an identity, and the guys take on that identity. The 13th Tactical Fighter Squadron was known as the Panther Pack. When we arrived at the party, it was a sea of pilots in black party flight suits. They wore white ascots imprinted with a black paw and an embroidered patch with their squadron logo—a black panther affixed to the front of their flight suits.

Pete started introducing me. "This is Angel, our new club officer." Everyone was friendly and welcoming. They flattered me with comments like "You sure look better than Hightower," and "How did Mendellson get so lucky all of a sudden?"

At the party I found out that Pete had originally had orders assigning him to another base in Thailand, but he had already decided he wanted to fly with 13th TFS. When the plane stopped at Udorn, he got off, went straight to personnel, and had them change his orders. I'm not sure how he did that. But he was a pilot, and pilots have pull.

Pete was a fighter pilot, but he wasn't the stereotypical kind whose bravado and confidence came from knowing he was one of an elite group of men flying the hottest planes on the planet. He had a quiet strength about him, one that came from knowing who he was. He didn't have a need to boast about it. It was evident from his interactions with the other squadron members that they respected him. I assumed he'd probably make full colonel someday. He wasn't in the Air Force to play the games one had to play to make general; his passion was flying.

After the party, Pete walked me back to the BOQ. When we got to the bottom of the stairs I said, "Pete, I had a great time tonight. Your squadron sure knows how to have fun. Thanks so much for including me."

"Of course," he said, "Why not? We're glad you joined us."

I gave him a quick kiss on the cheek and hurried upstairs. He never asked if he could come up, which was a nice change. His shyness made him even more attractive.

I knew that Pete was married, but it didn't really matter since the rules were different for him. He was PCS without his wife and family. To everyone at Udorn, he was as good as single. He continued to take me to all the 13<sup>th</sup> squadron events, and I always got to sit at the 13<sup>th</sup> Panther Pack table in the bar. I'd become an adjunct member of the squadron, which was a big deal. In the Air Force, there are the pilots and the "support pukes," and I was "support puke." You're nobody in the Air Force unless you're a pilot, and even then there's a pecking order. The fighter pilots are on top, and the cargo pilots, or "trash haulers," are on the bottom. I couldn't be a pilot, but I could do the next best thing and hang around with them. Interacting with them made me feel like I was part of the action. I got to hear firsthand what was really going on. Pete made that possible.

I now seemed to have a choice between two *tealocks*. Both men were married, but according to the rules—everyone was single in SEA. I could have a clandestine affair with a full colonel on his way to making general, or an overt one with an ops officer whose only desire was to fly and make it home alive. Being a woman in SEA was proving to be much more complicated than I'd imagined, but maybe it didn't have to be. Maybe I'd have a *tealock* or two.

*Surprises are foolish things. The pleasure is not enhanced and the inconvenience is often considerable.*

—Jane Austen, English writer (1775 - 1817)

# The General's Surprise

As THE WEEKS PASSED at Udorn, I came to realize that operating a club in a war zone was very different from running one Stateside. One major difference was the absence of families. No wives were here to rein in their husbands—no one around to care what the guys did at night. Hiring strippers for *sawadee* parties was simply a part of my job—part of keeping the troops' morale high. So, I didn't even bat an eye when the A-B-Triple-C Squadron's (ABCCC)[1] project officer came in to book a party and asked how much a stripper cost. "Twenty-five dollars," I said as I pulled out a party requisition form and wrote, "one stripper, 1900 hours, $25" in the box marked "miscellaneous."

I hadn't come in to supervise the *sawadee* party, but instead I left Sergeant Russell, the night manager, in charge. The morning after the party, I stood at my desk and read the notes in the night manager's log. "The ABCCC *sawadee* party—nude girl came out of a cake—sat on General Searles' lap—general's staff confiscated everybody's camera—removed the film—the general and two colonels left pretty pissed off—be in later tomorrow to fill you in on details."

I immediately picked up the phone and called Sergeant Russell. I surmised the Wing Commander and Base Commander had already heard about the incident at his morning stand up briefing and the Base Commander, in turn informed my boss, Major Anastasio, who was, at this very moment, probably on his way over here.

I finally reached the sergeant. "Good morning, Sergeant Russell, this is Captain Pilato."

"Morning, ma'am, I know why you're calling," he said.

"You got it. OK, fill me in on the fiasco that happened last night."

"Well, Capt'n, a couple of officers brought in this big cardboard box shaped like a cake and set it in the middle of the dining room floor. The stripper was inside. Then everyone filed into the bar and started drinking a lot of drinks."

"Yes, go on—then what?" I said.

"The stripper was in that cake the whole time they were at the bar and during dinner. After dinner, the Squadron Commander got up to say his hails and farewells. Then a young officer got up and said, 'We have a special performance tonight for our birthday-boy captain,' I didn't get his name, and before anyone knew it, she broke through the top of the cake bare-ass naked."

"You mean she had absolutely nothing on?"

"That's right, ma'am."

"Oh, my God! What happened then?"

"The stripper started bumping and grinding. Everyone was whistling and hollering. She started walking around and then sat on the first lap in front of her—General Searles. Then the cameras started flashing, and the general stood up with a jolt, and—"

"Nevermind," I said. "It all went downhill from there."

"Yes, ma'am. The stripper seemed surprised that the general wasn't pleased she'd picked his lap. The general said something to his aides. Then they went around to everyone who had a camera and ordered them to remove the film. They took the film and stormed out behind the general. That's about it, Captain."

"Well, I think that's quite enough. We're gonna have repercussions over this one. You can count on it."

"Sorry, Capt'n. There was nothing I could do. It all happened so fast. I don't think anyone planned on her sitting on the general's lap!"

"I know. It's not your fault. Thanks for filling me in."

No sooner had I hung up the phone when in walked my boss.

"I heard you had some excitement here last night!" Anastasio said with an insipid smile.

"Yes. You heard right. The boys were at it again. God, how could they do anything so stupid? Letting that stripper come out of that cake bare-ass naked and sit on the general's lap. And then, to add insult to injury, they took pictures! What were they using for brains?" I said in a raised voice.

"You know what they are using for brains, Angel!" he said, rolling his eyes. "Now the Base Commander wants a full report."

"That figures," I said. Then I started laughing and shook my head. "General Searles is such a prune face. He hardly ever comes to the club except for official events. He's probably still in shock!" The general set himself apart from the troops and wasn't very friendly. In fact, he hadn't said more than good evening to me the whole time I'd been here, and that's only because I greeted him first.

I continued, "I can only imagine the headline in the *Stars and Stripes* newspaper if they get a hold of this: AIR FORCE TWO-STAR GENERAL GETS A REAL PIECE OF CAKE!" Major Anastasio started laughing too, but then checked himself. "This is no laughing matter, Angel." But it was hard to stifle our grins.

Then Major Anastasio's face became serious. "Angel, you are not going to like this, but General Searles has sent down word that there'll be no more nude dancers in the club, no more strippers, no more Topless Tuesday, no more…" As he continued, all I could hear was no more, no more. All I could think of was that I would be blamed for all of this. The guys would think that I'd gone along with it and that I hadn't stuck up for their rights. Or worse yet, they would think it was the excuse I needed to cut out all their fun stuff.

"But Major Anastasio," I interrupted, "How can he do that?"

"Well Angel, he's a two-star general. That's how."

"I know that, but he doesn't have to be here to take the flack. I'm going to have to listen to these guys bitch and moan about losing their fantasy girls!"

In the months following the incident, it was determined that the club would be allowed to have go-go dancers, but they had to remain onstage and keep all their clothes on. The guys harangued me incessantly with their complaints. Every time I was confronted with a question about why they couldn't have their strippers, I gave them a rapid-fire response. "Look guys, don't blame me. Blame General Searles and those numb nuts from the A-B-Triple-C Squadron who let this whole thing get out of hand." I repeated this response so many times that I sounded like a barker at a carnival.

It didn't matter. They weren't hearing it. One pilot's remark stuck with me. "Angel," he complained, "I bet, if Hightower were still here, he'd get the strippers back!" Bull's eye!

Behind the scenes, I was doing everything I could to get the general's boys to have him rescind his edict. I confronted them every time they came into the club. I even went to the Base Commander and the Wing Commander to see if they would intercede. But the fact was, they had more important matters to consider: running air operations, reporting target results, and notifying next-of-kin their son or husband was KIA, MIA, or a POW. The chance of a reversal was extremely slim.

Still, while I was aware that more important matters needed to be dealt with, I also knew that my fight was symbolic. As a WAF running an o-club, many people figured I just didn't have the *chutzpah*[2] to fight this one, let alone win. I was going to show them I could do it, and getting their strippers back would be my proof.

[1] ABCCC (A-B-Triple-C) was an integral part of the Tactical Air Control System. It was the airborne command and control communications squadron that flew the C-130s. It functioned as a direct extension of ground-based command and control authorities. Its primary mission was providing flexibility in the overall control of tactical air resources, maintaining positive control of air operations, and communications to higher headquarters. http://www.globalsecurity.org/military/systems/aircraft/ec-130e-abccc.htm.

[2] *Chutzpah* is a Yiddish word meaning backbone or more succinctly "balls."

*What we can do and want to do is projected in our imagination, quite outside ourselves, and into the future. We are attracted to what is already ours in secret. Thus passionate anticipation transforms what is indeed possible into dreamt-for reality.*

—Johann Wolfgang von Goethe, German writer, philosopher (1749 - 1832)

## It's Time

THE WING COMMANDER WAS intent on building a patio at the o-club. My predecessor had managed to avoid the project by assuring the Wing Commander it was next on his list. Now it was on my to-do list, and the Wing Commander started in on me. "Angel, it sure would be nice to have a patio for the pilots to have their *sawadee* parties."

I couldn't imagine why he thought the pilots, in their sweaty flight suits, would want to spend time outside. It seemed they were always trying to escape the heat and high humidity by retreating to the comfort of the air-conditioned o-club. But the Wing Commander wanted a patio, and by God, he was determined to get it. I liked Colonel Gabriel and wanted to please him, so I told him the patio was my top priority. I said, "Consider it done." I thought, *how hard could it be?*

As president of the o-club advisory council, Colonel McHale wanted to make sure the project was going to happen this time. After all, he wanted to please the commander, too. He came into my office one day after lunch and said, "Angel, I wanna talk with you about where you are with the plans for the commander's patio."

"Yes, sir. I've drawn up a rough sketch of what I think would work, and I can show it to you. I think Colonel Gabriel is going to like it. When would you like to do that, Colonel?" I replied eagerly. "Did you wanna look at it now?"

He said, "I don't have time right now. I'm sure you've done a lot of work on it, and I'd like to see how it's progressing. How about coming over to my hootch tonight at about 2100 hours, and we can discuss it then."

"You want me to come over to your hootch?" I said, somewhat taken aback.

"Yes, I'll be free then."

"OK then, I guess I'll see you tonight," I said and thought, *going to his hootch to talk business seemed innocuous enough.*

"Which one is your hootch?"

"It's across the street from your BOQ, right next to the Wing Commander's, the third one down."

A few minutes before nine o'clock, with the patio plan under my arm, I left my BOQ room and headed for his hootch. I knocked on the door, and he opened it with a warm smile. "Hi, Angel, come on in."

"Good evening, sir."

"It's Tim, remember?"

"Yes, of course—Tim." I knew he'd given me permission to call him Tim, but as a captain I was uncomfortable calling a colonel by his first name. There was always a chance that I'd slip up in public and say, "Hey, Tim—how's it goin?'" I stepped into his living quarters. "So, this is how the other half lives," I said as I surveyed his domain.

"I'll show you around, but let me fix you a drink first. What'll you have? It's a gin'n tonic, isn't it?"

"Yes, that's right, sir—I mean, Tim."

I leaned up against the counter of his galley kitchen, set the patio plan down, and watched him while he mixed us a drink. The first swallow was a little heavy on the gin, but I continued sipping it as he gave me the grand tour. Another colonel's hootch adjoined his, but its entrance was around the back. He had a separate bathroom and a bedroom with a double bed. The living room was sparsely furnished with a couch, coffee table, a couple of vinyl covered chairs, and end tables. Although it looked like a traditional G.I. issue room, he certainly had more space than my 11 by 13 BOQ room.

We discussed the plans for the patio for all of ten minutes. He liked the concept for the design and encouraged me to move ahead with it. He told me the Wing Commander was excited that his project was finally moving ahead and that it would be completed during his tour of duty. He fixed me another drink and invited me to sit down on the couch. I did, and he sat down right next to me. He drank some of his bourbon cocktail and then put it down on the coffee table as he moved closer to me. I felt what was coming. He put his arm around my shoulder and said softly, "It's time." He brought his hand to my cheek and started covering my face with soft kisses.

"It's time?" I mumbled. We wrapped our arms around each other, and I eagerly returned his kisses. We moved into his bedroom where we couldn't get our clothes off fast enough. I'm sure the drinks made me more vulnerable. However, this encounter merely fulfilled a fantasy that I'd imagined from the first day I met him in Hawaii. He knew it, and I knew it. It had just been a matter of time.

This was the first of several rendezvous to come. Sometimes we discussed our work, and sometimes we didn't talk at all. Often I'd go to his hootch late at night, unannounced. I'd check from my BOQ window to see if his staff car was there. If the coast was clear, I'd hurry out of my room, dash across the street, tiptoe up the wooden stairs of his hootch, and slip in the front door without making a sound. I felt like a cat burglar who got her thrills not from stealing, but from knowing she might get caught. I found my way through the sparsely lit living room and into his bedroom. Only the sound of the overloaded air-conditioner hummed in the background. The reflection from the outside floodlight streamed through the small window and onto his bed.

As he lay there, he didn't look like a commander-in-charge, but just a man asleep in his powder blue nylon pajamas. On the nightstand was his command post brick,[1] a reminder that he was in fact a commander-in-charge. His uniform hung neatly on hangers on the door hooks; his shiny black shoes were under the chair; and his military flight cap was on top of the bureau ready for the coming day.

Before the first light of dawn, I'd kiss him good-bye, check to be sure no one was around, and scurry back to my BOQ room where I'd try in vain to recapture a few hours of lost sleep.

Tim McHale was the first man I got involved with at Udorn. He and I were never seen alone in public. He was on his way to becoming a general, and he wouldn't put his career at risk by getting caught in a fleeting affair. No, he was too smart for that. If we had been stationed together on a base in the States where he was with his wife and family, we may have flirted, but we would never have slept together. He would never have done anything to jeopardize his career or publicly disrespect his wife. Even so, his charisma would still have captivated me, like it did everyone else. I would have gone overboard to do a good job for him with the hopes that he'd notice me.

Many a commander caught breaking "the rules" inevitably paid for his indiscretion with the loss of any further advancement in the Air Force. I understood our arrangement. This was strictly a frivolous wartime romance. I was infatuated with him and flattered by his attention. And I knew the rules.

---

[1] Command post brick is a two-way radio carried by the commanders to communicate with each other and the command post. And it looked like a brick!

*It's the constant and determined effort that breaks down all resistance and sweeps away all obstacles.*

—Claude M. Bristol, American writer, WWI soldier (1891 - 1951)
From *The Magic of Believing*

## The Commander's Patio

COLONEL GABRIEL WAS JAZZED about the patio becoming a reality. The problem was that in my eagerness to prove I could get the job done, I told the colonel that I would have the patio completed by his birthday on January 21st. It was almost November. What was I thinking?

I knew that in order to get the patio built, I'd need some help. I started with Khun Ack, my maintenance man. He was a pleasant man, stood about five-foot-three, and always had the kind of smile on his face that made me wonder what he was up to. I took him outside, walked him around the o-club backyard, and told him about Colonel Gabriel's plans for a patio.

"He wants a covered patio for people to eat outside, a Bar-B-Que, and a garden," I explained.

"Yes, ma'am, bar-bee-q!"

Khun Ack spoke English fairly well, but sometimes things got lost in translation, especially with me talking at New York speed. "Yes, Khun Ack, a Bar-B-Que. You know, an outdoor fire to cook food like steaks, ribs, and hamburgers?"

"Ah yes, Kapton." He said, nodding his head.

"OK, Khun Ack. Can we do it?" I asked.

"Yes, Kapton. Can do easy."

With his commitment, the patio started to take shape. What evolved from my sketchy drawing and our brainstorming sessions was a plan complete with an eight-foot round Bar-B-Que grill, a cement floor, a new fence around the yard, a roof made out of ribbed, plastic panels that extended out from the club's main roof, and a garden with a water pond around the acacia tree. Tim McHale and the advisory board approved the final plans, and we were on our way.

It wasn't long before I encountered the first of several roadblocks. I guessed that Hightower had realized all this and decided it wasn't worth his effort. Now, I was on the hook.

I asked Khun Ack how many men we would need to build the patio.

"Maybe five or six, Kapton. I have friends who are carpenters. We can hire them." This was good news. If he were to supervise this entire project, he'd need a crew who could follow his directions.

I went over to the Civilian Personnel Office, which was in charge of hiring all the foreign nationals and keeping our agreements with the Thai government concerning their employment. I told the head of personnel, Mr. Martin, about the patio project and dropped the commander's name with the hopes that it would speed up the process.

"No, you can't hire any carpenters because the officers' club doesn't have any slots for carpenters," he said. "The regulation requires that if you want to create a slot for a full-time carpenter, you'll have to write a job description to justify the position. And then we'll have to get it approved."

"Oh, boy, I need five or six," I said. "How long does it take to get a job description approved?"

"Three to four months."

"Three to four months!" I said with a shocked look. "I'll be PCSed out of here by then!" I thought for a moment and said, "OK. Can I hire some part-time help?"

"Yes, but not carpenters because—"

"Yes, yes, I know," I interrupted. "The o-club doesn't have a slot for a carpenter. OK. Can I hire janitors?"

"Yes, but you can only hire part-time janitors because you already have your allotted number of full-time janitors, and you'd have to justify the need for another full-time position."

"I see, and that'll take three to four months." I was getting more frustrated by the minute, as I kept searching for the right questions that would yield the right answers.

Finally I said, "OK, I get it. I'll get back to you."

I decided to hire two part-time "janitors," two part-time "dishwashers," and two part-time "bus boys." I filled out the job requests and sent them to Civil Personnel in staggered intervals. On each job request, I wrote, "English

Not Required." None of Khun Ack's men could speak English, and they didn't need it because he'd be translating for them. If English were required, it would delay the process further because all "English Required" new hires had to be tested for their level of fluency.

When the request for the janitors was sent over to personnel, Khun Ack went with two of his friends to complete the application process. Then, the kitchen cook went over with the part-time dishwashers, and the dining room supervisor went with the last two busboys. They all got hired, and we were over the first hurdle.

Getting the supplies for the project presented another challenge. Regulations required that all supplies be bought from the United States. A purchase order had to be submitted to base procurement with the specifications for the item. Procurement then went out for three competitive bids. After the bids were received and reviewed, a vendor was selected, and an order was placed. Then we'd wait for the item to be delivered, which could take months.

Khun Ack knew where to get everything we needed quickly from sources off-base, but to do that we needed a written justification. We had to make a clear case that the item we wanted to purchase "on the economy" (off-base) couldn't be obtained from sources in the States in a reasonable amount of time. We got around this requirement by writing the specifications so tight that it was impossible for procurement to find the item in the States in the time we needed it.

This worked perfectly for getting the ceramic tiles for our Bar-B-Que grill. While I was in Bangkok, I found some white square tiles with a blue pattern that would look great. I attached a sample of the tile to the purchase order. There was no way procurement could fill this request from the States, so they gave us permission to purchase the tiles off-base. With the approval in one hand and Thai *baht* in the other, I headed to Bangkok to bring back the boxes of tiles. After a few more incidents like that, procurement just winked and gave me approval for all my requests. We also got some items through "midnight requisitioning"[1] and bartering. It was surprising what a person could get done with a case of cold beer and a petty cash fund with receipts labeled "supplies!"

As the work progressed, I thought of other improvements that would enhance the design of the patio, like a window on the side of the building.

I thought it would be nice for people eating in the o-club dining room to be able to look outside onto the patio and garden. I suggested this idea to Khun Ack, and he said, "Can do easy, Kapton." He proceeded to have his men cut out a six by three-foot hole in the outside wall. When the Base Civil Engineer came in for lunch and saw the gaping hole in the wall, he said, "Angel, just what do you think you are doing?" The Base Civil Engineers (CE) were responsible for maintaining all the buildings on base and approving any, and all, changes to the building's structure. Also, the regulation stated that any change had to be accompanied by the appropriate paper work.

I looked perplexed and said, "You know, there isn't one window in the dining room, and I thought a window would add a nice touch."

"You've gotta have a work order submitted to do any changes to the building. Don't you know that?" he said.

"I'm sorry, sir. I got so excited about the idea that I sorta got ahead of myself. I'll fill out the paperwork and hand-deliver it to you this afternoon."

"And I suppose you'll want me to approve it after the fact?" he sighed.

I gave him a sheepish smile, hesitated a little, and said, "Yes, sir, that sure would be kind of you." One thing I'd figured out in the Air Force was—it's always better to ask for forgiveness than permission. That little circumvention cut six weeks to three months off the approval process.

One day when I was in downtown Udorn, I saw a building with rock siding I liked. I asked Khun Ack if he knew where we could get rock like that for the o-club. "Yes, Kapton," he replied. "I have a friend who can get them."

Everything in Thailand was about bringing a friend some business. As a thank you for spreading the wealth, this friend gave the person who brought him the business a little kickback money. This was added on to the cost of the bill, and no one was the wiser. The military didn't sanction such arrangements, but that's the way the Thais did business. I looked at it as a referral fee. Even with a referral fee, the items would cost less to purchase on the economy than having them shipped in from the States. After all, we weren't ordering a $900 toilet seat. I wanted to get this patio done on time, and if that meant Khun Ack got a small gratuity, well so be it. Without him, this patio wasn't going to be built.

We hired a few more "busboys" to take down the old fence in the back yard and erect a new one. We hauled in dirt from God knows where (no doubt from one of Khun Ack's friends) to landscape the yard and put in a garden.

I found a portable electric fountain that could be placed in the little pond Khun Ack's men built around the acacia tree. I directed Khun Ack to run an extension cord up the tree and connect it to the electricity that operated the hanging lights on the patio ceiling. Things looked like they were coming together, but I was still crossing my fingers that we'd be ready for the grand opening on Colonel Gabriel's birthday. Every time I looked out my office window and saw what still needed to be done, I'd ask Khun Ack, "Are we going to finish all this on time?" He just kept saying, "Yes, Kapton. No problem. Yes, Kapton. No problem."

Three days before the opening, Khun Ack came in with a concerned look on his face and said, "Kapton, the bar-bee-q grill!"

I looked up and said, "What's the matter with the Bar-B-Que grill?"

"We need 24 tiles to finish."

"What? Two dozen tiles! Khun Ack, I bought those tiles in Bangkok. How am I gonna get them up here in time for you to install them? Maybe they won't even have the same tiles!"

He didn't say anything except, "We need 24 tiles, Kapton."

I called my secretary into the office and said with a sense of urgency, "Pip, you've gotta go to Bangkok to get these tiles today. Find out when the next plane leaves for Bangkok." Fortunately, the Royal Thai Airlines had regular flights to and from Bangkok out of Udorn. "Do you think you can find the place?" I asked as I searched through my desk drawer to find the card with the address on it.

"Yes, Kaptan, I will find it." Khun Ack handed her one of the tiles, and she was off. She found the ceramic shop, and luckily they still had the tiles. That night, she arrived back on the last plane with Khun Ack and his men waiting to put the remaining tiles on the Bar-B-Que grill. For the next two days, the workers rushed to put all the last minute touches on the patio.

On January 21st, we were ready. As we awaited the commander's arrival, everyone gathered around for the ribbon cutting celebration scheduled for 1730. The Bar-B-Que pit was fired up and ready to serve a free steak dinner with all the trimmings to hundreds of hungry officers. At about 1715, I looked around for the scissors to cut the ribbon, and they were nowhere in sight. I asked Bob Barnett to hustle over to the Base Exchange to buy a pair of scissors on the double. He returned just as the commander's staff car pulled up to the officers' club.

I greeted Colonel Gabriel with a huge smile and escorted him outside to his brand new patio. He stepped up to the ribbon. Khun Ack and all his troop of part-time dishwashers, janitors, and busboys stood close at hand. The commander smiled and thanked them for their hard work as Khun Ack translated. Their faces beamed with a sense of pride and satisfaction. The commander and Khun Ack held the ribbon and I handed the scissors to the commander. The crowd clapped as the ribbon fell to the ground, and then everyone rushed for the buffet line. The smell of juicy barbequed steaks filled the air, and it did indeed seem like a down-home backyard Bar-B-Que. Tables were set on the patio and out on the lawn to accommodate the crowd. The little fountain sprayed water up in the air, and a myriad of colorful orchids hung from tree branches and patio eaves.

We served about 300 people that night. Colonel Gabriel ate dinner with some of the aircrews. When he was finished, he walked over to me and with a big smile said, "Angel, you did one hell of a job getting this patio built. Your o-club troops did a super job. I know the officers are going to enjoy many fun times out here. It's going to be a good morale booster, and you made it happen."

Elated, I stood up and said, "Thank you, sir. I hope this was a happy birthday for you."

"It couldn't have been better."

"Many more birthdays, sir."

I was so happy that the commander was pleased. Now that the patio was completed, I had to admit that the commander was right. The patio turned out to be a wonderful addition to the club and a fun place for many a *sawadee* party.

---

[1] Midnight requisitioning means permanently borrowing something from somewhere else on base—in other words stealing!

# The Commander's Patio

The Commander's Patio – Before

The Commander's Patio – After

Bar-B-Que with all the tiles in place

# The Commander's Patio Ribbon Cutting Ceremony

Wing Commander and all the patio builders
"The Janitors" – "The Dishwashers" – "The Busboys"

Khun Ack, Colonel Charlie Gabriel, Captain Angel Pilato

*'Friends can be said to 'fall in like' with as profound a thud as romantic partners fall in love.*

—Letty Cottin Pogrebin, American writer, women's rights advocate, founder *MS* magazine (1939 - )

# Fast Friends

CAPTAIN LEO TARLTON THOMAS, JR. was the quintessential Southern gentleman. He was a charming, good-looking fighter pilot with jet-black hair and hazel green eyes, a great sense of humor, and a Kentucky drawl to go with it. Women found him so attractive it was rumored they'd often trip him to get his attention. All these qualities, plus the fact that he was an Academy graduate put him in line to be one of the Air Force's rising stars.

This was Leo's second combat tour in Vietnam. His first tour was at Takhi Air Base in the F-105s. He flew with the Triple Nickel squadron, but his primary duty was serving as the Wing Commander's Executive Officer. His official duties involved managing the commander's administrative affairs, planning the commander's gatherings, and a host of other duties as assigned. Aside from his official duties, he kept the commander informed of any "unofficial" news or problem areas on base. As Wing Exec, this put him up close and personal with the commander, which positioned him for a below-the-zone promotion and his pick of future assignments.

One of Leo's primary functions was serving as a gatekeeper for the Old Man, a term used affectionately by the troops to refer to the Wing Commander. So, if you wanted to see the "Old Man," you had to get past Leo. That was of no concern to me. Anytime I wanted to see the commander, I just came right in and said, "Hi, Leo, I need to see Colonel Gabriel," and he'd reply, "Go right in Angel. He always has time to see one of his good-looking WAF officers!"

Leo's affable, laid-back manner made it a pleasure to assist him whenever he needed something. One afternoon he came into the club and said, "Hi, Angel. How's my favorite club officer doing?"

"I'm doing everybody I can and the easy ones twice," I said with a grin.

"And how's my favorite Exec Officer?"

"Couldn't be better," he replied.

"What can I do for ya today, Leo?"

"Colonel Gabriel is having dinner on Friday for some brass, and he wants some white wine that sounds like poosay!" He said smiling and raising his eyebrows.

"Oh, he does, does he? I think you're looking for Pouilly Fuisse, a white burgundy from France."

"That's it. Do you have any?"

"Let's go over to the package store and see what we've got in stock." When we got there, I perused the shelves and said, "Boy, Leo, this is your lucky day. I can't believe it, but here it is, the last bottle of Pouilly Fuisse," and handed it to him.

Leo said, "Good on ya, Angel. You made it easy for me. After this event I'm goin' on R & R to see that new baby boy of mine."

"That's great. So tell me, when are you taking off?"

"After this party for Gabriel, I'm flying one more combat sortie on Sunday. Then on Monday I'm headed back to the good ol' U.S. of A. to see my Leo Tarlton Thomas the Third." He said with a proud father's smile.

"That's coming right up." Then I counted on my fingers and said, "That's four days and a wake up." A "wake up" is what they called the last day on a person's tour of duty. "Does the little tyke have your green eyes?" I asked.

"No, the wife says they're brown. I couldn't get leave when Kay had the baby and now he's seven months old. I can't wait to see him. I'll be teaching him to fly soon."

Grinning, I asked, "Leo, am I ever gonna see some pictures of the kid?"

"I'll take some when I get home. I had a couple when he was a newborn, but you know they all look alike—red and wrinkly. The little rascal is getting bigger now, and I'll probably be able to tell who he looks like when I see him."

"I'll bet the kid is a cutie, if he looks like his dad!"

"That remains to be seen, Angel. I've gotta say, you are a bigger b-s'er than some of these fighter jocks you serve around here."

"Well, Leo, I've learned at the feet of masters!" I quipped.

"OK, kiddo. I'll see ya when I get back. Thanks for taking care of me with the special wine for the Old Man. Charge this to Gabriel's account."

"No problem, anything for you and Gabriel. Have a good trip. Give that kid a hug from me. And don't forget the pictures, Leo. See ya later."

That was the last time I saw Leo. On Sunday, December 19, 1971, we got word that we'd lost another aircrew. It was Leo Thomas and his navigator, First Lieutenant Daniel Poynor, 25 years old, from Enid, Oklahoma. They were downed by heavy artillery fire over Laos, about five miles north of the city of Ban Na Mai. What we soon learned about Poynor was that he'd come in from Clark Air Base to train with the Triple Nickel, and this was his first combat flight. He'd had to sign a waiver to fly combat missions because his older brother, David, had been killed in1965 in a F-105 training accident.

Laos is a landlocked, mountainous, and thickly forested country about twice the size of Pennsylvania. For practical and political reasons, the U. S. military denied being in Laos. Declared "neutral" by a Geneva Accord in 1962, which stated no foreign personnel were to operate in Laotian territory. However, the U.S. violated that rule, as did China, Thailand, and North Vietnam. The CIA operated a "secret war" in Laos. With the unofficial approval of the Royal Lao Government, Air America pilots regularly bombed North Vietnamese forces that came across the border into Laos.

I heard that Air America pilots wore gold bracelets when they flew over Laos. If they were shot down and survived the crash, they could use them as barter. Another, more ominous rumor was, if a pilot survived a crash, they took no prisoners. They executed him on the spot.

The Pathet Lao insurgent forces were allied with North Vietnamese communists and supported by the Chinese. They were in a constant struggle with Hmong tribesmen over who should rule Laos. They continued to fight to overthrow the Royal Lao Government, which was aligned with the U.S. The Lao Government supported the recruiting and training of some 30,000 indigenous tribesmen in an attempt to strengthen anticommunist strongholds.

The U.S. committed hundreds of millions of dollars to the war effort in Laos against the Pathet Lao, which was unsuccessful. In 1975, the Pathet Lao took control of the country, ending a six-century old monarchy. Estimates are that the tonnage of bombs dropped by U.S. bombers between 1964 and 1973 exceeded the entire tonnage dropped over Europe during WWII.[1] Today, evidence of the bombing remains in the form of huge land craters, undetonated bombs, and ordinance embedded in the landscape.

Information about Leo's crash was intermittent. All we were able to find out was that he was flying the lead aircraft on a strike mission over a heavily fortified artillery site. His plane had been struck down in an area called the Plain of Jars which got its name from the hundreds of huge, ancient, gray stone jars that dot the landscape.[2] This diamond-shaped region in northern Laos spans about 500 square miles and is covered with rolling hills, high ridges, and tall elephant grass on the flatlands.

The Forward Air Controller (FAC), Eddie Pickel, had given Leo the coordinates for the target. Apparently, he didn't have a good fix on the target and his wingman, Major Roger Carroll[3] heard him ask for a clarification. As the aircrews flew overhead, heavy artillery fire kept blasting at them from all directions. Suddenly, the transmission ended, and Leo's aircraft exploded. His wingman looked for evidence of parachutes, but none were seen. Radio calls were sent out, but none were heard.

After we heard the news, several of us sat around my tiny BOQ room drinking Mateus Rosé wine. Our conversation revolved around our collective disbelief that this could have happened to Leo. After all, he was one of the good guys. Yes, all the guys who got killed in this war were good guys, but we didn't know them as well as we knew Leo. We were hopeful that we'd hear good news of Leo and Dan's survival and rescue.

Even though the FAC reported he'd witnessed a 37mm missile hit Leo's aircraft straight through the cockpit, Colonel Gabriel was optimistic and declared the crew MIA. For nine days, rescue crews flew over the crash site hoping to pick up a radio signal from the aircrew and looked for any evidence that they might have survived. Their efforts yielded no results, and on December 28th, with the urging of Leo's Squadron Commander, Joe Kittinger, Colonel Gabriel pronounced Leo and Dan KIA.

When I heard this news, I was distressed and went directly to the commander's office and said, "Colonel Gabriel, why did we stop looking for Leo? He could still be out there. How can you just declare him KIA?"

"Angel, it's been ten days and there's been no sign of them. We've done all we can. You know I thought the world of Leo and I'd like to think he's still alive, but it doesn't look that way. Besides Angel, it's better for the family this way."

"What do you mean?" I said.

"MIA keeps the family from moving on. KIA closes the door on any hope that they're still alive. It's the best thing to do."

"I see. So what you're saying is that odds are he's dead, and we're not going to find him—right?" I said.

"Yes." He said with a somber look.

My eyes welled up as I quickly turned and exited his office. A cold chill ran though my bones. Until now, the war seemed to be taking place somewhere else, but it had just become personal. There wasn't anything fair about this war, or any war for that matter. A pilot could get shot down on his first mission, his 100th, or maybe never. The whole thing was a crapshoot.

As I drove back to the club, I thought of Leo's wife, Kay. At first, when she received the news that he was MIA, she must have remained optimistic. Now, instead of meeting Leo at the airport with his new baby boy in her arms, she'd be getting a "regret to inform you" visit. A dark blue staff car would drive up to her house. She'd be holding the baby in her arms, and her body would stiffen with the realization of why the car was there. She wouldn't want to open the door, even though she knew she must. The Chaplain and the Personal Affairs Officer would deliver the dreaded news and leave her with a report that stated her husband "could not have survived."

That was the thing about plane crashes. The crew went down with the aircraft. For Kay, there would be no flag-draped coffin returning home, no twenty-one-gun salute, no burial, and no real closure. His body was God knows where in Laos, in commie territory, with no prospect of recovery. With no grieving rituals, the loss process seemed incomplete, almost like the loved one wasn't dead, but merely permanently out of touch.

When you watch a war movie, it's easy to fantasize about the glories of war, but it's different when it becomes a reality. With this new awareness, I wasn't sure I could make it to the end of my tour. A little part of me had gone down with Leo. No, I hadn't known him for that long, but we had become fast friends. That's the way it was in the Air Force. You got to know people quickly, and you either liked them, or you didn't.

Colonel Gabriel scheduled a memorial service at the base chapel, maybe because Leo was his Exec Officer, or maybe because I kept bugging him. I can't remember if we had any other memorials on base that year. If there were, the chaplain would have been pretty busy. Maybe I just didn't go to any of them. For me, most of my memorial services were held in the bar.

Twenty-three years later, in 1994, with the cooperation of the Laotian government, evidence of Leo and Dan's remains were unearthed at the crash site. Found there were the ejection seat harness buckles, parachute riser release fittings, oxygen masks, bayonets, and a dog tag. A statement by the Deputy Assistant Secretary of Defense (POW/MIA Affairs) James W. Wold, to a Congressional Subcommittee on June 28th, 1995 read, "All the evidence indicated that the crew members were in the aircraft at the time of impact."[4]

Leo remains, and his crewmate, Dan, were returned to the U.S. and buried with full military honors at Arlington National Cemetery. Assembled there were many of Leo's fellow Academy graduates, officers who had been stationed with Leo and Dan, Leo's mother, Liz Thomas Grant, his sister, Susan Hebel, and his widow, Kay McKinney, who had remarried. Leo Tarlton Thomas III, stood by the casket with tears in his eyes mourning the father he had never known. The only person missing was Leo's father, who had died on Leo's birthday eleven years earlier. The crew was awarded the Silver Star and each family was handed a folded American flag.

A total of 572 Americans were lost in Laos and as of June 11, 2011, 328 are still unaccounted for.[5]

[1] Excerpts from *The Vietnam, Cambodia and Laos Handbook*, Michael Buckley, Moon Publications, 1998.

[2] The urns are 13-14 tons each, about three feet high and made of sedimentary rock and granite. Created about 1,500 years ago by people of the megalithic iron-age and may have been used as burial urns. *Laos Keeps Its Urns*, Russell Ciochon and Jamie James. http://www.uiowa.edu/~bioanth/laoskeep.html.

[3] Major Roger Carroll was shot down on September 21, 1972 in a mission over Laos.

[4] U.S. Dept.of Defense. http://www.defense.gov/news/Jun1995/m062695_m-144-95.html.

[5] For currents stats on Vietnam War unaccounted for check http://www.dtic.mil/dpmo/vietnam/statistics/

F-4 Phantom loaded to hunt MiGs

Capt. Leo Taulton Thomas, Jr.
KIA Dec. 19, 1971

*No memory is ever alone; it's at the end of a trail of memories, a dozen trails that each have their own associations.*

—Louis L'Amour, American writer (1908 - 1988)


## Stop the Bombing for Bob

CHRISTMAS WAS A FEW days away, with not much to celebrate. Holidays, especially Christmas, bring a host of expectations and a host of upsets. No one was going home, and in this predominantly Buddhist country, there were no signs of Christmas—no holiday music playing in the shops downtown— no Christmas trees with packages wrapped in neat little bows—no chestnuts roasting on an open fire. It was just another day to get through, like every other day in a war zone.

My secret rendezvous with Colonel McHale continued sporadically. His door was always unlocked. He left it up to me when and if I wanted to come over. I couldn't resist the excitement of our affair. Here, under the cover of a war, we could get away with doing things we'd never get away with Stateside.

I continued to go the 13th Squadron events with Pete Mendellson and he wasn't going home for Christmas either. During his tour at Udorn, his wife had another baby. We congratulated him and celebrated the birth by smoking cigars and toasting with drinks in the bar. Pete was sweet and attentive. We complimented each other; he was the introvert, and I was the extrovert. I enjoyed the connection he gave me to the world of fighter pilots.

During the same time, I started seeing more of Captain Bob Barnett, who was in my special services squadron. He was the only single guy in my life, and I thought he might provide me with a shot at a real relationship. We spent many nights in downtown Udorn at a local nightclub with our boss Major Anastasio, who had a thing going with a Filipino singer named Cora. I spent the time getting to know Barnett, and although he couldn't compete with the infatuation I had for fighter pilots, he seemed like an OK guy. He was handsome and fun. He told me the Minnesota Vikings had drafted him, which was no small feat. When he realized that he'd never play first string, he decided to join the Air Force where he thought he might be able to do some good. I thought that was admirable. He'd been accepted into pilot training but was disqualified because he'd developed an ulcer.

Barnett was in charge of arranging a military transport plane for the enlisted troops to go see Bob Hope[1] who was coming to Thailand to perform at Ubon Air Base, about 200 miles Southeast from Udorn. Bob Hope had been entertaining the troops overseas during the holidays since 1941. I admired his commitment and was disappointed I wouldn't be able to see him in person.

At the last minute, Major Anastasio called and said, "Angel, there's one seat left on the plane. Do you wanna go?"

Although I felt a little guilty about taking a spot from one of the enlisted troops, I jumped at the chance. It would be a welcomed break. "You bet I would. When does the plane leave?" I was told the plane was leaving in an hour, so I flew out the door and headed for Base Ops to catch the transport.

The event was packed to overflowing with enthusiastic troops wanting to see Bob Hope and the celebs he'd brought with him. When we got to the staging area, Barnett said, "I wanna get closer to the front of the crowd so I can take some good pictures. Who knows? Maybe I'll be filmed as part of the audience and be seen on TV back home on Bob Hope's Christmas Special!"

"Great," I said. "I'll stay back here, and we'll meet up after the show."

It was evening and the huge crowd sat on the ground in front of the open-air stage eagerly waiting for the show to start. A warm breeze blew through the audience. It was the time of year between November and February when the humidity wasn't too high and the temperature was pleasant.

Then Les Brown and his Band of Renown started playing *Thanks for the Memories* as Bob Hope ambled on stage wearing a flight suit, a baseball cap, and clutching a golf club in one hand. The troops spontaneously rose to their feet clapping, whistling, and cheering with a deafening din that went on for several long minutes.

Once the cheering died down, Bob Hope brought out Vida Blue, a hotshot baseball player from the Oakland A's. They sparred back and forth making baseball jokes, which the crowd enjoyed. I turned to some kid sitting next to me and asked, "Who is this guy?"

He responded with an incredulous look, "Vida Blue? He's the southpaw pitcher who was named the 1971 American League's MVP and won the Cy Young Award."[2]

"Oh, I see, thanks," I responded blankly.

The guys thought it was great having some baseball star there, but the only names in baseball I was familiar with were Babe Ruth, Mickey Mantle, and Joe DiMaggio—a nice Italian boy who'd made good, as my mother would say.

Bob Hope then introduced eight of the Hollywood Deb Stars—gals who were selected every year as some of Hollywood's rising stars. As they strutted on stage in their miniskirts, it was clear they weren't chosen for their talent and acting ability alone. They sang a medley of pop songs with Bob Hope and did a little soft shoe number. Their long hair bounced in unison with their breasts to the beat of the music, as the troops whistled and carried on.

Jim Nabors, the beloved character who played the bumbling gas station attendant Gomer Pyle on the *Andy Griffith Show,* did some corny bits with Bob Hope, making cracks about the commies and the commanders. The crowd howled.

I sat behind the lighting crew's equipment and noticed someone handling huge cue cards that Bob Hope and his guests were reading. I don't know why, but that struck me as strange. I guess I had the impression that Bob Hope talked to some folks on base before the show about the latest incidents and personalities and then he'd incorporate those ideas into his shtick. When I'd seen him on TV, it appeared like he'd memorized all his lines, or was ad-libbing. He made it look so easy that I never thought he needed cue cards.

Bob Hope's next guest was Jan Daley, a Miss California nominee. Wow! That was the reaction she got from the audience of love-starved guys. Her long, blonde, wavy hair fell down around her face and accentuated her curvaceous body. What we didn't know was that her father had been killed attempting to rescue some American POWs in North Vietnam. Because of that she was trying to get her own USO troupe together to perform for the POWs there. Daley and Nabors sang a duet, and much to my surprise, Nabors didn't sound anything like his hillbilly character. His melodic baritone complimented Daley's voice beautifully.

When Daley asked for a volunteer from the audience, the boys stampeded. She seemed to pick the shyest G.I. from the crowd and brought him up on stage. She asked him his name and put her arm around him, held his hand, and started to sing in her sweet and sultry voice, "Where do I begin to tell the story of how great a love can be." She continued singing and cozying up to him. The airman could hardly look at her. He kept stepping from side to side, glancing down at the stage, and blushing from ear to ear.

As the crowd watched the interactions between them, they were living vicariously and loving every minute. Their deafening whistles and exuberant clapping muffled the sounds of jets roaring off the runway, headed for more bomb runs over North Vietnam.

When she finished her song, Bob Hope came back onstage but was interrupted by the rumbling of F-4 engines blasting off. He stopped the show and said, "I thought the Commander said there wasn't going to be any of that tonight!" The crowd responded with more clapping.

I got the feeling that Bob Hope didn't like the war either, or maybe he just didn't like his show being disrupted. He and the other celebs had given up their holidays with their families because they knew we were away from ours. Even though Americans back home were not supporting the troops, these stars were, and we showed our appreciation.

At the end of the show, Daley sang *Silent Night* and asked the crowd to join in. We started singing the words:

*Silent night, holy night*
*All is calm, all is bright*
*Round yon Virgin Mother and Child*
*Holy Infant so tender and mild*

The audience became still and serene. When we got to the last line, *Sleep in heavenly peace,* there wasn't a dry eye in the crowd. Chills went up and down my spine, and my stomach tightened. I thought, *what am I doing here? Was this war really worth it?* As the show ended, and the crowd exited, I saw Barnett walking toward me. He was crying too. He put his arm around me and said, "God, Angel, I can't believe it."

"Bob, what is it? What happened?" I said.

"It's Leo, he's dead—gone in an instant."

"I know Bob, it sucks. I can't believe it either."

This cold jolt of reality made me even sadder and continued to bring tears to my eyes. We left the show and walked out with our arms around each other. For us, it was truly a silent night.

[1] In 1969, President Johnson awarded Hope the Presidential Medal of Freedom for his service to the Men and Women in the Armed Forces. Bob Hope died in 2003 at the age of 100. His final USO tour was in December 1991, when he visited the troops deployed in Operation Desert Shield in Saudi Arabia and Bahrain. In 1997, President Clinton, along with approval from Congress, made Bob Hope an honorary veteran.

[2] The Cy Young Award is an honor given annually to the best pitcher in the Major Leagues. Commissioner Ford Frick first introduced the award in 1956 in honor of Hall of Fame pitcher Cy Young who died in 1955.

*Disenchantment, whether it is a minor disappointment or a major shock, is the signal that things are moving into transition in our lives.*

—Sir William Throsby Bridges, British general (1861 - 1915)

# Take This Job and Shove It

WITH CLOSE TO 850 o-club members, every member thought it was *his* club. And because they suffered from this illusion, every guy expected his demand be met instantaneously. "Where did you dig up that band, Angel?" "Where are the cigars, Angel?" "Can you get another popcorn machine, Angel?" "The bartenders are too slow, Angel."

At first, I met the challenges and complaints that arose at the club with a get-it-fixed attitude and a sense of humor, but all that changed as the problems started to mount. Supplies ran short or were unattainable. The procurement regulations made it harder to get supplies in a timely fashion. Orders got lost, stolen, or sent to the wrong base, and we'd often run out before the next order was delivered.

The food at the club drew the most complaints. "This steak is overcooked, Angel." "The spaghetti is like mush, Angel." "Why are you always running out of tacos, Angel?"

The Thais did the best they could to reproduce American food, but I constantly fielded complaints. They had a hell of a time with Mexican night. Many of the pilots had done their pilot training in Laredo, Texas, where they'd gotten a taste of authentic Tex-Mex cuisine, and they loved it. It was their comfort food. Of course, now these gringos were all experts, and someone always seemed to be schooling me on how the enchiladas or tacos were supposed to taste. When we ran out of tortillas, I had to cancel Mexican night, and I thought there was going to be a full-scale rebellion. "How could you run out of tortillas, Angel? What does it take to get tortillas for Christ sake?"

That was it. I decided that come hell or high water I wasn't going to run out of tortillas again. The next time Tim McHale went to the Philippines and asked if I wanted him to bring me back anything, I said, "Yes, bring me back a case of tortillas." Within the next week, he returned with a case of tortillas that he'd put in the nose of his F-4. That held off a rebellion for a little while.

Because the club was open 24 hours a day, and the pilots flew missions at all hours of the day and night, breakfast was available at anytime. This generated the "grits incident." A pilot stormed into my office and said, "Angel, the menu says grits, and when I come in here at 0300 I expect to have grits." I apologized, but it didn't seem to matter. I felt like everything was my fault, and I guess it was. After all, I was in charge.

It wasn't just the pilots who complained about the food. One morning, one of the commanders wanted Eggs Benedict. I explained that we couldn't get English muffins in Thailand, and he suggested I teach the Thais how to make them. He even had his secretary find a recipe for English muffins.

Making English muffins from scratch is no easy task. It requires starting the yeast at the right temperature, proofing the dough, kneading it, and then grilling the dough. No, I wasn't going to take on teaching the cooks how to make English muffins. It wasn't a priority—it wasn't even going to make the list. Besides, I didn't like that commander.

Thankfully, the bar didn't get too many complaints as long as the popcorn machine kept popping. When I tried to raise the price of martinis from 25 to 30 cents, because a martini had more vodka than a regular mixed drink, a colonel went straight to the Wing Commander and complained. "What is she trying to do? She can't raise the price of martinis." That guy probably died with the first dollar he ever made. The Wing Commander said, "Angel, just leave the price the way it was. It's just a nickel." The price promptly went back to 25 cents.

Then there was the non-smoking table. One day Fred Olmsted, alias "Broadway," obviously a man ahead of his time, came in and said, "Angel, I think we ought to have a non-smoking table in the dining room. A few of us don't smoke, and I'd like to eat without getting smoke blown in my face."

"Fred, are you crazy? Do you want these guys to run me out of town? It's bad enough that they think a woman shouldn't be running an o-club in a war zone, and that they think I stopped the strippers. If I do something as bizarre as set up a non-smoking table, they'll think it's some girlie thing. Before you know it they'll be worried I'm going to make the bar waitresses wear long skirts."

"No, Angel, don't mess with those miniskirts! Christ, Angel, I'm just asking for one table in the whole damn dining room. Come on, it's not a big deal," he insisted.

"Forget it, Fred. It's not going to happen on my watch. Besides, you, me, and Mendellson are the only ones who don't smoke like fiends."

"Well there's ah…"

"Sorry, Fred," I interrupted. "I'm not going to put any more restrictions on these guys. Besides, majority rules."

"Sounds like you're the majority, Angel."

"Well, you got that right!" I said with a smirk.

"All I can say, Angel, is no guts, no glory."

Telling him no didn't stop him. He kept cajoling me for the non-smoking table, and I just kept on saying, "No! And hell no!"

In most cases, rank has its privileges, but that wasn't the case the night Lieutenant Colonel Perkins attended a party and couldn't get a drink at the "colonels only bar." Most likely, this incident was what put me over the edge. He was the Vice Base Commander and I figured he suffered from a short man's complex. Either that or his ill humor stemmed from the realization that he knew he was never going to make full colonel.

The officer who scheduled the party had asked me to set up a special bar for full colonels so they could get their drinks more quickly. I set it up and told the bartender, "This bar only for colonels—officers with birds on flight suits," as I pointed to my shoulder where the bird insignia would be. "Other officers go to main bar—OK?"

When Lieutenant Colonel Perkins went up to the colonels' bar for a drink, the bartender, seeing that Perkins had a silver oak leaf on his flight suit and not an eagle, told him, "Sorry, sir, this bar for colonel only. You go main bar." This did not sit too well with Perkins. He just kept insisting the bartender give him a drink. When the bartender wouldn't comply, Perkins immediately tracked down the night manager and told him to "Get Captain Pilato over here, on the double."

I knew I was in for it when I saw him pacing the floor like an angry bull ready to charge. Before I could finish saying, "Good evening, Colonel Per—," he launched into a verbal attack.

"Angel, I wanna know why I can't get a drink at the colonel's bar?"

"Well, sir, I'm so sorry for the misunderstanding. You see, sir, the intent was…"

He kept pointing his finger at me and said, "It's about time you teach your bartenders how to recognize a colonel."

This was the same guy who registered a personal complaint about the shoes I wore when I was in my civilian clothes. They were a pair of comfortable, wooden cowhide clogs I'd purchased while I was in Austria.

When I relayed this incident to McHale, he said, "Angel, you shouldn't take this guy so seriously. He's a mosquito. Forget it. You have to keep your eye on the alligators and not worry about the mosquitoes."

I said, "What? Mosquitoes? Alligators? What are you talking about?"

"Angel, alligators are the guys that can take a big bite out of your butt, someone like me or the Wing Commander. Angel, we think you're doing a great job. That's all you have to worry about. Forget Perkins, he's a mosquito—a small nuisance."

All of this, combined with Leo's untimely death, added up. I'd had it. I had to get out of there. I was sick of having to prove myself every time I turned around. I was sick of listening to all the bitching and moaning and being expected to be on duty 24/7. I was trying so hard, and I was exhausted from all of it. Maybe I was being a wimp, but something snapped. Then all I could think was, *you can take this job and shove it.*

So, one day at the end of December, I walked over to the personnel office, asked for the papers I needed to resign my commission and had my Squadron Commander sign them. At the end of my tour, I'd be out of there. From that day on, it was a countdown to my last day, and it couldn't come quickly enough.

*Anytime you suffer a setback or disappointment, put your head down and plow ahead.*

—Les Brown, American motivational speaker (1945 - )

## Sevens, Eights—It's Too Late

TIM MCHALE KNEW I'D turned in my papers to resign my commission and leave the Air Force. Whenever we met for a drink in his hootch, our conversation would always end up with him trying to convince me not to leave.

"Angel, I think you ought to reconsider leaving the Air Force. You've got a good job with a salary a woman would have a hard time matching in civilian life. Colonel Gabriel said he'd get you an assignment anywhere you wanted to go."

My emphatic response was always, "No. No. And hell no! I've had it. I want out of this hell hole."

"You know, Angel, the Old Man and I think you've done a hell of a job."

"Tim, this has nothing to do with you or Gabriel. I couldn't have asked for two better commanders. You guys are the best. If you could guarantee me that I'd work with you or Gabriel I'd stay in, but you can't. Besides, I'm too frustrated with everything and everybody. I'm tired of having to justify every decision I make, of dealing with all the bureaucratic restrictions that make it almost impossible to get even the simplest supplies. I'm sick of the dust, the dirt, the Thais, the rain, the mud, and our guys dying for nothing. To put it plainly Tim, this whole place—this whole war—is totally fucked."

"Well, I guess that about covers it. Angel, I know it hasn't been easy for you, but you've got a good future ahead of you in the Air Force. I think you ought to reconsider."

"Thanks, Tim, I know you mean well, but I'm leaving. That's it. There's nothing you can say that will change my mind. Besides, if I did stay in the Air Force, I'd probably never get promoted anyway."

The more he used logic to cajole, the more I used emotions to resist.

Maybe I was tossing the baby out with the bath water, but there didn't seem to be anything salvageable. I had to get out of this environment. It was clear that I was in the wrong place, and although my stance was unwavering, he was still determined to change my mind. After all, he knew what was good for me.

One afternoon, I got a phone call to report to McHale's office immediately. Although I didn't think there was any cause for concern, I still felt a twinge in my stomach, the kind I used to get when one of the nuns would say, "Angelica, I need to see you after school." Nevertheless, I was curious about the sense of urgency. When anyone got a call to report to the commander's office, it usually wasn't to chitchat.

When I entered the outer area of his office, I said hello to the secretary and announced, "Captain Pilato here to see Colonel McHale."

"Go right in, he's expecting you."

I walked into his office and attempted to maintain some appearance of military formality, I whipped him a casual salute and a quick, spirited greeting, "Good afternoon, sir." He returned my salute with very little expression, "Come in, Angel. Sit down." I sat down on the couch in his office.

"Angel, I wanna talk to you about our OERs." Unbeknownst to me, he had solicited my records from personnel to review my Officer Effectiveness Reports, which was the Air Force's term for an officer's performance review.

"Yes, sir. What about 'em?"

The usual spark that we shared seemed to be gone. "Angel, I can't believe these ratings. They're all over the map—sevens, nines and even an eight." He had put all my OER rating numbers down on a sheet of paper and had evaluated them to determine what my chances for promotion were if I did decide to stay in the Air Force.

He continued in a stern voice, "Angel, awhile back when you mentioned that you thought your OERs probably wouldn't get you promoted, I wanted to see for myself. All I can say is what have you been doing for the last five years?" His tone of voice evoked earlier reprimands from my father chastising me for my less than exemplary grades in high school.

Clearly, Tim was angry with me. I just sat there with a pained look on my face. It was like someone had punched me in the stomach. Here was a man who was at the top of my list both professionally and personally, and I felt I'd disappointed him. I imagined that after seeing my OERs he thought less of me, which added to my anxiety. I got a lump in my throat and couldn't respond. If I had, it would have been accompanied by a flood of tears.

I remembered that one time at McHalae's hootch I had confided in him about some challenges I was having at the o-club. A particular lieutenant colonel was giving me a hard time, and I broke down and cried. He told me "Angel, stop crying. This is the very reason women can't fly airplanes—they're just too emotional." I figured that my little breakdown had set back the entire female population to pre-19th Amendment.[1] No, I wasn't going to do that again and reinforce his view of women being too emotional.

He saw my agonized expression and realized that I might be on the verge of tears. Not wanting that, he immediately responded with, "Never mind, never mind, you don't have to answer that question."

Thank God, I'd gotten a reprieve.

"I know what you've been doing. You've been doing your job, but not taking care of your report card. You're such a hard worker, Angel. If you'd been reporting directly to me, I would have promoted you to major, below-the-zone."

I still couldn't say anything. He just kept looking at the sheet of paper in front of him trying to make sense out of the numbers. "It looks like you'd get to a base, piss off the commander, then he'd realize you were a good troop, and he'd give you a good rating. You can see it. It's all right here: down, up, sevens, nines."

To understand how the OER rating system worked, here's a sample of a couple of officers' Rating Factors:

| KNOWLEDGE OF DUTIES | | | | |
|---|---|---|---|---|
| SERIOUS gaps in his knowledge of fundamentals of his job. | SATISFACTORY knowledge of routine phases of his job. | WELL INFORMED on most phases of his job. | EXCELLENT knowledge of ALL phases of his job. | EXCEPTIONAL understanding of his job. EXTREMELY well informed in ALL phases of his job. |
| ☐ 5 | ☐ 6 | ☐ 7 | ☐ 8 | ☐ 9 |
| JUDGEMENT | | | | |
| DECISIONS and recommendations often wrong or ineffective. | JUDGEMENT is usually sound but makes occasional errors. | SHOWS GOOD JUDGEMENT resulting from sound evaluation of factors. | SOUND logical thinker, considers ALL factors to reach accurate decisions. | CONSISTENTLY arrives at right decision even in highly complex matters. |
| ☐ 5 | ☐ 6 | ☐ 7 | ☐ 8 | ☐ 9 |

Additional Rating Factors included: Performance of Duties, Effectiveness in Working with Others, Leadership Characteristics, Adaptability, Use of Resources, Writing and Oral abilities, and Military Qualities.

On the reverse side of the OER were two sections called:

- **Overall Evaluation:** Compare this officer with other officers of the same grade. It had ten boxes ranging from Unsatisfactory to Outstanding, 1 through 10.
- **Promotion Potential:** There were four boxes ranging from 1 through 4, with 4 being the highest.

As he continued, I desperately tried to get rid of the lump in my throat, but I couldn't seem to swallow. However, I did manage to hold it together.

"Angel, you know the Old Man thought you did a hell of a job getting his patio built. How could that asinine boss of yours, Major Anastasio, ever give you an eight and a two? Good God, an eight and a two are the kiss of death for getting a promotion. Why didn't you use your ace and tell us about this? You knew Gabriel and I would have never signed off on this OER."

I was quickly getting the picture. It wasn't the descriptive words in the OER that counted it was the numbers. To get promoted, an officer needed to get all nines, or what they called a "firewall OER" which meant Xs all the way down the right side of the page. Humiliated and embarrassed, I realized I was probably the only officer in the entire Air Force that didn't know how the "real" system worked. McHale now knew how dumb I was.

Finally, I found my voice and said reluctantly, "I didn't know how it worked. Besides I didn't wanna take advantage of you or ask for any special favors." Why would a woman ask for what she wanted or speak up for herself? If she did, she would be labeled as aggressive and unfeminine, a braggart with a poor upbringing.

"For God's sake Angel, you wouldn't be taking advantage of anybody, you'd be getting what you deserved, which is an outstanding OER. Well, damn it! Gabriel and I should have looked at your OER, but we only reviewed the rated officers, majors, and above."

Then he hit me with another blow, "Angel, you know you were right. If you did stay in the Air Force you'd have a hell of a time getting promoted with these ratings."

Now, even if I wanted to withdraw my resignation papers, it would be impossible. The joke was on me. Instead of me deciding to leave the Air Force on my own, "Xs" on a sheet of paper had decided it for me. It was totally ludicrous. I couldn't believe how naïve I'd been.

The final zinger came when the Wing Commander entered the office. Any self-esteem I might have had left was about to evaporate like water spilled on hot pavement. Tim decided to involve Colonel Gabriel in this conversation. Now he was going to know how dumb I was, too! I just sat there totally mortified. Tim handed Gabriel the sheet of paper with the numbers he had scratched on it and said, "Charlie, what would you think of an officer who had OER ratings like these?"

Gabriel took a moment to look it over, and I thought, *is this really necessary?* He shook his head and responded, "God, I sure hope this guy isn't assigned to us!" That did it—one last punch in the stomach—it was a TKO. I'd never be able to face these guys again.

"Well, these ratings are hers," Tim said, as he looked right at me.

When Colonel Gabriel realized he'd just "stepped in it," he winced and quickly searched for something to remedy his faux pas. "Angel, I can't imagine anybody giving you OERs like these when you've got such great looking legs!" he quipped in his North Carolinian drawl.

At the time, his statement didn't offend me. Even today, after years of sensitivity training about comments that might be construed as sexist, I still don't consider what he said offensive. He was doing his darnedest to say something to make it up to me, and as far as I was concerned, he did the best he could. Besides, I liked him.

After Gabriel left the office, Tim turned to me and said, "I've tagged your personnel file. The next time your OER comes up for evaluation, it will be sent over here for Gabriel's review and endorsement. He'll make sure this doesn't happen again."

Tim, the champion of lost causes, was doing his best to make this right for me. Nice touch, but it was too late. Getting out of the Air Force was my only alternative. Even if I changed my mind, one outstanding OER wouldn't erase all the negative ones. I left his office and drove back to my BOQ room where the impact of the last hour hit me, and I started to cry. I realized not only was I dimwit, but Gabriel and McHale knew it!

A month later, my OER came up for review. When Major Anastasio sat me down to give me my review, he went on and on about how much I'd improved and what a great job I'd been doing. What a surprise! It was straight nines and a four in the "Promotion Potential" box.

Rather than leave well enough alone I blurted out, "Don't give me that bullshit, Major. The only reason you're giving me an outstanding OER was because you knew my records had been tagged to go to the Wing Commander's office." He denied it, but it didn't matter. I knew. After that, my OER was sent to Gabriel's office, and he endorsed it adding, "Captain Pilato has been exemplary in every respect." It ended with "Recommend Regular Air Force augmentation and promotion well ahead of her contemporaries." He signed it, "Colonel Charles A. Gabriel, Brigadier General Selectee."

The week before Gabriel was scheduled to leave Udorn Air Base, he asked to see me one last time. "Angel, I can still get you an assignment to wherever you wanna go. I think you're an outstanding officer."

I said, "Charlie, I'll stay in if I can be your general's aide."

"Angel, a one-star general doesn't get an aide until he has two stars."

"Sorry, sir, I can't wait that long!"

I knew he thought the outstanding OER would encourage me to change my mind, but it didn't. There was no recovering. But I learned a valuable lesson, and in future jobs I never lost another raise or promotion.

---

[1] In August of 1920 the 19th Amendment to the Constitution was ratified giving women the right to vote.

SECTION THREE

# Fun and Games

*Laughter is the closest distance between two people.*

—Victor Borge, Danish humorist, musician (1909 - 2000)

## Synergistic Smiles

DURING "OPERATION LINEBACKER," THE war escalated and more squadrons rotated in from the States. The bar was always abuzz with a mix of TDY pilots and our squadrons. One afternoon, I was in the o-club lobby when someone walked up behind me, put his hands over my eyes, and said in a thick Southern accent, "Angel, you WOP female club officer." There was no mistaking that voice, and I immediately started laughing.

"Don Newell, you son of a bitch," I said as I spun around and saw that it was indeed Don, one of my former sweeties from Germany. I had met him when his squadron was temporarily reassigned to Bitburg while the runway at Hahn Air Base was being repaired. He was a typical sweet-talking fighter pilot who always played the game to make a score and had a sense of humor that made him easy to be around. He knew he had surprised me and a huge grin covered his face. "Angel, how the hell are ya? I've gotta say, you're still as good lookin' as ever."

"Looks like you're still losing your hair!" I said jokingly.

"Come on, Angel, don't be so hard on me. Aren't you glad to see me?"

"Of course I am," I said, giving him a bear hug. "Hell, I can't be too easy on you, Newell, or you'd be disappointed. When did you get here?"

"Let me buy you a drink, and I'll tell ya," he said.

"OK, you got it," I agreed, and we headed for the bar.

We ordered a couple of drinks, and Don proceeded to fill me in. "I ferried an F-4 here from the States. After I got here, I caught the C-47 transport to Ubon because I'd heard you were stationed there. When I got there, I went over to the o-club and asked for you. They said, 'There's no Captain Pilato here, she's at Udorn.' I couldn't believe it! I high-tailed it back to the flight line just in time to jump back on the C-47 as it headed back to Udorn, and here I am."

I was grinning and shaking my head the whole time. "Don, that's a riot! It's an easy mistake to make. Ubon/Udorn. It all sounds the same to me! I'm glad you made it." We continued drinking, laughing, and catching up on each other's lives, which didn't take too long. I was getting out of this God-awful place, and he was eager to continue flying those exciting, yet terrifying, missions over North Vietnam in his F-4 Phantom.

Then he asked, "Do you wanna have some dinner?"

"Yeah, I'm getting hungry."

"Do you wanna eat here at the club?"

"Hell no, I eat here every day. Let's go to the Royal Thai Restaurant. It's off-base and within walking distance."

"OK then, let's go," he said, still smiling.

We walked over to the Royal Thai. We ordered some of those wonderfully crunchy spring rolls. While I was wolfing them down, Don reached down and unzipped the leg pocket of his flight suit, he pulled out a small box and said, "I've got something for you." In the box was a beautifully mounted butterfly that was a velvety ebony color with an iridescent lime-green border encircling its six-inch wingspan. The name printed on the back was *O. brookiana-Malaysia,* a butterfly that I found out later was being hunted to extinction.

"Don, this is the most gorgeous butterfly I've ever seen. Where did you get it?"

"At a flea market in the Philippines outside of Clark Air Base. When I found out that you were stationed over here, I knew I had to get it for you. I remembered you told me that you collected butterflies as a kid, and I thought you might like it."

"Like it? Don, I love it. It's absolutely beautiful." I leaned over and gave him a quick kiss on the cheek. "I can't believe you remembered I collected butterflies. This was so sweet of you," I said as I continued to admire my treasured gift.

"Well sometimes I even impress myself!" he replied with a pleased look.

We were both light-hearted and enjoying the moment, like we had been transported from this place to another, less precarious one. Our smiles were synergistic. They were the kind of smiles that come from the delight of giving and receiving. I thanked him again for being so thoughtful. I set the butterfly on the table where I could admire it while we finished our meal.

We walked back to the base and up the stairs to my BOQ room. I invited him in because I knew what he wanted. I couldn't say no. Why would I? I liked him, and we'd had a spontaneous and fun evening together. It wasn't long after our lovemaking that the door opened, and in walked my roommate and her *tealock*.

Don looked up and said nonchalantly, "Hi! How's it going?"

It was clear they were embarrassed. "Sorry, we'll see ya later," they said and quickly left.

Don and I started laughing again, and I said, "Welcome to the war zone!"

Don took a deep breath, "I guess it's time for me to leave." He zipped up his flight suit and gave me a kiss. "Thank you, Angel."

Still smiling, we gave each other a long, hard embrace. I wondered if I'd ever see him again. One never knew.

Years later, I decided to find out what had happened to Don. I hoped he'd survived the useless war and was happy. I tracked down his phone number and called him. He recognized my voice immediately and said, laughing, "Is this that WOP WAF club officer?" Don Newell married a wonderful nurse and is a happy grandpa. I still have the beautiful butterfly. It's hanging in my kitchen.

*I realize that humor isn't for everyone. It's only for people who want to have fun, enjoy life, and feel alive.*

—Anne Wilson Schaef, American psychotherapist, activist (1934 - )


## Skits and Tits

ENTERTAINMENT AT THE O-CLUB consisted almost exclusively of skimpily clad go-go girls in bikini panties and pasties. In an effort to mix things up a little bit, I came up with an idea. Each month a different squadron would create a skit and perform it at the club. I got my idea approved by the Advisory Council, and with the chairman's endorsement, all the Squadron Commanders were on board.

The 432nd Support Squadron, my squadron, was first up. A group of us got together and came up with a skit that parodied the Air Force regulations and how they affected what happened on base. The civil engineers set up a call center desk with a sign that read, "If CE can't fix it—it ain't broken." Personnel spoofed paperwork mix-ups that had people sent to the wrong squadrons or getting their tours extended a year. One officer wore a huge, cardboard sign, cutout in the shape of a pilot's wing pin that read, "Prince."

Bob Barnett rode in on a motorcycle wearing a "Burn Some Shit" t-shirt and asked, "Where's personnel, I gotta get drug tested." Someone appeared to be testing beakers of urine (ginger ale) for drugs and came out and shrieked, "Holy crap—all the tests came out positive!" A group of talented officers composed a song, accompanied with some neat guitar playing. We took a fun hit at everyone and everything, and the laughs rolled in from the crowd. It was a huge success. Now it was up to the other squadrons to top our performance.

The following month the Triple Nickel Fighter Squadron did a take-off of a tape that was circulating in the war zone at the time called, *What the Captain Means.*[1] It simulates a news reporter from the States who interviews one of the fighter pilots about his views on his involvement in the war. The Wing Information Officer is on hand to ensure what the pilot says is interpreted correctly for the media. The Triple Nickel's Captain Mike Cooper played the pilot.

**Reporter:** Captain, what's your opinion of how the F-4 Phantom performs?

**Pilot:** It's so fucking maneuverable you can fly up your own ass with it.

**Information Officer:** What the captain means is that he has found the F-4 highly maneuverable at all altitudes, and he considers it an excellent aircraft for all missions assigned.

**Reporter:** I suppose, Captain, you have flown a certain number of missions in North Vietnam. What did you think of the SAMs (surface-to-air missiles) used by the North Vietnamese?

**Pilot:** Why those bastards couldn't hit a bull in the ass with a bass fiddle. We can beat the shit out of them—there's no sweat.

**Information Officer:** What the captain means is that the surface-to-air missiles around Hanoi pose a serious problem to our air operations and that the pilots have a healthy respect for them.

**Reporter:** I suppose, Captain, that you have flown missions to the south. What kind of ordinance do you use, and what kind of targets do you hit?

**Pilot:** Well I'll tell ya, mostly we aim at kicking the shit out of Vietnamese villages, and my favorite ordinance is Napalm. Man that stuff just sucks the air right out of their frickin' lungs and makes a son of a bitching fire!

**Information Officer:** What the captain means, is that air strikes in Vietnam are often against Viet Cong (VC) structures, and all operations are always under the positive control of Forward Air control or FAC. The ordinance employed is conventional 570-pound bombs and 20-millimeter cannon fire.

**Reporter:** I suppose you have spent a night in Hong Kong. What were your impressions of the oriental girls?

**Pilot:** Yeah, I went to Hong Kong. As far as those oriental broads, well, I don't care which way the runway runs—east or west, north or south—a piece of ass is a piece of ass.

**Information Officer:** What the captain means is that he found the delicately featured oriental girls fascinating, and he was very impressed with their fine manners and thinks their naïveté is most charming.

**Reporter:** Tell me, Captain, have you flown missions other than over North or South Vietnam?

**Pilot:** You bet your sweet ass I've flown missions other than over North and South Vietnam. We get flak[2] nearly every day from those fuckers over there—they throw everything at you but the frickin' kitchen sink. Even the goddamn kids got slingshots.

**Information Officer:** What the captain means is that he has occasionally been scheduled to fly missions in the extreme western DMZ (Demilitarized Zone)[3], and he has a healthy respect for the flak in that area.

**Reporter:** I understand that no one in the 13th Tactical Fighter Squadron has got a MiG yet. What seems to be the problem?

**Pilot:** Well, you screw head, if you knew anything, the problem is those dipshits at 7th Air Force. They must think we're some kind of simple bastards. You should see some of the FRAGS[4] they give us. If we got fragged by pecker-heads at 7th for those fuckers in the MiG valleys, you can bet your ass we'd get some of those mothers. Those glory hounds at the Triple Nickel get all those FRAGS while we settle for fighting the frickin' war. Those Triple Nickel mothers are sitting on their fat asses killing MiG's, and we get stuck bombing the goddamn cabbage patches and a few frickin' supply trucks.

**Information Officer:** What the captain means to say is that all the target selection is performed at the 7th Air Force Tactical Air Control Center at Tan Son Nhut Air Base near Saigon. They try to spread the targets around to the various units according to the unit's capabilities. Some units are assigned the job of neutralizing enemy air strength by hunting out MiGs, and other elements are assigned bombing missions on interdiction of enemy supply production points and mobile supply caches.

**Reporter:** Of all the targets you have hit in Vietnam, which one was the most satisfying?

**Pilot:** Well shit, I'd have to say it was getting fragged for that frickin' suspected VC vegetable garden. I dropped Napalm in the middle of the fuckin' cabbage patch, and my wingman splashed it real good with six of those 750-pound mothers and spread the fire all the way to the frickin' beach—along with the carrots.

**Information Officer:** What the captain means is that the great variety of tactical targets available throughout Vietnam makes the F-4 the perfect aircraft to provide flexible response.

**Reporter:** What do you consider the most difficult target you have struck in North Vietnam?

**Pilot:** The frickin' bridges. I must have dropped forty tons of bombs on those swaying bamboo mothers, and I ain't hit one of the bastards yet.

**Information Officer:** What the captain means is that interdicting bridges along enemy supply routes is very important and quite a difficult target. The best way to accomplish this task is to crater the approaches to the bridges.

**Reporter:** Did you have an opportunity to meet your wife on leave in Honolulu, and did you enjoy the visit with her?

**Pilot:** Yeah, I met my wife in Honolulu, but I forgot to check the calendar, so the whole five days were frickin' well combat proof—a completely dry run.

**Information Officer:** What the captain means is that it was wonderful to get together with his wife and learn first hand about the family and how things were at home.

**Reporter:** Thank you for your time, Captain.

**Pilot:** Screw you, why don't you bastards print the real story instead of all that crap.

**Information Officer:** What the captain means is that he enjoyed the opportunity to discuss his tour with you.

**Reporter:** One final question, Captain, can you give me your overall impression of this war?

**Pilot:** Well, if the IG's, the VIP's, the staff assistant weenies, and all the rest of those sons of bitches would get the hell out of the way and let us fight this war, it wouldn't be too bad. But frankly, I think it's a fucked up war.

**Information Officer:** What the captain means is it's a fucked up war!

The crowd roared in agreement at one thing that night, "It was a fucked up war!"

The following month the A-B-Triple-C squadron, known as the "Alley Cats," had a solo act. A captain came in his white robe and black belt and broke a stack of bricks with one karate chop. It was a crowd pleaser. The guys yelled out, "Way da go! Shit Hot!"[5] I just looked on and thought, *Ouch! How does that guy do that?*

The 14th Tactical Reconnaissance Squadron was next, and they wanted me to participate. I said, "No way. You guys are on your own. Listen, guys, as soon as I get up on that stage some dickhead is going to yell out, 'Angel, show us your tits,' and that will be the end of it. Frankly, I'm sick of that crap." They kept after me until finally I said, "OK. What do you want me to do?"

"It's simple Angel, just wear a blouse and those hot pants of yours and walk across the stage and wave at everybody."

It sounded doable. The night of their skit, I waited in the wings until they called for me. I started across the stage like a rock star walking down the red carpet waving to the paparazzi. Sure enough the whistling started and, as if on cue, someone shouted, "Angel! Show us your tits!" The crowd started laughing and joined the mantra, "Show us your tits!"

I knew I could count on some smart ass to say that. It was as instinctive as a cat pouncing on a mouse. But this time I was ready for them. I paused a moment and then opened my blouse wide enough for them to see. The crowd went wild. They started whistling, clapping, and tossing popcorn. I couldn't stop smiling. Much to their surprise, pinned to my t-shirt under my blouse was a huge sign covering my bosom. It read, "MY TITS." I walked off the stage, and no one ever asked to see my tits again.

[1] "What the Captain Means" was composed by Lieutenant Colonel Joe Kent, who was the Information Officer for the 12 TFW at Cam Ranh Bay and recorded in 1966. Kent played the Wing Information Officer and Colonel Travis McNeil, 12 TFW Director of Operations played the part of the captain. I looked for someone who had a copy of the tape for years, and in 2006 I was lucky enough to get a copy tape from Kenneth L. Weber who wrote a book entitled *What the Captain Really Means*. In 2008 I found the entire scenario played on the Internet. I have taken the liberty to combine and modify it a little. No letters of complaint please.

[2] Flak is a nickname for antiaircraft guns (AAA).

[3] DMZ (Demilitarized Zone) refers to a combat-free area between two enemies. The DMZ in Vietnam was at the 17th parallel and was created by an agreement know as the Geneva Accords of 1954. It separated the North Vietnamese Communists from the South Vietnamese Nationalists.

[4] FRAG is a term used to describe a fragmentary portion of the operational war orders. Each unit in SEA was assigned and responsible to carry out a FRAG each day. Every unit wanted the best piece of the pie.

[5] Shit Hot means great job. Over the airwaves pilots would say Sierra Hotel, because FCC prohibits using naughty words. When communicating over the radio airwaves, every letter of the alphabet is represented by a word. A is alpha, B is bravo, S is Sierra, and H is Hotel. How Shit Hot came to mean great job? I have no idea.

# Hanging Out at Angel's Truck Stop

Captain Mike Cooper
and bar waitress, Yao

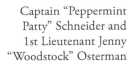

Captain "Peppermint
Patty" Schneider and
1st Lieutenant Jenny
"Woodstock" Osterman

## "Skit & Tits"

The 432nd Combat Support Group roasts the pilots and all…

*Dare to be naive.*

—Richard Buckminster Fuller, American architect, inventor (1895 - 1983)


## It Pays to Advertise

IN THE MILITARY EVERY insignia, patch, ribbon, or pin has a meaning. Patches indicate the squadron and command a person is in, ribbons specify campaigns fought in, Presidential Unit Citations won, and commendations awarded. Pins indicate paratrooper, pilot, or navigator status.

In keeping with this tradition, the pilots started showing up at the o-club with an unfamiliar pin on their flight suit lapel. It was a small metal circle with an arrow pointing at an angle, inward towards the center, Ⓛ. One afternoon, a group of us were sitting around the 13ᵗʰ squadron table in the o-club bar. Major Matt Kinsley was sitting across the table from me, and I noticed he had one of the circle pins on his lapel.

"Matt, what's that pin you're wearing?" I asked him.

He said, "This one?" pointing to the small circle.

"Yeah, that one."

He gave me a Cheshire cat grin and responded, "I'm safe."

With a puzzled look I said, "You're safe?"

He laughed, which triggered the other guys to join in. Instantly, I knew the boys understood what Matt meant, and I didn't. They loved to play one-upmanship games, and as hard as I tried to keep up, they were usually ahead. It was my own sense of competitiveness and ego that trapped me into thinking I might be able to keep up. The more I tried to outwit, out joke, out gross, out think, out dance, or out drink, they always seemed to have the edge. This insatiable desire to win with this crowd was like trying to run a marathon in combat boots.

They all sat there waiting for my response. Even though I knew I'd stepped into his well-laid trap, like a fly drawn into a spider's web, my curiosity got the best of me and I said, "OK, Matt, I give. What d'ya mean you're safe?"

Our *pas de duex* had everyone's attention, as they eagerly waited to hear Matt's response and see the expression on my face when he told me.

"Angel, it's an inverted male sign." Then with a slight pause and a mischievous grin he added, "Get it?" His group of supporters started to chuckle at the puzzled look on my face. It reminded me of my senior year in college when I went to my sorority sisters' dorm room and saw a stuffed animal with condoms on all four legs. As I touched them, I asked, "What are these rubbery things?" The sisters roared with laughter and couldn't believe they had to explain what those rubbery things were.

Those same pangs of naïveté returned, but my brain couldn't process fast enough. My reputation was at stake. They were about to score again. I was sure they were timing how long it was taking me to figure this out. The clock was ticking as I thought of all the possible scenarios: *an inverted male sign and he said, "He's safe." It can't mean he's not going to have sex any more. No. Never. Not Matt. His libido was too active. Inverted male sign...his penis is gone! Ludicrous. Heavens no, He wouldn't be smiling.*

Finally, the light came on and my expression changed. "I get it, Matt! You've been neutered!" Everyone busted into laughter. I heard a couple of comments like "It's about time, Angel" and "Way da go! Matt." The guys clinked their beer bottles together with Matt's, continued to drink, and enjoyed the fun of it all.

I shook my head back and forth, and replied, "Matt, you're bad. As for the rest of you guys, I said, pointing a scolding finger at them, "You aren't much better. You just continue to encourage him!"

I could have spared myself this embarrassment and asked Pete Mendellson in private what the significance of the circle pin meant. We could have had a private chuckle over it, but my impetuous and inquisitive nature had its drawbacks.

Matt continued in a confident tone and pointed to his pin, "You know, Angel, it's good to let a girl know that her guy isn't playing with a loaded gun. You know...that he's shooting blanks."

Trying to be nonchalant, I responded, "Yeah, Matt, I guess it pays to advertise."

While in Thailand, it seemed that some of the guys decided they'd take the opportunity to get a vasectomy. As it continued to grow in popularity, they started calling it "the operation." Who knew what their motives were?

Maybe they thought it was convenient to do it while they were away from their wives. Maybe it was peer pressure. Maybe they didn't want to wear condoms anymore.

In Matt's case it wasn't just for his wife. I'm sure he didn't want any accidents with his *tealock* either. Pete Mendellson got "the operation," too. He and his wife had decided they didn't want any more surprises. Of course, this was good news for me. It meant no worries, no rubbers, and no mistakes when I was with Pete.

About a week later, Dean White, a big, burly, cocky pilot who fancied himself a lady's man, came into the bar. As he walked over to the 13th squadron's table, his gate seemed a tad slow, and he had a slight limp. He sat down ever so carefully and ordered a drink. Pete Mendellson and I and some other fighter jocks were at the table. I looked over at him and asked in a concerned tone, "Dean, what happened to you? Why are you limping?"

He said, "I'm recovering from 'the operation.'"

Even though Dean wasn't one of my favorites I was curious. "Oh, I see. When did you have 'the operation' Dean?"

"On Monday," he replied.

It was Friday, and I was puzzled why Dean was still limping and in apparent pain. I said, "Gosh Dean, it seems like it's taking you a long time to heal. Maybe you need to go back to the flight surgeon and get it checked out."

"No, it's OK, it just takes time," he said.

Then without skipping a beat I said, "Gosh! It didn't take Pete that long to recover!" The entire group started laughing, except Dean White. Pete's face turned beet red as he said, "Good going, Angel. You got him."

Score one for me! But of course, I was still behind.

*I love it when a plan comes together!*
—*The A-Team,* American television show (1983 - 1987)

# McHale's *Sawadee* Party

WHEN I FOUND OUT Tim McHale was returning to the States to be the Wing Commander of Beale Air Force Base in Sacramento, I wondered, *who was going to protect me from the ever-present "alligators."* He'd done a lot to teach me the ropes, and for that, I was grateful. Now he was leaving five months before me.

Others on base were disappointed about his departure, too. As Vice Commander, he'd arrived here with a notable record, but he wasn't a fighter pilot. This made the other pilots skeptical about whether or not he could cut it in the cockpit. Their concerns were soon dispelled after McHale flew a few check rides with the pilots in the F-4D. Word got around that he was disciplined, capable, and a quick study, which won him the respect of the fighter jocks.

There was a definite pecking order within the pilot ranks. Fighter pilots considered themselves number one. Then came the "reckie" (reconnaissance) pilots, the bomber pilots, the tanker/refueler guys, and lastly the cargo pilots or "trash haulers." Then there were the helicopter pilots, who were low on the totem pole unless you needed to be rescued. Then they became number one.

A huge Wing *sawadee* party was planned for him the night before his departure. We had a week to plan the party, so we had plenty of time to do it up right. I called a preliminary meeting with Sergeants White and Bradshaw, along with the Thai supervisors in charge of the waitresses, kitchen staff, and bartenders, to give them detailed instructions of how the party was to be carried out. We discussed the menus, the flowers, the ice carving, the waitresses' attire for the evening, the table settings, and of course, the cigars. The club was going to be inspection clean—even the men's room was to be spotless.

The staff gathered in the dining room. "We are going to have a big *sawadee* party next Thursday night for Colonel McHale. He's going back to the States," I announced.

Dang, the head waitress, said, "Ooh Kapton, he go home too soon. He number one."

"Yes, Dang, I know. We'll all miss him. That's why I want this party to be very special."

Then Dang said something that seemed to come out of nowhere, "Kernol number one for you, Kapton?" It might have been an innocent inquiry, but her eyes twinkled a little, as if she knew McHale and I were *tealocks*. She may or may not have known, but I was pretty sure she was the occasional *tealock* of the Wing Commander, Colonel Gabriel. Nevertheless, my response was, "Yes, Dang, Colonel McHale is number one," and went on giving instructions.

"There's going to be about 300 officers and guests coming."

"That *mak mak*," said Dang.

"Right, and we're going to have to squeeze everyone into this dining room," I said, surveying the room. "We'll need to use all the round tables we have and set them for ten. It'll be a tight squeeze, but that's the only way we'll be able to fit everyone. We'll use the rectangular tables to make up the difference. Dang, do we have enough green tablecloths for all those tables?"

"Yes, Kapton, we have. You want white napkins? We have *mak mak*."

"OK, good. That'll work. OK, Sergeant Bradshaw, you'll need to take care of the head table. Set it up on the wooden risers over here," I said, pointing to the front of the dining room. "Put two eight-foot rectangular tables with ten chairs and have the wicker princess chair in the center for Colonel McHale."

"You got it, Capt'n," responded Bradshaw.

I continued doling out commands. "Dang, drape the head table with white tablecloths and put green tablecloths on top with white napkins. Brad, hang our eighteen-foot *sawadee* banner behind the head table. I've got another six-foot banner with Colonel McHale's name on it being painted. When it gets here, hang it above the *sawadee* banner, and make sure they're both centered."

"Can do easy, Capt'n," was Brad's quick reply.

Then I turned to Sergeant White, my kitchen supervisor, who was a hard worker. The conditions he worked under made his job difficult, but he and his Thai troops consistently delivered top-notch results.

"Sergeant White!"

"Yes, ma'am!" he said as he straightened up, his pen poised and ready to write down everything that was needed.

"Here's what I want for the menu. For the appetizer, let's have a lobster tail with drawn butter. For the entrée, a tenderloin of beef filet mignon wrapped in bacon. Make the baked potato stuffed with cheese, and let's have buttered green beans with slivered almonds. And for God's sake, keep 'em green, don't overcook 'em. Of course, we'll need a green salad with ranch dressing, rolls and butter, and I think we need a special dessert. Let's do a flaming baked Alaska."

"Yes, ma'am," he nodded, writing down everything as fast as he could. He hesitated a moment and then interrupted, "ma'am?"

"Yes, Sergeant White, is there a problem?"

"I don't think we have any lobster tails in the freezer or enough eggs for the baked Alaska," he responded.

"Eggs—call the NCO club and see if we can borrow some from them. Tell 'em we'll replace 'em next week when our order comes in. As for the lobster tails, I'll call the manager at Clark Air Base and ask him to put some lobster tails on the next KC-135 transport out of the Philippines into Utapao."

"Who's gonna pick 'em up from Bangkok, ma'am?" he asked with a distressed look.

"I'll call Mr. Ling. He'll do it for us!" Mr. Ling was our local Chinese merchant who could get anything from anywhere—for a price. He'd gotten our carpeting in here from Hong Kong and even shipped an elephant to a zoo in the States. How they found him, or vice versa, I have no idea, but he was always trying to be helpful.

"Supon, I'm going to need an ice carving."

"Yes, Kapton. Can do!"

Earlier that day I'd gone to the Base Information Office to look for a picture of a SR-71 Blackbird, McHale's signature aircraft. I wanted Supon, our head cook, who was great at copying anything, to make an ice replica of the SR-71. I'd taught him how to make an ice carving of the F-4, and he'd done a superb job of creating them for special parties. Now, I was going to ask him to create another work of art and hoped he could pull it off.

I turned to Supon, handed him the picture of the SR-71 and said, "Supon, you think you can do an ice carving of this plane?"

"Oooh, Kapton, this beautiful plane! How big you want?" he asked with slight apprehension.

"The same size as the F-4 carvings that you do so well—about three feet," I said. I extended my arms out to show him and eagerly awaited an affirmative response.

He smiled and said, "OK, Kapton. I can do for you."

"Great Supon. You're number one. I know you can do a good job," I said but still thought it wise to keep my fingers crossed.

I asked if there were any questions. There weren't any, so I said, "OK, let's make this party number one!"

Sergeant Bradsaw replied, "We'll get right on it, Capt'n—no sweat—can do easy!"

During the next few days, the *sawadee* party was my top priority. My involvement was continual. Supon was freezing the large blocks of ice for the ice carving. Mr. Ling was picking up the lobster tails from Bangkok in a truck filled with ice, and the flowers were ordered. The sign with Colonel McHale's name on it was rolled up in my office along with boxes of after dinner cigars and a few tiparillos for the ladies. The final count for the party was 325, and things looked like they were coming together.

On the afternoon of the party, I met with Dang in the dining room and showed her how I wanted the tables set. Afterward, I jumped into the club pick-up and drove to downtown Udorn to get a manicure and pedicure and to have my long brunette hair done up in a French twist. Every time I went into this open-air salon, everyone was smiling and happy. I wondered, *how could they be so happy? Didn't they know there was a war going on right next-door?* They were fascinated with the *falong* with the hair on her arms. They stroked the thin layer of hair and said, "Oooh *sway mak, sway mak.* Very beautiful."

I couldn't imagine why they liked it. I'd always found the hair on my arms distasteful and one of the negatives of my Italian heritage. Their arms and legs were free from hair, which I envied. Three women worked on me: one on my hair, one on my feet, and the other on my hands. I was finished in about an hour. I gave them ninety baht, an equivalent of $4.50 in U.S. dollars, which included the tip. With my hands together in a prayer position and with a slight bow I said, *"Kop kun kah,* thank you, and *sawadee kah."*

They smiled, returned the bow, and said, "You look *sway mak,* very beautiful, *kop kun kah sawadee.* Have fun at party tonight."

I returned to the club and headed straight to the kitchen to see how things were progressing. When I saw Supon's carving of the sleek replica of the SR-71 aircraft, my eyes lit up and I exclaimed, "Supon, you did a great job! It's beautiful. *Sway mak mak!*" Just one minor detail remained—he had to assemble it without it collapsing.

Supon was all smiles. "Thank you, Kapton. You like?"

"Absolutely. You number one, Supon. *Kop kun krup."*

About an hour before the guests were scheduled to arrive, Supon and his three kitchen helpers placed the ice carving, its pedestal, and the ice base onto a cart and rolled it out to the patio. A draped table with a shallow metal drip pan lined with white cloth napkins was set up for the assembly. A 10-gallon soup pot, about two-feet high and 18 inches in diameter, was used to freeze the base for the ice carving. The base had started to thaw away from the sides of the pot, which allowed them to turn it upside down into the drip pan. A one-foot high rectangular pedestal was attached to the circular ice base by sprinkling it with table salt and pressing shaved ice around the bottom of the pedestal until it fused together. With the pedestal and base in place, the test would now be to secure the body of the SR-71 to the pedestal. Two of the men got up on chairs, as the other two cautiously handed off the SR-71 ice carving to Supon and his partner.

Supon rapidly fired out instructions to his staff. I didn't understand any of it, but I was sure from the frantic tone of his voice and his body language, he must have been saying, *alright you guys, you better get this right, or we're all screwed!* They positioned the heavy SR-71 upward at about a 110-degree angle and balanced its weight on the pedestal. Again, salt and shaved ice were quickly used to affix it to the top of the pedestal. They all continued to hold it in place until the shaved ice solidified.

We all held our breath in anticipation to see if this precariously assembled ice sculpture would stay in place. After several long minutes, he gave the command. They slowly and carefully removed their hands and stepped away from the table.

*Voilá!* They'd done it! We all clapped and smiled. I exhaled a grateful sigh of relief. I went over to the crew and said, "It looks great, absolutely beautiful, *sway mak mak.* Great job! Thank you, thank you, *kop kun krup."* I said with my hands in a prayer position. They were all beaming with pride. I turned to Supon and startled him with a bear hug.

With 45 minutes before the party, I high-tailed it over to the BOQ to change. My talented Indian seamstress, Rashmi, had made an elegant evening dress from a sketch I had given her with only my measurements. She was like Cinderella's fairy godmother, who transformed a char maid into a vision of beauty. It was a sleeveless, long, black silk pant-dress, with a low-cut v-neckline accented with silver-colored beads and sequins. After a quick shower, I applied my makeup, slipped into my evening dress and stepped into my glass slippers, a pair of black sandals, and dashed back to the club.

I walked through the club with an eagle eye to make sure everything was perfect before the first guests arrived. It was. The candles were being lit, and a beautiful centerpiece of chrysanthemums, carnations, and orchids graced the head table. The waitresses looked stunning, dressed in their traditional, multi-colored, long Thai dresses.

"Everything looks beautiful, and you all look *sway mak,"* I told them.

They smiled and responded with "Kapton, you look *sway mak mak,* very beautiful, Kapton."

Pete Mendellson arrived shortly before the others. He was my official *tealock* and my escort for the evening. He greeted me with, "Wow! You look absolutely gorgeous."

"You like it?" I said as I spun around so he could see every inch of me.

"Yeah, you look great," he said, beaming.

He looked dashing and handsome in his jet-black party flight suit.

I said, "Thanks, so do you. We match, Pete." I stood by his side, and put my arm through his, and proceeded to the outside patio for the cocktail hour.

"I have all the 13th squadron's tables right up in front."

"I guess the 13th has some pull around here!" he said, grinning.

I told him, "Sweetie, you're the one who's got the pull."

At 1830 hours, the officers and guests began to arrive. The ice carving was the center of attention. The officers gathered around for a closer look and snapped pictures. The ice sculpture was quickly thawing in the night heat, and as it did, the ice became more translucent making it even more impressive.

When McHale came in and saw it he said, "Angel, you really outdid yourself. This is absolutely amazing."

"Thank you, sir, I'm so glad you like it. The Thais worked very hard on it." I replied with a radiant smile. He and I stood next to the ice carving as the base photographer took our picture. He leaned over and whispered, "Come over tonight. I'll be waiting." I smiled and reluctantly said, "OK." For the rest of the evening he attended to his guests, and I returned to Pete's side.

The party was packed with well-wishers, brown-nosers, and back-slappers. Everyone knew that this below-the-zone colonel was headed for his general's star, and they hoped with a little luck they could ride along on his coattails. He was keenly aware of who was sincere and who wasn't, but he accepted all their kudos modestly.

At the end of the meal, the lights were lowered and the cooks rolled out the cart with the frozen baked Alaska, the *pièce de résistance*. The kitchen staff had spent hours cracking dozens of eggs, separating the yolks from the whites, and whipping them into a stiff meringue. They assembled the frozen baked Alaska by starting with a white sheet cake, layering it with strawberry, vanilla, and chocolate ice cream. Then spreading the meringue over the top and sides, which sealed the ice cream and kept it from melting when it was flambéed.

The lights were dimmed as the crowd awaited the show. This was the club's first attempt at a flaming baked Alaska. The kitchen staff started warming the brandy in a stainless steel ladle, swishing it around over a lit can of Sterno. The fumes quickly ignited the brandy, which was ceremoniously poured over the dessert setting the meringue ablaze and turning it a beautiful golden brown. Everyone clapped at the gourmet delight. I exhaled. My part of the evening was complete!

Pete leaned over, put his arm around me, and gave me a hug, "Good going, Angel, everything was Shit Hot." All the guys at the table give me thumbs up. I beamed and returned the thumbs up, "Thanks, guys." I squeezed Pete's hand and said, "Thanks, Pete, you're a love," and gave him a kiss on the cheek.

Before Colonel McHale began his farewell speech, several officers stood up and spouted a barrage of good luck toasts. One Squadron Commander raised his wine glass, and said, "Here's to Colonel McHale, our Shit Hot

Vice Commander. Our loss is Beale's gain." Everyone stood up, raised their glasses, and responded with, "Here! Here!"

Then McHale got up to give his farewell address. "I wanna thank everyone who has made my tour at Udorn, short as it was, a memorable one. The officers and NCOs I've worked with are among the most professional and committed in the Air Force. I'm very proud to have been a part of such an outstanding Wing." Then he went on to talk about the U.S. military's part in the war. "Some day history will regard the United States' involvement in Vietnam as helping a small nation win its independence. All of you have played a significant role in protecting our democracy and that of all the free world." As I listened to him, I realized that he really believed it. I guess you'd have to if you were a career military officer on your way to becoming a general. On the other hand, I'd come to believe that this war was going nowhere, and the sooner I got out the better.

At the end of the party, Colonel McHale went into the kitchen and thanked all the employees for a job well done. They were surprised and honored that he had come to thank them. Smiling, they said, "You welcome, sir, you number one."

He said, *"Sawadee,"* and went to the bar to mingle with the guys who wanted to buy him a farewell drink. Shortly afterwards, he left for his quarters.

Pete hung around at the bar waiting for me to finish. "Do you want me to walk you back to the BOQ?" he asked. Knowing what that meant I said, "No thanks, Pete, not tonight. I'm exhausted." The truth was I had other plans.

# *Sawadee* Parties

Captain Angel Pilato and Public Affairs Officer
with the famous SR-71 ice carving

F-4 ice carving

# Colonel Gabriel – End of Tour Flight

Top Row: Major John Mesenbourg, Captain Don Bullock, Colonel
Coleman Baker, Colonel Charles Gabriel, Captain Burke
Front Row: Major Dan Bowen, (Mystery Man?) Captain Steve Ritchie

Wing Commander Colonel Charlie Gabriel's *Sawadee* Party with
Colonel Scott Smith (left) and General DeWitt Searles (right)

*Didn't I make you feel like you were the only man, well yeah,*
*An' didn't I give you nearly everything that a woman possibly can?*
*Honey, you know I did!*

—Jordan Ragovoy, American songwriter (1935 - ) and
Bertrand Russell Berns, American songwriter (1929 - 1967)
From *Piece of My Heart*

# It's OK to Say I Love You

I THOUGHT THE PARTY would never end, and I was among the last to leave. I rushed back to my BOQ room to change out of my evening dress. I peeked through the drapes to ensure the coast was clear and then hurried to Tim's hootch.

I walked in and found my way to his bedroom. He had dozed off. I stood there awhile, watching him lying in bed wearing his blue nylon pajamas. This was the last night I was going to see him, in or out, of those blue pajamas, and I wanted to savor the moment.

I was going to miss the closeness we shared, the risky, late-night rendezvous, the stories we told about our lives, and the insights he'd given me about this man's Air Force. It had been a small way to escape reality and help me mark another day off my tour in SEA. I'd probably never see him again, and if I did, we'd have to act like we had never shared these private moments.

I noticed his command post brick on the nightstand. Even though he was leaving in the morning, he was still on duty. His uniform was neatly laid out on a chair next to his bed. His bags were partially packed and ready to go.

As the weight of my body touched the edge of the bed, he said in a sleepy but eager voice, "What took you so long?"

"I got here as fast as I could." I said as I tossed off my shoes and slipped out of my sundress.

I leaned over and started kissing him, as his hands moved slowly over my body he whispered, "God, Angel, you are so soft, and you feel so good."

The act of making love can be powerfully potent, especially when it's with someone who excites both your mind and body. The techniques of touch can be taught, but it is the mind that triggers the sensuous synapses between lovers.

We lay there side by side, locked in a warm, sweaty embrace. He unwrapped his arm, got up, and returned with a wet cool washcloth, which he gently passed over my body. It felt cool and refreshing.

Then he asked, "How about some ice cream?"

Chuckling, I responded, "Ice cream! That sounds great. What kind is it?"

"Chocolate."

"Hmm, that's my favorite."

"I know. That's why I got it," he said, smiling.

"Isn't chocolate your favorite, too?" I joked.

He brought in a small carton of ice cream and two spoons. We sat on the edge of the bed devouring it as fast as we could, trying to find some relief from the heat and humidity. The overworked air conditioner groaned on incessantly. It still wasn't enough to sufficiently cool the room, and the chocolate ice cream soon got soupy. A little spilled on the front of my body.

As I reached for the washcloth he said, "Wait a minute, let me do that." He leaned over and kissed off every drop. Goose bumps appeared on my arms, and we both laughed with sheer delight.

At about 0200 hours, exhausted from our passionate evening, we decided to try and get a little shut-eye. Time was running out. They'd be here at 0800 to pick up Tim and take him to Base Ops for his flight out. He wrapped his arm around me as I lay my head on his chest.

As our eyes became heavy with sleep, I broke the silence and whispered, "I love you, Tim." He pressed his arm a little tighter around me and said, "I love you, too." We both knew what saying that really meant. He'd explained it to me numerous times before. *Angel, I love you, but I don't want you to get the wrong idea. It means I love you for who you are, for right now. There can't be anything more. I hope you understand that.* Yes, I understood all too well. I knew the rules, and I'd assured him that his explanations were unnecessary.

Even though everyone was "single" in SEA, Tim was a career military man. Not only was he a married man, he was an Irish Catholic family man—a dutiful husband with a wife and children. He loved them and missed not being with them. He was concerned about being away from them because he knew his wife and the kids needed him. He justified his absence as an important sacrifice that he made to protect the world from communism and secure a democracy for the Vietnamese. Soon, he'd be back with his family who would be thankful that he'd been spared from being a casualty of this divisive war. Besides, the Air Force had bigger plans for Tim. As we drifted off to sleep we knew no explanation was necessary. We both let it be OK to say, "I love you."

*It is lucky that small things please women. And it is not silly of them to be thus pleased. It is the small things that the deepest loyalty, that which they need most, the loyalty of the passing moment is best expressed.*

—Joseph Conrad, English writer (1857 - 1924)
From *Chance: A Tale in Two Parts*

# Blue Pajamas

MORNING SEEMED TO ARRIVE only minutes after we had put our heads down. The alarm's shrill buzzer roused us from a sound sleep. Tim got up, kissed me on the cheek, and headed for the shower. I lingered in bed awhile, until I saw him get out of the shower and wrap a white G. I. towel around his waist. I got out of bed, slipped into my sundress, and stood by the entry to the bathroom. The steam from the shower added to the intense humidity of the bathroom. He lathered up for a shave and spread the shaving cream on his checks and neck, leaving only his lips showing.

There's something sensual about watching a man shave. It's like a mini-striptease. Each deliberate stroke of the razor peels off a small section of shaving cream, revealing the smooth, sweet-smelling skin underneath. He smiled and his eyes gleamed at my apparent fascination with this seemingly mundane, masculine task. It reminded me of when I used to sit on the edge of the bathtub and watch my dad shave while he took drags off his cigarette.

In the middle of the show, Tim leaned over and kissed me, leaving a little shaving cream above my lips. Strange, how this small but tender gesture seemed to please me and made me burst out with a euphoric giggle. He checked his watch, and I asked, "What time is it?"

"0730," he responded, as he finished the last stroke and wiped his face.

"The guys will be here soon, Tim. I should leave." I turned my back to him and asked, "Zip me up, please?"

He zipped me up and said emphatically, "No, Angel, I want you to stay."

"I don't think that's a good idea. They'll know I've been here all night."

"I don't care, they probably already know. There aren't any secrets on this base."

I felt awkward being there. What would the guys think of me? What would they think of him? Maybe they'd think I just got there ahead of them. Who was I kidding? They'd see the expression on my face, or his, and they'd know. But even so, I set my concerns aside and said hesitantly, "OK, Tim, if you insist."

Then he said, "Angel, who is going to look out for you when I'm gone?"

Without hesitating I said, "Pete Mendellson."

"Well, good. Pete is a good troop. I don't feel so badly about leaving now that I know you'll have someone to keep you out of trouble!" Then he added, "Angel, I know you said you didn't wanna come and see me off, but I want you to. It would mean a lot to me."

"Tim, I know people don't often tell you 'no,' but I'm not coming to see you off. I already told you that. Besides, too many people will be there. If they see me there, everyone will know we've been messing around." I was really thinking that if I went to see him off I'd probably do something silly, like cry. Then they'd not only know I'd been sleeping with the Vice Commander, but that I was a wimp! No, I wasn't going to the airport.

"OK," he said. "I'm disappointed. I really would like it if you came to see me off." As he continued getting dressed, he kept pressing me to change my mind.

"Tim, I'm here, aren't I?" I said with a touch of melancholy in my voice.

Then he saw I was about to get weepy on him, and he couldn't handle that again, so he said, "OK, OK. Have it your way."

He changed the subject and announced, "I decided to give Sooneepon a princess ring, and I put some money in this envelope for her like you suggested. She's been such a reliable maid. I hope this helps her out some." Then he turned to me and said, "I still don't know what to give you."

"Tim, I told you what I wanted."

We had talked about this before, and I really didn't like telling someone what to give me as a good-bye present. Hadn't his wife taught him what a woman likes? Hadn't he been in Thailand long enough to know what the guys gave their *tealocks*—one of those gold four seasons bracelets?

No, he didn't need to give me a gold *tealock* bracelet as a token of appreciation. I'd buy my own. Besides, asking for a gift of that magnitude was much too brazen a request. Secretly, I did think it would be a romantic gesture on his part, but I really didn't need one. After all, I'd have those memories of him. That was far more valuable than a bracelet.

"I know what you told me," Tim said. "I can't imagine you really want my pajamas."

"Yes," I said, "They'll remind me of you. I'll put them on, and you'll be in them, too."

He smiled, relishing my adoration. "Alright," he said. "They're yours." We both smiled, I kissed him and then started to choke up. The moment was interrupted by a knock on the door. His entourage had arrived to escort him to his flight back to the "real" world.

The hootch door opened and in walked Pete Mendellson, Dan Bowen, and a couple of the other guys from the 13th Panther Pack. They exchanged greetings and shook hands. The mood was quiet. They knew they were losing one of the good guys and would be stuck with that military misfit of a Vice Commander, Colonel Smith, and that thought made me shudder.

When Pete saw me standing there, leaning up against the kitchen counter, his look said it all. His suspicions had been confirmed. Now the entire 13th squadron knew I was McHale's *tealock*, too.

I smiled at everyone, tried to be nonchalant, and said, "Good morning, you guys. I'm glad the 13th is the one taking the colonel to the airport."

They picked up McHale's travel bags and carried them out to the staff car. I stood there in my sundress waiting for them to leave. Then one of the guys said, "Angel, are you coming with us?"

"No, it looks like you guys can handle it." I took in a deep breath, forced a smile, and with as little emotion as possible said, *"Sawadee,* Colonel McHale." I knew I couldn't say one more word for fear of the inevitable.

As Tim went out the door, he put on his flight cap, turned to Pete Mendellson, and said, "Pete look after her, will ya?"

"Yes, sir," Pete replied without skipping a beat. Tim walked down the stairs, got into the dark blue staff car, and never looked back

I stood in the doorway until the car was out of sight, then I took one more walk through his hootch. I looked around at all that was left: an empty room with the sheets all rumpled, wet towels piled on the bathroom floor, and a pair of blue pajamas on the edge of the bed. I picked them up, folded them neatly, and walked out the door.

A heavy feeling came over me. He was gone. I crossed the street to my BOQ room, with the blue pajamas held tightly to my chest. I shut the door to my room and burst into tears. I'd never see him again. Yes, he made general and not just one star; four stars were in his future.

*Good advice is always certain to be ignored, but that's no reason not to give it.*
—Agatha Christie, English mystery writer (1890 - 1976)

# Advice from Married Guys

AN AUTOMATIC SWITCH SEEMED to go off when I realized time was running out. It was like a time bomb waiting to explode. It just kept ticking and wouldn't shut off. After five years in the Air Force and at 29 years of age, my prospects for marriage had yielded zero results. Knowing that my liaisons with married men were futile, I had decided to focus on Captain Bob Barnett, who was single and seemed to be a likely candidate.

Bob and I had begun to do a lot of things together. We traveled to see the Surin elephant round up and the Bob Hope Christmas Special, went to movies on base, explored the local establishments downtown, slept together, cooked spaghetti in my BOQ room, and even went on R&R (rest and recovery) to Australia. Things seemed to be going well. I assumed the reason he had never said he loved me was because he was single and found it difficult to express himself.

I saw no reason to stop my liaison with Pete since I wasn't sure where my relationship with Bob was going. Pete Mendellson had no trouble, after a couple of scotches, expressing his feelings for me. Of course, I knew he was very much married and when we said, *I love you,* we both knew what it meant.

Then there had been Tim McHale. Even though I had wanted to believe it was merely an exciting wartime romance, I had developed feelings for him, but it was probably just infatuation. Sex was not the driving force in my relationship with Tim. Although, I suspect it was for him. I was attracted to his power, his charisma, and his dedication to the Air Force. Our clandestine love affair had been thrilling, but he was gone.

Both Pete and Tim knew I was seeing Bob, and although they never said it, I suspected their egos were a little crushed knowing they weren't my only *tealock.* Being faithful to a married man was the kiss of death. I needed to protect myself from getting too emotionally involved because eventually he would leave me and return to his wife and family. No, I wasn't anyone's fool. These escapades were simply wartime trysts. I was single, and I could sleep with whomever I wanted. After all, if the guys could do it, so could I.

Even though Tim realized that he didn't have much to say about my relationship with Bob, that didn't stop him. One night while I was at his hootch, he started in.

"Angel, I know you've been hangin' around with Bob Barnett, and I just wanna say, he's not the right kind of guy for you. He's too immature. You need a guy like me."

Rolling my eyes I said, "I know. I'd love a guy like you, but you're married, and Barnett isn't. And you know I wanna get married."

"I didn't mean me," he said, "I meant someone like me. Someone older and more mature, someone who can take care of you, and someone who can handle you."

"I don't need to be handled," I scoffed.

"I meant someone strong. You've got a mind of your own. You're a mover and shaker. You need someone who can keep up with you."

"I know that's what I need, but where are those guys? Most of them are married. You know, sometimes I think you just don't want me to see Bob because you want me all to yourself."

"Christ, Angel, that's not it at all. I just have your best interest at heart. I hope you'll think long and hard about this before you do anything you'll regret."

Even though Tim never talked to Pete about Bob Barnett, it seemed that they were both singing from the same hymnal. One evening, Pete decided to add his two cents worth of advice.

"Angel, I don't know what you see in Bob. He's a loser and a ground-pounder.[1] Remember the night he was playing touch football with the base team and the ref called a penalty on him? He bounced the ball on the ground and walked off the field in a huff."

"Yes, I remember. I know he's a little immature, but he's four years younger than I am—he'll grow out of it. The one big thing in his favor, Pete, is that he's single," I said, reinforcing the fact.

"Single! Right! Well that's about the only thing he's got going for him.

Angel, you need to find a single pilot, someone who's going places."

"Sure, Pete, easy for you to say. You're married and have a sweet wife and kids to go home to. I wanna get married, settle down, have some kids of my own, and be a normal, respectable woman," I replied longingly.

"Pete, I'd love to marry a fighter pilot," I continued, "but most of them are like you—married. And the ones who aren't, don't seem to be interested in me. Besides, Pete, it really isn't a crime not to be a fighter pilot. You know, Bob was selected for pilot training but had to drop out because he developed an ulcer," I explained looking for a point to pin my case on.

"Well, that figures. He couldn't cut it. He probably flunked out," Pete snapped as he took another swallow of his scotch.

"Pete, you don't understand. I'm not getting any younger. I feel like life is passing me by," I said somberly.

"I'm sorry, Angel. I know how much you wanna get married. I love you so much, and I just don't wanna see you get hurt."

I ignored all of Pete and Tim's advice and decided that Bob was my last chance. I was stubborn and my mind was made up. The fact that everyone was telling me I was wrong only made me cling harder to my opinion. Back then I thought maybe Tim and Pete didn't have my best interest at heart. Only later would I realize they did. I was getting out of the Air Force, my biological clock was ticking, and if I didn't land someone soon, I'd miss the chance to start having kids. I saw Bob's faults, but I wanted to believe I could make it work. He would grow out of his immaturity. After all, people can change, right?

At any rate, I wasn't taking their advice. Sometimes, you only figure it out after you end up in a spin, crash, and burn. And then, it's too late.

¹ A ground-pounder is another name for support puke or a non-pilot.

*And now how abhorred in my imagination it is!*
—William Shakespeare, English writer (1564 - 1616)

# The Snake and the Chicken

RECREATION FOR FIGHTER PILOTS revolved around three Fs and a D: flying, fighting, fucking, and drinking. These activities could be done separately but were usually combined. Drinking and fighting went well together, as typically one followed the other. Drinking and sex was a great combo, as long as you didn't have too much to drink. Drinking and flying was not advisable, even if a pilot sucked oxygen before getting into the cockpit.

These activities ranked among the highest forms of entertainment with fighter jocks. But in a war zone, when flying missions involved the possibility of getting your ass shot off, and women were in short supply, other forms of entertainment needed to be devised. They soon found another F that they could combine with drinking. Enter "Fresco," Captain Skip Sutton's pet python.

Skip kept Fresco in his hootch and on occasion hung him around his neck as he walked around the base. Where Skip got the snake, I wasn't sure, but they're common in the hot Asian jungles. Bi-weekly Saturdays with Fresco soon became a regular form of amusement for the fighter jocks.

Fresco was about 10 feet long, six inches in diameter, and weighed in at about 40 pounds. He was a mere baby compared to an adult that can grow to 30 feet and weigh upwards of 200 pounds. His smooth skin was olive green with brown saddle-shaped patterns outlined in ebony.

Pythons are in the boa constrictor family and get their name from how they kill their prey. They coil their bodies around their prey to suffocate it, and then swallow it whole. Boas can stretch their jaws wide enough to swallow an animal larger than their own head.

Skip held a "Fresco Feeding Fest" about every two weeks, because depending on the size of its last prey, a python can take several weeks to digest its food. On a hot, muggy, Saturday afternoon a raucous group of fighter jocks gathered outside on the patio, drinking cold beer and waiting for Skip and Fresco to arrive.

Shortly after the crowd had assembled, in sauntered Skip through the back gate with Fresco draped over his shoulders. The jocks welcomed him with whistles and loud cheers, "Here they come! Who hah! It's about time you got here." Skip unwrapped Fresco from his neck and set him down on the grass to settle him into his surroundings.

Meanwhile, Skip got everyone's attention. "Alright, you guys, listen up. Last time Broadway won the pool by estimating the kill time at three minutes, forty-five seconds. Who's going to beat that record?" The jocks started to deliberate among themselves.

"What's it gonna be this time?" "How big's the chicken?" "Hell! How hungry is Fresco?" The pilots peppered Skip with questions as they reached down, unzipped the pant-leg pockets on their flight suits and pulled out a few dollar bills. As they started bellowing out their estimated kill times, Skip quickly wrote them down on a small note pad and collected the money in his flight cap.

"OK, Chuck, you got three and half minutes. Cherry, what's your kill time?"

"Three minutes," Dan Cherry shouted back.

Skip headed over to Broadway and chided, "Broadway, are you in again?"

"Of course. You know these pussies can't beat my call on kill times. I say Fresco is pretty hungry today—this is gonna be a quick strike. I'm goin' for three minutes, ten seconds," he said and handed Skip two bucks.

"Wait a minute," said Cherry, "That's too close to my time."

"Tough rocks, you got ten seconds on me—try 'n beat it," Broadway fired back. Others continued shouting out their kill time estimates as Skip repeated them and gathered their cash.

"Any more bets before I close this off? OK. Hearing none, all bets are closed. Let the game begin," shouted Skip.

A couple of Thais carried in a bamboo cage with a small live chicken inside. They opened the cage door, reached inside, grabbed the chicken by the legs, pulled it out, and held it upside down. The chicken started flapping its wings and clucking frantically as it sensed its impending fate. Meanwhile, the other Thai tied a string around one of the chicken's legs and set it on the ground. The string was long enough so the chicken could walk around on the grass, but couldn't get away.

The guys began yelling, "Go get it, Fresco! Come on! Get it! Go for it! Get it! Go! Go! Go!" The chicken became frenzied with all the commotion and kept running around in circles. Soon the python's elliptical eye caught sight of the chicken and slowly began to slither toward his soon-to-be dinner.

"One minute thirty seconds down," hollered Skip.

As the sun and the beer worked their chemistry, the fighter jocks fired out more words of encouragement. "Get your ass in gear, Fresco!" "What's takin' you so long?" "I've got money on you—damn it!" "Get a move on, dickhead!"

Stealthily, Fresco moved in closer to his prey, then lunged for the chicken. As he did, the chicken attempted to fly away, but it was futile. The crowd yelled, "No! No! Get back down here! Come on—don't let it get away!" The Thai gave a quick jerk to the string attached to the chicken's leg and snapped it back down to the ground. The chicken was now directly in the python's line of sight. Fresco charged again and this time successfully caught it. Slowly and deliberately Fresco coiled his body around the terrified bird.

"Two minutes and twenty-five seconds!" yelled Skip. The snake systematically squeezed every ounce of life out of the chicken, then opened his jaws and devoured the lifeless body headfirst. Loose chicken feathers were scattered about—the aftermath of Fresco's lunch.

The crowd hollered out shouts of approval, "Good goin', Fresco!" "Shit Hot! Way da go Fresco!" "What's the time, Skip?"

Skip looked at his watch as the crowd eagerly awaited his announcement. "Three minutes and two seconds and the winner is," he quickly checked his note pad, "Dan Cherry by two seconds."

The crowd whistled and clapped and hollered boisterously. Skip took the pool of dollar bills out of his flight cap and handed it to Dan Cherry. "Great goin'," he said and gave Cherry a celebratory slap on the shoulder. "It's your turn to buy a round of drinks. As for the rest of you dicks, you'll have another chance to win again in two weeks." The jocks eagerly adjourned to the o-club bar to continue drinking. It was just another great day in paradise—except for the chicken.

SECTION FOUR
# MiG Killers

*The Air Force comes in every morning and says, 'Bomb, bomb, bomb.' And then the State Department comes in and says, 'Not now, or not there, or too much, or not at all.'*

—Lyndon B. Johnson, 36th President of the United States (1908 - 1973)

# Rules of Engagement

THE TERM "RULES OF Engagement" (ROE) in the military are not to be confused with a TV sit-com with the same name. The military defines rules of engagement (ROE) as "Directives issued by competent military authority, which delineate the circumstances and limitations under which the United States forces will initiate and/or continue combat engagement with other forces encountered."[1] The definition stresses the word competent, which seemed to be missing in the ROE that were in place during the Vietnam War.

Here's how a country prepares for a possible war. The military trains men (and now women) to be warriors who will be deployed to a war zone. These actions will ultimately result in people on both sides being killed. In the sixties, every male could be drafted for military service. If you had a problem with killing people or being killed, you either got a deferment or you went to Canada. Today, there is no draft, so if you disagree with what warriors do, then you don't volunteer to join the military. While I was in the military, I agreed with the philosophy that to win the peace you have to win the war. I thought we were the good guys, and if we applied enough pressure they, whoever "they" were, would come around to our way of thinking. That only seemed logical. After all, my father would hit us kids to get us to do what we were expected to do, and that worked. Surely, I assumed the same strategy could work on a larger scale.

With a readied military behind them, the President and Congress determine what country to invade and destroy, or what dictators to overthrow in order to spread democracy. Congress funds the war with our hard-earned tax dollars. The spin-doctors come up with a good slogan for the war like, "Operation Bring 'Em Freedom," because if you add the word freedom to anything, most Americans will buy it. Then the military is given the order to go get 'em.

Unfortunately, during the Vietnam War, the military was not able to determine ROE. The war was totally directed from Washington by President Lyndon B. Johnson, who often boasted, "Those boys can't hit an outhouse without my permission."[2] In my estimation, he and his cronies were ego-centered, control freaks. They seemed to be more concerned about their political image than the results their actions would have on the thousands of military men and women who put their lives on the line for Uncle Sam. One of the biggest culprits was Robert McNamara, the Secretary of Defense, who helped design the ROE and the Air Force's forbidden target list during the sixties. After he had served as Secretary of Defense for seven years, he came to the conclusion that the war was unwinnable. He wanted to stop the bombing in North Vietnam, but Johnson rejected his advice. Subsequently, McNamara left for "other opportunities." During the conflict, McNamara never spoke out against the war. If he had, he might have been an influential force in bringing the war to an end sooner. I believe his lack of integrity was responsible for the needless loss of thousands of lives. In 1995, in an effort to ease his conscious, he wrote *In Retrospect: The Tragedy and Lessons of Vietnam.* Unfortunately, it was too little, too late. But I guess he could have gone to his grave and never said anything.

The following restricted targets were part of the ROE that our pilots were up against during this hideous war. It appears from reviewing this list that the word competent could not be applied to the bureaucrats who devised this strategy.

- Any MiG base designated as a sanctuary. *(How could any MiG base be called a sanctuary? Isn't that where the MiGs were launched against our aircraft?)*
- Any MiG fighter jet not showing hostile intent. *(Wait a minute. If one of our pilots saw a MiG on his radar or in his check-six[3] position, guess what? They were out looking for him. What happened to the element of surprise?)*
- Any SAM (Surface-to-Air Missiles) site not in operation. The Russians installed SAM sites in North Vietnam. SAMs were launched to shoot down our aircraft.[4] *(How was anyone supposed to*

*know whether or not the site was operational? Were they supposed to post a sign?)*

This was like a game of baseball where one team played by the three-strikes-and-you're-out rule, and the other team played by you're out after one strike. Surely, the enemy knew our rules and were laughing all the way to their officers' club at the end of a good day of shoot 'em ups.

The guys talked endlessly about these restrictions, and I couldn't understand the logic of any of it.

"What do you mean, you can't bomb a MiG base? Isn't that where the MiGs are? Why are you only allowed to bomb vegetable trucks? God, you can get killed doing that!"

"Well, Angel," explained a pilot who was either very naïve or very brainwashed, "you see, if you bomb those vegetable trucks, that will keep the enemy from getting its food and slow down the war."

"That's bullshit. Get 'em where it hurts!" Of course, they already knew this and didn't need any woman club officer telling them the obvious.

The military became more frustrated with the inept war strategists who hindered the military's efforts to operate efficiently and safely. To counter these ROE, "protective reaction strikes" were devised. They would allow the fighters the option to strike only in three specific instances:

- When a reconnaissance aircraft appeared to be threatened;
- When antiaircraft artillery (AAA) and SAM sites threatened military aircraft operating near the borders of North Vietnam; and
- When "limited duration" raids were deemed necessary to counter buildups of enemy forces.[5]

These guidelines for "protective reaction strikes" sounded like a good opportunity to apply the concept of broad mental reservation. It was something I learned from one of the good sisters in Catholic school.

Sister Ignatius explained broad mental reservation during our class on the Ten Commandments. "Class, today we are going to discuss how you can obey each commandment when two commandments seem to be in conflict. As you know, the seventh commandment is 'Thou shall not bear false witness against your neighbor,' or more simply, 'thou shall not tell a lie.' The fourth commandment is 'Honor your father and mother' which means you must obey your father and mother."

We all listened attentively. "OK class, say your mother sees a salesman coming down the street soliciting door to door. She says to you, 'Mary, when he comes to our door, tell him I'm not home.' Now girls, you know lying is a sin, but you also know you must obey your mother. So, what do you do?" We all looked perplexed wondering how we were going to get out of this dilemma.

She continued, "When the salesman comes to the door and asks, 'Is your mother at home?' You can respond with, 'No, my mother isn't at home' even though you know she really is. Now, after you say, 'No, my mother isn't at home,' and the salesman walks away, in your mind you say, *she isn't home to see you.'* This is called broad mental reservation, and it can be used to save you from breaking the commandments. God knows all, even your innermost thoughts, and He will understand your circumstances and forgive you from this unintended sin of lying. In your heart you meant to tell the truth, but you had to obey your mother. For all intents and purposes, this was a clear case of broad mental reservation and not lying."

I thought this was brilliant and was sure Sister had studied law or watched *Perry Mason* to have come up with a strategy to save all of us from the extra time we'd have to spend in purgatory for lying. We all began using broad mental reservation when our parents asked us questions we'd rather not answer like, "Have you been out necking with that hooligan Sean O'Brien at the movies?" "No, Mom, I wasn't necking with him at the movies," *but I was necking with him in the back seat of his Chevy.* At the time, I thought only the Catholics knew about this marvelous concept.

But it seemed others had gotten wind of it, too. The fighter pilots definitely knew about it. "Yes, I'm single," *while I'm TDY at your base.* Even the civilian war planners seemed to know about broad mental reservation when they designed the "protective reaction strikes" which allowed pilots, under certain caveats, to bomb targets that might not be OK to bomb under normal ROE. I figured that if broad mental reservation was used, the revised guidelines to the ROE meant we could start bombing the hell out of the VC and wrap up this war in no time. I think that's what some high-ranking, military personnel thought, too. Go get 'em guys!

[1] The American Heritage Dictionary of the English Language, Fourth Edition, 2000 by Houghton Mifflin Company. Updated in 2009. Published by Houghton Mifflin Company.

[2] President Johnson supposedly said this. However, when I sent an inquiry to the Johnson Library to confirm this, they could not verify the actually date or document that quoted this.

[3] Check-six means look behind you. It refers to the 6 o'clock position on a clock.

[4] *Vietnam Memoirs*, Joe Patrick, March 31, 2004. http://80fsheadhunters.org/vietnam_memoirs. htm.

[5] Congressional Record—Senate, United States Senate, June 13, 1972, pages 20599-20600.
Congressional Record—Senate, United States Senate, June 14, 1972, pages 20754-20764.
Congressional Record—Senate, United States Senate, June 21, 1972, pages 21773-21779.

*To insure peace of mind ignore the rules and regulations.*
—George Ade, American humorist (1866 - 1944)

## Whistle Blower

AFTER PRESIDENT JOHNSON ANNOUNCED he would not seek re-election, Richard Nixon ran on a campaign promise to end the war. He won the election, but two years later it didn't seem like much progress had been made. Henry Kissinger, National Security Adviser, was holding secret peace talks in Paris in an attempt to negotiate a truce with North Vietnam. Hanoi rejected the terms and walked out, which gave Nixon a justification to increase the bombing campaign in the North and South along the DMZ. While all this was going on, Nixon planned a visit to China, a country that provided North Vietnam military weapons and supported reunification under Communist rule. Nixon was the first American President to visit China while in office, and his intention was to normalize relations.

If pilots could only strike targets under specified instances, then they needed to interpret the rules a little more liberally. Soon, the use of broad mental reservation was extended to the protective reaction strikes rule. They rationalized it this way:

- A pilot may only strike a target when reconnaissance aircraft appeared to be threatened. *(Since reconnaissance aircraft were unarmed, they were always threatened.)*

- A pilot may only strike a target when antiaircraft artillery sites threaten military aircraft operating near the borders of North Vietnam. *(These sites existed to shoot down our aircraft so they were always a threat.)*

- A pilot may only strike a target during "limited duration" raids deemed necessary to counter buildups of enemy forces. *(Couldn't the enemy always be building up forces, and therefore, it would always be deemed necessary?)*

Enter Sergeant Lonnie Franks, an intelligence specialist with two years under his belt, who was assigned to the Directorate of Operational Intelligence. His primary duties included providing intelligence information for the aircrews and the Wing Commander. Aircrews received updated maps and slides that indicated the location of friendly and enemy units and equipment, orders of battle, and location of reconnaissance targets useful on their way to fly missions over Laos and North Vietnam. The Wing Commander received a summary of the previous day's reconnaissance missions at his 0800 "stand up" briefing.

Franks understood the importance of generating accurate reports. Reconnaissance aircrews flew unarmed aircraft over enemy targets with fighter-bomber escorts. The "recce" crew had to fly at a precise air speed and altitude to get the required photos. However, since the fighter-bomber escorts did not have to fly straight and level, they could engage in "jinking"—flying in irregular patterns in anticipation of ground fire. Then, if fired upon, the protective reactive strike rule came into play, and the fighters could drop their ordinance on the enemy AAA sites.[1]

Franks also served as a debriefer who collected every scrap of information from the pilots when they returned from a mission. Debriefs could last an hour or longer depending on the nature of the flight. After the information was collected, an operational report 4 (OPREP 4) was generated, which was the official record of the mission.

Franks didn't know about broad mental reservation. He interpreted the ROE strictly by the book. So, when one of the aircrews gave him a disturbing answer to one of the questions after a routine mission, he didn't know what to do. When he asked them if they had received any hostile fire, they said, "No, but we had to report that we did." The escort crew had to report that they received hostile fire in order to justify their actions in case they had dropped their bombs. This was not an isolated incident. Over the next few weeks, preparing the OPREP 4s became increasingly more difficult and convoluted.

When Franks asked his superior what to do about the false reporting, he was told to "Just report what the aircrew tells you." He felt he could not go to anyone on base to report his concerns because they were all privy to it. He suspected that someone higher up the chain of command was authorizing these actions. So, he did the next best thing. He wrote a letter to Senator

Harold Hughes, from his home state of Iowa, stating that he had been forced to falsify reports. The Senator ended up submitting a sanitized version of the letter to General Ryan, the Chief of Staff of the Air Force.

At first it was not known who wrote the letter, because initially Franks was concerned about repercussions. His letter started a whole chain of events that led to a full-blown congressional investigation. Our base was crawling with IG personnel and congressional staff who interviewed those involved. They reported back that yes, in fact "some missions had not been flown in accordance with the ROE and there were irregularities in the operational reports."

When Major Pete Mendellson was asked about the unauthorized bombings he said unequivocally, "It was the only time I felt I'd ever done any good in this whole damn war." His unapologetic attitude did not earn him any accolades. In fact, it cost him any further promotions in the Air Force. I thought he was right. All others involved, including the Wing Commander Colonel Gabriel, responded with, "All we were doing was following orders."

But whose orders? Where did the buck finally stop? It ended up at the feet of General John D. Lavelle, who was the Commander of 7th Air Force in Saigon. He took full responsibility for the misreporting done under his command and ensured that it would not happen again. General Ryan told him that his application for retirement would be accepted. The Pentagon announced his retirement in the middle of an intense bombing period and said that he was retiring for health reasons at his permanent rank of major general (two stars).

This raised a red flag with the press, because although a general retires at his permanent rank of two stars, the President automatically recommends he be retired at his retirement rank, which was four stars for Lavelle. The President then sends a request to Congress for approval. However, in Lavelle's case, this was delayed for several weeks.

Suspicions were aroused about the real reasons for Lavelle's departure. Finally, General Ryan admitted he had asked General Lavelle to resign, which caused Congress to call for a full-scale investigation. Congress had the impression that the Vietnam War had generated so much dishonesty over three successive administrations that it was considered normal. Even the military had become highly suspect.

During the congressional hearings, Lavelle admitted that he had interpreted the ROE liberally but stated that he never exceeded his authority. He gave four reasons in his defense:

1. **Increase in Enemy Aggression.** It was well documented that MiG incursions had increased from 4 to 72 from one year to the next and surface-to-air missile attacks had increased from 20 to 200.

2. **Pressure from Above.** With the increase in the enemy build up, his superiors wanted him to be more aggressive.

3. **Rules of Engagement Made Obsolete.** Since the ROE were established in 1968 the North Vietnamese had developed more sophisticated technology for the radar detection used for their Surface-to-Air Missiles (SAM) sites. Prior to this development the North Vietnamese had to turn on their radar when they saw fighter aircraft approaching, which our pilots could detect. Because the new radar was always on, it could be assumed that it was always tracking our fighters. Therefore, using one's best judgment, our fighters could hit the SAM sites.

4. **A Commander's Moral Obligations to His Troops.** "All of my judgments were made as a field commander acutely mindful of my often anguishing responsibility for the protection of the lives and safety of thousands of courageous young airmen under my command."[2]

Lavelle said to Congress, "It is not pleasant to contemplate ending a long and distinguished military career with a catastrophic blemish on my record." He retired with the reduced rank of a two star in disgrace after being dragged through the mud.

In August 2010, shortly before this book was completed, General Lavelle was exonerated and his rank restored to four-star general, along with his honor. While researching historical records, Aloysius and Patrick Casey unearthed White House tapes and wartime military message traffic that indicated President Nixon was personally involved. Nixon had ordered Secretary of State Henry Kissinger and the U.S. Ambassador to Vietnam Ellsworth Bunker to relay to the combatant commanders in Vietnam (Lavelle) his approval to strike any Surface-to-Air Missile (SAM) site, whether or not it had locked on, and to characterize these strikes as "protective reactions." When asked, the former Secretary of Defense Melvin R. Laird admitted he had told the commanders to liberally interpret the ROE concerning protective reactive strikes. The new orders permitted hitting antiaircraft installations and other dangerous targets, whether they were activated or not.

On June 26, 1972, at a press conference, Nixon had been asked about General Lavelle's actions concerning the stepped-up assaults on SAM missile sites in the North Vietnam. Nixon told reporters, "It wasn't authorized, and it was proper for Lavelle to be relieved and retired."[3]

Unfortunately, Lavelle died of a heart attack in 1979. Some say he died of a broken heart. Lavelle's widow, Mary Jo, 91, and their seven children were relieved that his name had finally been cleared and his honor restored.

As for the whistle blower, Sergeant Franks, he still feels he did the right thing. However, he got out of the intelligence field and was assigned as a clerk-typist. He later applied for Officer Training School, and it was General Ryan who rejected his request.

[1] "An Affair to Remember?", Major Patrick R. Tower, USAF Academy, 1994 (approx) International Society of Military Ethics at http://www.pjsinnam.com\vn-history\vn-doc\lavelle. html/ http://isme.tamu.edu/Cases/Affair.html.

[2] "An Affair to Remember?", Major Patrick R. Tower, USAF Academy, 1994 (approx) http://isme. tamu.edu/Cases/Affair.html and the Congressional Record.

[3] "Obama Restores Honor to General Lavelle," Craig Whitlock, Washington Post, August 5, 2010. Also, see the Arlington National Cemetery Site that gives biographies of those buried there. http://www.arlingtoncemetery.net/jlavelle.html.

*In war there is no substitute for victory.*

—General Douglas MacArthur, WWII Field Marshall (1880 - 1964)

## Triple Nickel Delivers

ON THE MORNING OF February 22, 1972, I walked into the club to find the Triple Nickel's Jeep parked in the lobby. On top of the Jeep was a wood-carved elephant wearing a Triple Nickel hat. Painted on the window was "One for the Christians! Shit Hot from the Alley Cats." They were celebrating something. After I read the night log, I realized that the Nickel had shot down a MiG and had drunk until the wee hours of the morning. At first I was annoyed by the antics but soon realized what an important symbol this was to them and simmered down. A call from the Wing Commander telling me, "Not to sweat the small stuff," also helped.

With Operation Linebacker in full swing and the initiation of the "Protective Reactive Strikes," the lid was off on restricted targets. We were back in business and restarted bombing over North Vietnam. As a result, the Triple Nickel was the first to shoot down a MiG-21.[1] Major Robert Lodge and Lieutenant Roger Locher were the victorious crew. To celebrate, some fighter jocks, whom I'm sure were egged on by their wacky Squadron Commander, Lieutenant Colonel Joe Kittinger, decided to literally carry Joe's Jeep up a half-dozen stairs, through the swinging doors of the o-club, and park it in the lobby.

Kittinger, a redheaded wild man, sometimes still acted like a high school kid trying to get away with drag racing in his father's car. He was a man's man and didn't think the military was any place for a woman. He earned his outrageous reputation while doing test pilot experiments for the Air Force. In 1960, they wanted to determine from what altitude a crewman could free fall and still stay alive. Kittinger signed up for the job. He wore a pressure suit and layers of clothes to protect him from experiencing the severe cold at minus 94 degrees Fahreheit. At 102,800 feet, he jumped out of an open gondola, free fell for 13 seconds, and then his six-foot canopy opened to stabilize him. After four-and-a-half additional minutes, traveling at 614 miles per hour, almost the speed of sound, he descended to 17,500 feet where his regular 28-foot parachute deployed allowing him to land safely in the New Mexico desert. This feat proved to be historic and established that a man could survive a descent from high altitudes. It also put Kittinger's name in the aviation record books.[2]

Kittinger was an adrenaline junkie, always wanting to raise the ante. Some saw him as courageous and brave while others characterized him as flamboyant and a reckless risk-taker. I believed he was a little of both.

I decided to call Kittinger. "Good morning, Colonel Kittinger. This is Captain Pilato." Before I could get out another word, he started in on me, "Angel, before you tell me that my boys did some damage to the officers' club by driving our Jeep into the lobby, I just wanna let you know we'll get the Jeep out of your lobby in due time. But Angel, these guys deserve to celebrate a little. After all, this is the first MiG the Air Force has downed since 1968, and there's no need to get your tit in a wringer over a little Jeep parked in the lobby."

"You're absolutely right, sir. The fact is, Colonel, I was just calling to congratulate you and the Triple Nickel on your MiG kill and to say Shit Hot. And, go get 'em."

"Well…ah…thanks for the call," he said. I could tell my response had taken him by surprise.

"Just one thing. There's no problem with the Jeep being in the lobby. I'd like to ask you to have a couple of the guys come over and put a tarp under the truck to keep the engine grease from leaking on the carpet."

"Oh, sure, we can do that, and we'll have the Jeep out of there in a few days."

"Thanks, Colonel. Enjoy your day and your victory."

A week later, on March 1st, Kittinger and Lieutenant Leigh Hodgdon shot down another MiG-21—and in rolled the Jeep. That's how it all got started. Now the stage was set, every squadron that scored a MiG kill was going to want to park their truck in the o-club lobby.

On May 11, 1972, just seven days before he was to end his third tour of duty in SEA, Kittinger was shot down, captured, and became one of the 801

POWs held during the Vietnamese War. On March 23, 1973, after 321 days in captivity, he was released. Welcome home, Joe![3]

[1] MIG-21 is an advanced supersonic single-engine jet built by Mikoyan-Gurevich Design Bureau. It can travel more than twice the speed of sound and provided a formidable challenge to the F-4 Phantom.

[2] To read the full story of Kittinger's famous feat and his other aviation accomplishments, go to the U.S Centennial Flight Commission report. http://www.centennialofflight.gov/essay/Explorers_Record_Setters_and_Daredevils/Kittinger/EX31.html.

[3] Information on POWs from http://www.nampows.org.

Triple Nickel's truck parked in the O-Club lobby
after their first MiG kill since 1968

# Triple Nickel – Off They Go

F-4 Phantom Fighter Jet

Lieutenant Colonel Joe Kittinger,
Triple Nickel Squadron Commander
MiG Killer - POW May '72 to March '73

Marty Cavato

Triple Nickel mascot "Triple" catching
a ride on the Commander's Jeep

# Triple Nickel Celebrations Continue

Roger Locher

Triple Nickel plaque hung in the o-club bar to celebrate
Major Lodge's and Captain Locher's first MiG kill

USAF

Major Bob Lodge and Captain Roger Locher
Triple Nickel Celebs

*When a man becomes inebriated, any modicum of mild-manner virtue that he might have had turns into mayhem and mischief.*

—Angelica Pilato, Lieutenant Colonel, USAF (Ret.) (1942 - )

## Where Can We Park Our Truck?

I WAS GETTING USED to being awakened by early morning phone calls informing me of a "problem" at the officers' club. It usually had to do with a clong fight (guys running through the club chasing people with huge banana leaves), the Air Police arriving to stop a drunken brawl, or the o-club furniture being dismantled in preparation for a bonfire. This morning the call was from Pete Mendellson.

"Hello, Captain Pilato speaking," I said in a groggy voice.

"Hey, Angel! We did it! We did it! We shot down a MiG-21! We blew the son of a bitch out of the sky!"

Hearing the news that the 13th Squadron had downed a MiG instantly got my attention. "Shit Hot, Pete! That's great. I'm glad to hear it. But Pete, it's 3 o'clock," I said as I squinted at the clock on the end table.

"Jesus! Is it that late?" he slurred.

"Yes, it is." Then I asked, "Who got the kill?"

"Fred Olmsted and Gerry Volloy. It's their first kill and our squadron's first since 1968," he said exuberantly. "Can you believe it?" The kill had happened earlier in the day on March 30th, and they were still celebrating.

"Pete, this is great news, but I'm going back to sleep now. I'll celebrate with you tomorrow. OK?"

"Wait a minute Angel. Wait a minute. Remember, you told us we could park the truck in the club lobby if we shot down a MiG?"

"Yeah, Pete, I did. If you want to park the truck in the lobby, go ahead. Just put a tarp underneath the engine to keep the oil from leaking on the rug, OK? I'm really happy to hear the news, but I've gotta get some sleep. Bye."

"Wait a minute, don't hang up. I'm sorry I woke you up, but I knew you'd wanna know. There's one small problem."

"And what's the small problem, Pete?" I said now fully alert.

"Well...ah," he continued, "when we started to drive the truck up the stairs, we couldn't get it in the front door and now it's stuck in the doorway."

"It's stuck in the doorway! Good grief. I can't leave you guys alone for a minute. How did that happen, Pete?"

"Well, ah, we thought we could get it through the door. Fact is, Fred measured the front of the truck and the doorway and figured we had enough clearance," Pete explained.

"How the hell did he measure it?" I asked rather sarcastically.

"Well, Christ Angel, he eyeballed it. How d'ya think he measured it?" he said like it was a given.

"Pete, can't you guys just back it down the stairs?" I asked. At this point, exhausted, I hoped I'd be able to go back to sleep when I hung up.

"We can't," he said. "It's jammed, and besides, we have to get it into the lobby."

"Jammed? Good grief!" I could hear the guys yelling in the background, "Tell her we wanna knock the wall down!"

"Look, Angel," Pete persisted, "it's pretty important we get this truck parked in the lobby tonight because the Triple Nickel already has two MiG kills under their belt, and they parked their Jeep in the lobby. Don't forget, Angel, you said we could park our truck in the lobby if we shot down a MiG. We're gonna get this truck into the lobby tonight, if we have to knock the wall down."

I realized the conversation was going nowhere fast. Besides, trying to negotiate with someone who was smashed was, as the pilots would say, "like pissing in the wind."

"OK, Pete. Listen up. You're right—You're totally right. I did say you could park your squadron truck in the lobby," I said. "What d'ya think about this idea? Leave the truck where it is. In the morning I'll call the guys at Civil Engineers and have 'em knock the wall down. OK?"

"But, Angel," he persisted, "we've got enough guys here. We could have that wall down in a few minutes. All we need is a couple of sledgehammers. It'd take no time at all, and then we could drive her right in," he insisted.

Then, before I could respond, I heard him shout out, "Hey guys, who's got some sledgehammers?"

"Pete, wait a minute—wait a minute," I pleaded.

"Yeah, Angel. I hear ya. The guys are going for some sledgehammers."

"Hold on a minute, Pete. I don't think that's necessary. I think it would be a good idea to wait until morning and then let CE do it," I insisted.

The guys in the background were prodding Pete. "Tell her we're driving this son of a bitch into the club tonight. Come on Pete, tell her we can do it."

He snapped at them and said, "Shut up, you guys, Angel's trying to say something."

In as empathetic a voice as I could muster at that hour, I said, "I know you want to get that truck in the lobby tonight and show those Triple Nickel guys you scored a MiG kill. And I know you could probably knock out that wall in no time. But please let me call CE in the morning, and I promise you, I'll get it done. Just leave the truck where it is, and I'll handle it tomorrow. Once CE gets there, you'll be able to drive your truck right into the lobby. No need to mess with it tonight. OK? What d'ya say? You know you can count on me." All the time I was thinking, *if I can get them to just leave the truck right there until morning, they'd sober up, come to their senses, and realize the whole thing was a bad idea.*

"Angel, CE will take forever to get this done. We want it in the lobby now," he said as his band of brothers continued to egg him on.

"Pete, you know I've got connections over at CE. I can have them over at the club ASAP. They'll bring the right tools for the job, and they'll have it done in no time flat. Just let me handle it. Please?" I was envisioning the ramifications of this event. If they knocked down that wall, their MiG kill might be minimized by a reprimand, or at the very least, some hand slapping. Who knew? Plus, the club's front entrance would be a disaster.

With some reluctance Pete slurred, "OK, OK. Then you'll call CE in the morning and tell 'em to knock down this wall. Right?"

"Sure, Pete, absolutely. No problem. I'll take care of it. Go back to celebrating, or better yet, go get some sleep. OK?"

Pete yelled back at the guys, "There's no problem guys. Angel's gonna call CE in the morning, and they're gonna knock out this damn wall for us. Then we'll drive this baby right into the lobby."

I heard their cheers through the phone, "Way d'go, Angel. Shit Hot!"

"Thanks Angel, you're the best." Pete said. Then he whispered into the phone so no one could hear, "I love you."

"I love you, too, Pete. Now can I get some sleep? I'm going back to bed."

"Angel?" Pete hesitated, "Do you want some company?"

"No, Pete, not tonight."

With the few hours left until morning, I tried to go back to sleep, but to no avail. Shortly afterwards, I heard some noise on the street below my BOQ window. It was Pete and the boys from the 13th calling my name out, "Angel. Angel. Pete's out here and wants to come up and play. Angel. Angel," they continued.

That was it. I got up, went out on the balcony and picked up a pail of water that had been collecting from the dripping air conditioner and tossed it over the balcony. It landed square on top of Pete and the group. I yelled out, "Good night, boys!" and slammed the door and hopped back into bed.

The next morning the truck was still partly on the stairs, with the front end jammed in the doorway. Everyone had to go around to the back door to get into the club. Some of the non-pilots grumbled. "These jocks are at it again." "Why the hell do we have to use the back door?" "What's goin' on around this place?" "Those guys are out of control."

In the morning, CE came over to the club, but it wasn't to knock down the wall. They were there to fix a leak in the kitchen. I filled the sergeants in on what had happened and why the truck was there, "I don't know how I kept them from knocking down the wall. Maybe it was because they were all too drunk or because they couldn't find any sledgehammers."

Just then I looked out the window and saw Pete coming toward the club. I turned to the CE crew and said, "Here comes Major Mendellson from the 13th. Just go along with me on this one, will ya?" They agreed.

Pete walked into my office and I said, "Hi, Pete, how's it goin'?' The troops from CE are here to knock down the wall. They said it wouldn't take too long and then you can drive your truck right on into the lobby."

He looked a little surprised, "Well, that's what I came over to talk to ya about," he said with a sheepish look.

Before he could continue I said, "See, Pete, I told you not to worry. I knew if I called CE and told them what needed to be done, they'd come right over. Isn't that right, Sergeant?" I said and turned to get his response.

"That's right, Capt'n. We've got the equipment right outside in the truck, and we're ready to go. It'll probably take a half-day or so. After we knock down the wall, we'll have to put up a new door jam and order some new double doors. We can put some canvas up over the entryway until the new doors get here. By the way, Captain, are we charging this work to the o-club or the 13ᵗʰ Squadron?" This guy was going along with the ruse better than if I'd written a script for him.

Finally, Pete interrupted, "Wait a minute—hold on—Angel. That's what I came over for. We've got a tow truck out front. They're gonna hitch it up to our truck and get it off the front steps."

"You mean you've changed your mind?" I asked with an innocent smile.

"Well yeah, I think it's best if we remove the truck, seeing that folks haven't been able to use the front door. I think we might have been a little overly enthusiastic last night."

"You mean this morning, don't you?" I retorted and turned towards the CE guys.

"Well, sorry, guys. I guess you're not needed here after all. Sorry for the inconvenience. Thanks for coming over so quickly, guys." I gave them a wink and a smile. "Why don't you guys go back to the kitchen and have Sergeant White give you a case of cold beer for your trouble."

"Way da go, Capt'n. Thanks. Any time we can help out just call us," they said, eager to get their prize for a "good performance."

The tow truck hitched up the pickup truck, and a half hour later off it went. The front door was back in use and the pilots were on to their next MiG kill.

The practice of driving the squadron's truck into the club became routine, and the pilots nicknamed the o-club "Angel's Truck Stop." I started calling the monthly newsletter the *Truck Stop News*. Pete even had a sign made that said, "Angel's Truck Stop." They hung it on the front of the o-club. Unfortunately, someone stole it. I never did get it back.

From February 21 to August 28, 1972 when I left Udorn, 29 MiGs had been shot down.[1] Our 432ⁿᵈ Fighter Wing shot down a total of 21. The Triple Nickel accounted for 11; the 13ᵗʰ Panther Pack had seven; and three were credited to the TDY Squadrons deployed at our base. During that same time period, the Air Force reported 34 KIAs and 17 POW and MIAs.[2]

During the Vietnam War from 1964 to 1975, there were 58,266 American deaths and approximately 2,500,000 dead on both sides[3]. 1,678 American MIAs still remain unaccounted for.[4] In the end, Communism would prevail in Vietnam, but while we were there, we hoped it wouldn't.

[1] MiG kills and models were taken from *U.S. Air Force Combat Victory Credits Southeast Asia,* Albert F. Simpson, Historical Research Center, Air University, March 1974.

[2] Numbers derived from: http://thewall-usa.com/summary.asp.

[3] The number of actual dead on both sides varies from a variety of sources.

[4] Unaccounted for numbers are from Department of Defense http://www.dtic.mil/dpmo/vietnam/statistics/

13th TFS truck stuck on the O-Club stairs
after their first MiG kill since 1968

*There is a peculiar gratification on receiving congratulations from one's squadron for a victory in the air. It is worth more to a pilot than the applause of the whole outside world. It means that one has won the confidence of men who share the misgivings, the aspirations, the trials and the dangers of aeroplane fighting.*

—Captain Edward 'Eddie' Rickenbacker, American WWI Air Ace (1890 - 1973)

## It's A Shit Hot Day!

ANY DAY A PILOT shot down an enemy MiG was a day to celebrate. On April 16, 1972, our Wing shot down *three* MiG21s, and that was a Super Shit Hot Day! The 13th Squadron shot down two, and the 523rd, a TDY fighter squadron, shot down one. Everyone rushed to the o-club to congratulate the victorious fighter pilots like they were triumphant warriors entering the coliseum on their chariots. Our celebration didn't quite resemble the pomp and ceremony of Rome, but it was one hell of a party. The atmosphere at the o-club was exhilarating. The crowd was jubilant and playful, and the MiG killers were euphoric. Two white sheets painted with congratulatory messages hung on the red velvet curtain on the stage in the bar. One sheet painted in blue read:

> **13th Shit F----ing HOT!**
> **C.B. Dan & Jeff**
> **Broadway & Stu**
> **Twofers**
> **Kill a Commie 4 Christ**
> **April 1972**

Translated:

Shit F---ing Hot: The superlative of Shit Hot
Congratulations to the 13th TFS.

C.B. Dan & Jeff: Major Dan Cherry & Captain Jeff Feinstein
The pilot and the navigator who shot down a MiG

| Broadway & Stu: | Captain Fred Olmsted & Captain Stuart Maas Second crew of MiG killers |
|---|---|
| Twofers: | Two kills for the 13th Fighter Squadron |
| Kill a Commie for Christ: | It's OK to kill people if their political or religious beliefs disagreed with yours. |

These types of slogans are used to indoctrinate the warriors on both sides, to make it easier for them to fight and kill each other. Today our battle cry might be "kill a turban head for Christ" and theirs, "kill an infidel for Allah." The other sign painted in red said:

**S. H. 523rd**
**Jim and Mike**
**(Null & Void)**
**13th Trained**

Translated:

| S. H. 523rd: | Shit Hot. Great Job 523rd Fighter Squadron. |
|---|---|
| Jim and Mike (Null & Void): | Captain James Null ("Null") the pilot and his navigator Captain Michael Vahue ("Void") |
| 13th Trained: | The 13th Fighter Squadron was taking credit for getting this crew up to speed! |

The booze was flowing. The pilots were being doused with beer and *Cold Duck* and decorated with floral leis. Dan Cherry, a fighter jock in every sense of the word, was hoisted onto the shoulders of one of his squadron buddies and paraded around the bar. He was grinning from ear to ear. His disheveled hair and overgrown moustache were dripping with a mix of sweat and *Cold Duck*. He wore his trademark red bandanna, held a beer in one hand, and waved at the cheering crowd of admirers.

Dan was on his second tour in SEA. His first tour was at Korat Royal Thai Air Base in 1967 flying the great F-105 Thunderchief, affectionately called the "Thud," where he racked up 100 combat missions. That could have been enough of an accomplishment, but he decided to return to SEA to stay in the action and upgrade to the F-4.

Born in Ohio, the buckeye state and home of many military heroes, Dan would be joining the ranks of WWI fighter ace Eddie Rickenbacker, WWII fighter ace Dominic Gentile, and NASA astronaut Neil Armstrong. He'd chosen the Air Force because he wanted to be an aviator. He was a fun-loving, likeable guy who was the life of the party at every squadron event. One night, after a few too many, Dan was seen jumping into the pool at the Charoen Hotel off-base bare-ass naked with everyone clapping and cheering. His motto was, "Live today, who knows if you get tomorrow."

Captain Fred Olmsted nicknamed "Broadway" after the legendary quarterback "Broadway Joe" Namath of the New York Jets. He even looked like him, but it was Namath's bravado that Olmsted most emulated. In 1969, Namath shouted down a heckler who was chiding him about his upcoming game against the favored Baltimore Colts. He said, "We'll win the game. I guarantee you. We'll win the game." He needed a miracle to pull that off, because the Colts were touted as the greatest football team in history. But on game day, Namath led his Jets to defeat the Colts. Olmsted, by comparison, would say, "Damn it! I came here to win this war, and by God that's what we're going to do."

Olmsted was raised by a single mom in California, graduated from the Air Force Academy in 1964, and joined the Air Force to do two things: fly jets and take down the commies. He was smart, dashing, and had the makings of an outstanding fighter pilot. Initially he became a T-38 training instructor, but that was just too boring. He was itching to go where the action was and volunteered continuously to go to SEA. He couldn't reconcile the fact that he was in the States while many of his comrades were POWs. He'd been trained to fly and fight and felt it was his duty to do his part to end the war and help free them. Udorn was his second tour in SEA; his first tour was at Cam Rahn Bay, Vietnam in 1969.

He was in love with his F-4 and flew it with the passion and fervor of an obsessed lover. He once told me enthusiastically, "Angel, flying an F-4 is like having an orgasm, sometimes better." He played 4-5-6s until 0200, drank vodka like it was water, ran with the Thai women until 0500, and was ready to fly at 0700. When he slept wasn't certain.

Broadway's flight suit was drenched. His hair cascaded down his forehead as he puffed on a stogie. Colonel Gabriel, the Wing Commander, shook his hand and patted him on the shoulder. This was Broadway's second MiG kill, and he was basking in all the glory. His success came not from being lucky, but rather from skills he'd honed from his 300-plus combat missions at SEA.

Today was a true hero's party. The guys drank enough booze to drown an entire squadron or two. This celebration with their friends would be the only party these pilots would have. There wouldn't be any big hoopla back home to congratulate them for their courage and flying prowess. No, the press was reporting body counts and fueling the antiwar movement. The majority of the public had become antiwar and turned their rage toward the military. These guys were portrayed as baby killers, along with anyone else who was in the military. Their victory might get a few rounds of applause at the Veterans of Foreign Wars hall.

But why spoil the moment? As the pilots said to me, "Hey, Angel, don't knock it. It's the only war we've got!" This was the only place where a pilot could fly and fight and put his training into action. After all, getting promoted was tough enough. Flying in the war zone got you points and shooting down MiGs got you *big* points. These pilots were among the elite few who got to fly one of the best fighter jets of its time. For that privilege they embraced the challenge, danced with danger, and pushed themselves and their machines to the max.

It all sounded exciting and exhilarating, but when I seriously thought about it, it was downright scary. When a fighter pilot took the controls, he had to figure out how to outwit his opponent, lock in on the target, and fire his missiles before the other guy knew what hit him. If not, he could be the one blown to kingdom come.

It was a numbers game. No matter how well trained a pilot was, he could always end up being outmaneuvered by a fighter who was quicker on the draw. Of course, a fighter pilot doesn't think much about that. If he did, he would never get into the cockpit. It was a deadly game of target practice, one he was determined to win. It required him to think of himself as better than his rival. One wrong call, one screw up could cost him and his backseater their lives. This accounted for the fighter pilots' cocky, competitive, confident attitude. Or maybe it was just his way of coping with danger.

While we toasted and drank, there was another deeper thought that never crossed our minds. What about the North Vietnamese pilots who were blown out of the sky? Their families would be crying tonight, not celebrating. No one was thinking about the other guys that day. The pilots never saw the other airman's face. There was no mangled body or bloody evidence to confront them. It was all very sterile.

Even if we did think about it, we rationalized it. The other guy was a commie, and it was better to blow him away before he got you or one of your buddies. That's how the game was played. Ultimately, it always ended with one winner and one loser. When a pilot flew a mission, he had to think he was going to win. If he didn't, it could cost him his life. It seemed like a high price to pay for the joy of flying, but we weren't thinking any deep thoughts. We were too busy enjoying the moment. We had won this game of target practice, and we were celebrating, having fun, and drinking ourselves into oblivion. There was no need to think about anything else. And we didn't.

On that day, Dan Cherry certainly would never have imagined the scene 36 years later, when he would meet his former opponent, Nguyen Hong My, who was the pilot in the MiG-21 he'd shot down. Hong My had ejected and for a split second, Dan had seen him hanging from his chute as he glided to earth.

In 2008, Dan, now a retired brigadier general, went back to Vietnam to shake the hand of his former foe. Both men had tears in their eyes when they showed each other pictures of their families, children, and grandchildren. Dan held Hong's grandson in his arms and thought that if things had gone differently on that day in 1972, there would be no baby smiling and reaching for Dan's hand.[1]

---

[1] To get the full story of the reunion, read "Above and Beyond: My Enemy, My Friend," *Air & Space Magazine,* May 01, 2009. http://www.airspacemag.com/history-of-flight/Above--Beyond-My-Enemy-My-Friend.html. Also read *My Enemy—My Friend,* General Dan Cherry, Aviation Heritage Park, Second Edition, 2009. It's a wonderful story.

## It's a Shit Hot Day! Congratulations!

MiG Killers celebrating at the O-Club

Major Dan Cherry on top

Captain Jim Null riding high

Captain Jeff Feinstein on right

Captain Fred "Broadway" Olmsted in middle

# MiG Chasers - MiG Killers

Marty Cavato

September 9, 1972
Top: 1st Lieutenant Dwight Cook*, partly cut off 1st Lieutenant Bob Carley*
Top Right: Captain Marty Cavato, with mustache
Bottom left corner: Captain Billy Graham
Clockwise from bottom: Captain Bryan Tibbitt*, 1st Lieutenant Bud
Hargrove*, Captain Mike Francisco, Captain Bill Dalecky,
Captain John Madden, shaking hands with Captain Terry Murphy
and Captain Chuck DeBellevue (6 time MiG killer)

* Dwight Cook, Bob Carley, Bryan Tibbitt, and Bud Hargrove
were killed shortly after this photo was taken

Lieutenant Colonel Jack Rollins, Captain Angel
Pilato and Major John Mesenbourg

"Panther Pack" on the fabulous F-4

Marty Cavato

July 8, 1972
Back row: Captain Bryan Tibbett, Captain Steve Ritchie,
Captain Chuck DeBellevue, 1st Lieutenant John Hamm
Front row: 1st Lieutenant Bud Hargrove, Captain Dwain Houck,
1st Lieutenant Tommy Feezel, 1st Lieutenant Bob Hornack

# End of Tour Splash Down Celebrations

Colonel Charlie Gabriel, Wing Commander and
Major Dan Bowen, Executive Officer

Major Dan Cherry gets hosed

No one escapes the hose

Major John Mesenbourg survives his dunking

*You can never go home again, but the truth is you can never leave home, so it's all right.*

—Maya Angelou, American poet and writer (1928 - )

# The Phone Call

I WAS SEVEN MONTHS into my tour, and I remembered what Bob Grimaldi, a sergeant who worked for me at Bitburg, had said. "Captain, if you wanna see the Orient, take thirty days and go see it. Mark my words; you're going to hate that place. You'll be sorry if you're stuck there a whole year." He tended to be somewhat negative and overly dramatic, so I ignored his counsel, even though he had spent a year in Vietnam. Besides, one tends to ignore advice unless it agrees with what you're thinking.

It wasn't long after I'd gotten to Udorn that I'd become disillusioned and turned in my request to resign my commission. How would I ever finish my last five months? I'd volunteered for this assignment, I wanted to be part of the action, and now I felt trapped. If I was going to make it, I needed to suck it up and hang in there. I thought a lot about why I hated it so much. I wasn't getting shot at, languishing in the trenches, or experiencing the blood and guts of war. So, what the hell was my problem? Things that wouldn't have bothered me before became annoying and overwhelming. It was like pulling a thread on a hem; things just started to unravel.

It began with the expectation that a club in a war zone could be run like one in the States. Then, there were those ridiculous restrictions on procurement, running out of supplies all the time, and the cultural differences to work around. The club members complained continually about everything and anything. I took it all personally, like I was a failure and not able to live up to their expectations. What I didn't realize was that they were transferring their unhappiness about the war, their missions, and their assignment onto me. We were all experiencing the same conditions, and everyone dealt with their frustrations in different ways.

I was tired of having to translate everything over and over again to the Thais, who I was sure understood me but were just trying to get away with something. I no longer found the Thai food interesting and tasty. It was boring, and it was the only food we could get off-base. The countryside wasn't green and exotic, but ugly and dirty. The muddy roads riddled with potholes became unbearable, along with the vendors who were always hawking their goods. I no longer saw kids on the street begging for money sympathetically, but as mini-marauders who'd steal from you any chance they could.

The only escape I had was the bar or the bedroom, which brought its own type of misery. The bar room brawls, the drinking late into the night, the sex— it all became banal. Then, the overriding anxiety that loomed over everything was the possibility that another pilot might be declared MIA, KIA, or POW.

As I continued to mull it over, I realized it wasn't only the things that were happening here, it was my isolation from the familiar that had gotten to me. I longed for the things that were of comfort to me. I wanted to go to Dandrea's, a neighborhood Italian restaurant in Rochester that Mom used to take us kids to on Friday nights for the best beer-battered fish fries. It was our way of fulfilling the no meat on Friday requirement imposed by the Catholic Church. I wanted to watch some inane television show like *Rowen & Martin's Laugh-In, The Mod Squad,* or *Hogan's Heroes.*

I hungered for one of Mom's traditional Italian macaroni and sauce dinners (it wasn't called pasta until Italian became hip). Her tomato sauce would simmer on the stove all day until the meat on the braised spareribs loosened from its bones and the fennel-spiced sausage and meatballs became succulent. That aroma always made me salivate. I'd come into the kitchen smiling, eager to taste her delicious sauce. It was sad to think that she was gone, and I'd never again experience the wonderful food that made me long for home and for her.

Mom was the glue that held our family together. Dad was lost without her, and I knew he was worried about me but would never let me know. I wanted to reassure him with a hug, laugh at his corny jokes, and argue with him over the price of anything. He always thought everything was too expensive.

My brother and sister were thousands of miles away at college in New York City and Long Island. They were lost without Mom's constant encouragement, and being so far away I wasn't much help. My sister Nancie was obsessed about passing her math course. The way she related it, I thought for sure she wasn't going to pass. Her anxiety transferred to me, and I felt guilty because I couldn't be there to assist. But when she ended up getting an "A," I figured she didn't need help in math; she was just a little short on confidence and moral support.

My older sister, Marianne, was in California with her husband and three-year-old son. I wasn't very close to her. Her schizophrenia had driven my mother to despair and depression. Her condition made the rest of us fantasize that maybe we were adopted. The only way I could escape my wacky family was to leave, but now I was missing them.

It was 1972, and we didn't have the internet, e-mail, cell phones, or text messaging. Television on overseas bases was non-existent. The only way to get news was through the military's *Stars and Stripes* newspaper, which was one-sided. To stay in touch with family and friends, we had to use snail mail, but who made time to write?

I longed to hear the familiar voices of my family and friends. Before I left the States for Europe in 1968, I thought the best way to keep in touch was through voice tapes. I gave my parents a small reel-to-reel tape recorder, and I'd tape news and send it off to them. They'd listen to it, tape the family news over it, and send it back. By the time I'd left for Thailand in 1971, technology had improved. I bought my father, brother, and sister a cassette tape recorder to send news back and forth. It took time to fill up a tape, and by the time we listened to our tapes the news was old, but hearing their voices did bring some sense of connection.

I thought it would be great if I could have a real conversation with them. I decided to talk to Colonel Martin, the Base Communications Officer. He was instrumental in getting a phone installed in my BOQ room shortly after I arrived, which very few officers had. If you wanted to get hold of anyone, you had to wait until you saw him. I asked Colonel Martin, "Colonel, do you think there's any possibility that you can get a call through to the States for me? I'd really love to talk with my family."

"I think we can give it a shot," he said. "We'll need some time to arrange it. Once we do, you'll need time to let your family know when the call will be coming through."

"That'd be great! How about Easter? That's three weeks away. Is that enough time?"

"Sure, that'll work. I'll get it set up for you," he said, smiling.

"That'd be a perfect time to talk to all my family. My brother and sister will be home at my dad's house on college break. Colonel, thanks so much. It'd mean so much to me. Wait 'til I tell 'em. They'll be so excited," I said.

"OK, Angel. Glad to do it for you."

Before he left, I thanked him again, threw my arms around him, and gave him a huge hug.

A few days later, he gave me a heads up that the plan was a go. At midnight on April 2, 1972, Easter Sunday morning, I went over to the officers' club excited and ready to talk with Dad, Nancie, and Charles. It was six p.m. in Rochester, and they were eagerly waiting, too.

Telephone calls to the States were done through MARS, the Military Affiliate Radio System, which was set up by the Department of Defense. MARS used civilian licensed amateur ham radio operators to augment the military's local, national, and international communications. Phone transmissions were done by patching calls through from one ham operator to another until they reached the landlines in the States.

When it was time, I called over to the communications squadron. The sergeant rapidly answered, "432nd Tactical Telecommunications Squadron, Sergeant Stevens speaking."

"Good evening, Sergeant Stevens, this is Captain Pilato awaiting my call to the States."

"Yes, ma'am. Hold on a minute. We're going to get ready to patch you through. What's the number in New York?"

I quickly told him the number, "716-454-5443." It took awhile. Finally, I heard the phone ringing. It sounded like it was a million miles away in outer space and reverberating in a tunnel. I thought the use of the word MARS was appropriate.

Dad answered the phone, "Hello! Over." I had instructed them that after every sentence they had to say "over" to let them know they had to switch over to the other person to talk.

"Hello, Dad. How are you? Over." It was great to hear his voice. My words echoed back over the lines, and there was a lot of static.

"Good, Doll! How are you? Over." More echoing and more static, then we were disconnected.

The sergeant came back on the line and said, "Hang on, ma'am, I'll try it again." I waited and waited until I heard the far away ring of the phone. This time Charles answered. "Hello, Angelica, over."

"Hello, Charles. How are you? Over." Again it took a long time for my greeting to reach him.

"Good, how are you? Over," his voice rippled back. Then we were disconnected again.

The sergeant sounded frustrated when he came back on line, "All right," he said, "we'll try it one more time."

"Thanks, Sergeant. I know you're doing everything you can," my voice was cracking just a little.

On the third try, Nancie got on the phone. We went through the same routine and then we were disconnected for the last time. The sergeant said, "I'm sorry, ma'am, that's all I can do for you."

"Thanks for trying. It was good to hear their voices, even if it was only for a few moments." I left the club via the back door and cried all the way back to my BOQ room. That was the only time I talked to my family the entire year, and I was one of the lucky ones.

*I know that I shall meet my fate*
*Somewhere among the clouds above;*
*Those that I fight I do not hate,*
*Those that I guard I do not love;*

—William Butler Yeats, Irish Poet (1865 - 1939)
From *An Irish Airman Foresees His Death*

## Two More Brass Name Plates

FROM THE AIRCRAFT WINDOW the geometric patterns of lush, jade-green rice paddies seemed to blend into the horizon, broken only by an occasional thatched-roof house on wooden stilts. These innocent images of the Thai landscape, with its hand-worked farmlands, were soon replaced with the stark contrast of a sprawling U.S. military air reconnaissance wing. As we rapidly approached the mile-long concrete runway, we saw massive aircraft hangers that housed F-4 Phantom fighter jets, brown wooden hootchs with gray tin roofs, rows of fighter pilot trailers, and a multitude of rectangular cement buildings. I was returning from my monthly club manager's procurement meeting in Bangkok. After eight months of being stationed at Udorn, every time I returned to base, I was greeted with some kind of crisis, either at the officers' club or with some dreadful incident on base.

Pete Mendellson was at base ops to pick me up. I rushed over to hug him and planted a quick kiss on his cheek. His shy, reassuring smile was a comfort to me. He was my rock. Today something was different. My exuberance was instantly squelched when I saw his expressionless face.

He feigned a smile and said, "Hi, Angel. It's good to have you back," as he grabbed my bag and remained silent. I didn't want to ask him how things were, for fear I'd hear bad news. But I wasn't much for leaving well enough alone either. So, I broke the silence.

"Pete, what's up? I can tell something's up. You're not yourself." He walked around to the rear of the truck with me trailing close behind.

As he tossed my bag into the back of the pickup he stopped and looked at me with a forlorn expression. "Angel, we lost Bob Lodge and Roger Locher today."

My heart sank. "Oh, my God, two more! What happened this time?"

"They were shot down by a MiG-19.[1] They think Lodge went down with the plane. One of the other pilots in the flight thinks maybe Locher got out, but they couldn't confirm whether or not they saw his chute deploy before the plane hit the ground. They didn't hear any radio contact."

"Where did they go down? Maybe they can go back and see if they're still alive and get them out," I said, hoping against the odds.

"They're in North Vietnam, deep in enemy territory, about 330 miles north of the DMZ which is almost right on top of Hanoi," Pete said and kept his eyes straight ahead as he drove.

"What are we doing so far into enemy territory?"

"We're bombing the hell out of it. That's what we're doing there!" he said as he tightened his fists around the steering wheel.

"When will this war ever end? It's totally fucked! That's what it is—totally fucked! And that's the only way I can describe it." I exclaimed.

Pete shook his head, almost as if he agreed with me. Of course, he was frustrated with this war, too. But being a fighter pilot, I'm sure his answer for ending the war was to suspend those ridiculous target restrictions, go in there, bomb them to kingdom come, and win the son of a bitch!

Then in a subdued tone he said, "You know, those guys were in hot pursuit of their second MiG-21 when they were hit by the MiG-19. Today's MiG kill was Lodge's third! Boy, he was good." Silence filled the truck as Pete and I drove the long distance around the runway back to the officers' club for dinner.

It was May 10, 1972, and we had resumed heavy bombing in North Vietnam (NVN) because of increased activity along the DMZ. As a result of these actions and our promise to support the South Vietnamese, President Nixon reneged on his campaign promise to end the war and retaliated with renewed violence.

In addition, on May 4th, the Paris peace talks were canceled indefinitely. As part of an increased offensive to show the Communists we meant business, Nixon authorized a campaign called "Operation Linebacker." It was intended to systematically restrict the North Vietnamese (NVN) from external sources by mining major NVN harbors and bombing major military and supply facilities. It was the first major NVN offensive since 1968 and the most intensive air-to-air combat battle launched by the U.S. in the history of the Vietnam War.

On the first day of the campaign, a highly coordinated air strike by a multitude of F-4s from several air bases was launched against the Paul Doumer rail and transport bridge and the Yen Vien railroad yard, targets strongly fortified by the North Vietnamese. The Paul Doumer Bridge, built by the French and opened in 1902, was named after the Governor of French Indochina, Pol Doomâr. It was renamed the Long Bien Bridge in 1954 after the Vietnamese defeated the French. The Vietnamese saw it as a symbol of French colonialism, and now the North Vietnamese used it as a strategic asset to move supplies and equipment from China to Hanoi and on to the Haiphong Harbor. There were 1,300 miles of rail lines, a mile of which traveled over the Paul Doumer Bridge.

During the war, this bridge became an infamous target for U.S. forces and a major symbol of resistance by the North Vietnamese. The bridge was like an anthill; level it to the ground on one day, and the next morning it's rebuilt again. It was one of the key targets submitted by the Joint Chiefs of Staff to Secretary of Defense Robert McNamara in the mid-sixties. However, some of these key targets were never implemented because the U.S. didn't want to escalate the confrontation with the Chinese or the Soviets.

Back in 1967, as part of an operation called "Rolling Thunder," the bridge was put on the target list and was bombed, causing serious damage. Undeterred, the North Vietnamese repaired the bridge, and now it was back on the target list. This time the objective was the same as before: to drop the bridge, disrupt the railroad lines, and hit as many Surface-to-Air Missiles (SAMs) and antiaircraft artillery (AAA) sites as possible.

On May 10th, they were ready and waiting for us, almost as if they knew our coordinates. Our fighters were met with a barrage of SAMs, as they flew over the terrain on their way to the targets and then were intercepted by an onslaught of Soviet MiGs. Two of the eight airmen shot down that day were from our base and the Triple Nickel Squadron.

Paul Doumer Bridge wasn't dropped that day; it was only damaged. The North Vietnamese rapidly erected a pontoon bridge a few hundred yards away while they repaired the bridge, which only caused them minor inconveniences. Ten months later on March 4, 1973, in a strange twist of fate, a train engine with a huge picture of Ho Chi Minh tied on the front roared across the bridge. On board were our released POWs on their way back to freedom.

Major Bob Lodge, 30, graduated from the Air Force Academy in 1964 and made major below-the-zone. Becoming a major was pretty good for a guy who was denied entry into the Air Force because of his slight build the first time he applied. At the Academy, he was an ardent student, had an aptitude for flying, and ended up at the top of his class. He was a serious-looking guy who didn't smile much, but Lodge knew his stuff and had a love for flying that went back to his teenage years.

Lodge was a competent, experienced air-flight tactician who was respected by his fellow pilots. He prepared for his missions with the skilled precision of a professional. Unlike most of the other fighter jocks, he wasn't much of a drinker or schmoozer. He pretty much kept to himself. In fact, sometimes the guys would joke about him being a loner. The guys would say, "You know, Angel, you gotta wonder about a guy who doesn't smoke, drink, or mess around a little."

On the other hand, Captain Roger Locher, 25, was a sweet Midwestern Kansas boy and a weapon systems operator, or GIB (guy in back), as they were affectionately called. Roger was the antithesis of Bob. He had a warm, friendly smile and was more outgoing. Both guys were from the noted Triple Nickel Fighter Squadron, which had a long history of flying fighter aces. Because of its high number of MiG kills, the Triple Nickel earned the reputation of being the "World's Largest Distributor of MiG Parts." Together, Lodge and Locher had more than 400 combat flight hours, and they were considered one of the best aviator teams in SEA. For them to take a hit was devastating to their squadron and to all of us.

The Triple Nickel scored an unprecedented day with three MiG-21 kills but also took the most hits. What started out as a crackerjack day for the fighter pilots, with a perfectly planned and executed mission, ended not with a celebration in the o-club, but with a solemn reminder of the hazards of war. No one knew Lodge and Locher's fate and a subdued atmosphere permeated the bar.

Losses were not discussed at length. Once the facts were known and stated, that was it. It reminded me of an evening news flash. *Today, in a massive air strike over North Vietnam, an F-4 Phantom jet was shot down, two men missing in action, names are not being released until notification of the next of kin. Now, on to sports.*

One of the unwritten commandments of being a combat fighter pilot is "Thou shalt not dwell on death too long." Drink a toast to the missing airman, be glad it wasn't you, and goddamn it man, get on with it. And, yes, keep the drinks coming. To fly one of those exhilarating, powerful F-4 jets, you had to have what Tom Wolfe would later characterize as, "The Right Stuff."

Because I was a support person, my access to the inner circle was limited, which made getting any details about what happened to Roger and Bob difficult. I picked up bits and pieces of information from conversations around the bar. I guess that was one of the advantages of being the club officer, if it could be called an advantage. The rest of the details I got from Pete, who was privy to more of the facts.

Apparently, Bob Lodge and Roger Locher, whose call sign was "Oyster One," were the flight leaders of four F-4s with a mission to penetrate deep into North Vietnamese territory. The intent of the MiG Combat Air Patrol (MIGCAP) was to draw out enemy aircraft, engage them in combat, and keep them occupied while others proceeded to bombard the strategic targets. As predicted, MiG-21s emerged from every corner of the sky and homed in on our F-4s. Lodge and Locher were ready and poised for the attack, and an aerial dogfight ensued. They fired off their sparrow warhead missiles, many of which didn't always fire as advertised, and shot down a MiG-21.

Lieutenant John Markle and Captain Steve Eaves, Oyster Two, followed suit and shot down another MiG-21. Captain Steve Ritchie and Captain Chuck DeBellevue, Oyster Three, also scored a hit on a MiG-21. The mission was going as planned and looking good. "Sierra Hotels" were heard all over the airwaves.

While Lodge and Locher continued in hot pursuit of the Soviet MiGs, a MiG-19 appeared at their 10 o'clock position. They were unaware of the impending danger fast approaching because their attention was focused on scoring another hit on the MiG-21 directly in front of them.

John Markle, Oyster Two, blasted an urgent call over the airwaves, "Bob! Reverse right. Reverse right. Bandit behind you. Bandit behind you!" Lodge and Locher charged ahead chasing the MiG-21 well within their sights.

They fired on it and missed. Almost simultaneously, the MiG-19 closed in on them firing 30 millimeter rounds into the rear of Oyster One's fuselage causing flames to rapidly disperse throughout the rear of the aircraft. From the backseat, Roger Locher shouted over the airwaves, "We're hit! We're hit! It's getting hot back here, we've gotta eject. We've gotta—"

That was the last the other pilots heard from Oyster One before they saw the jet take a steep nose dive and crash, sending clouds of dark, black smoke billowing up from the ground. With the loss of their flight leader, and surrounded by MiGs, the rest of the F-4 flight decided to cut their losses and jettison out of there. One of the pilots thought he might have seen Locher's chute open before the plane hit the ground, but the smoke was so dense and their exit so swift that he couldn't be certain. Even though they only heard Locher's voice before the crash the Wing Commander declared both Lodge and Locher as MIA.

When something like this happened, I wanted to talk about it until I wore the subject out. I thought that if I asked the right questions, I might get an answer that justified why something this terrible happened. I wanted to cry. Cry a lot. But military women didn't cry. At least, you never let anybody see you cry.

The next night while we sat around the bar drinking, I started asking Pete more details about the downed crew. "Pete, do you think there's a chance that Lodge and Locher are still alive?"

"We can only hope, Angel. But they only heard Roger Locher's voice before the crash."

"Well maybe Roger is still out there. If he survived, what do you think his chances are that they'll find him?"

"Hard to say—who knows? Maybe, if the Charlies[2] don't get him first!" he said as he downed his Scotch on the rocks.

I continued asking Pete questions, like he had some kind of crystal ball. "If they do find him, do you think they'll be able to get him out?"

"Christ, Angel! I don't know! He's not exactly in a convenient location! They're deep in enemy territory, probably on the side of a mountain where it's dense with 40 to 50 foot high trees and thick with impenetrable brush."

I decided it was best for me to stop talking and concentrate on drinking. I could only imagine that if they were able to parachute out in that thickly forested terrain, it might be a good place for a flyer to hide, but not so easy for a search and rescue crew (SAR) to extract him. In the valley there were rice paddies, water buffalo pastures, and North Vietnamese civilians who were eager to collect a high ransom for picking up an American G.I. flyboy.

My silence was momentary as I searched for more answers. "Pete, do you think Bob Lodge was alive when their plane was hit?"

"Don't know. They were hit in the rear of their aircraft," he replied in a somber tone.

"Maybe the blast could have knocked Lodge unconscious or killed him instantly," I added.

"Well, Lodge was in the front of the aircraft and Locher was in the rear, but who knows? He might've gotten knocked unconscious, but it doesn't seem likely. Besides, Locher's voice was the only one they heard on the radio before the crash," he said, repeating the facts he had already given me.

"If he wasn't unconscious or killed instantly, then he would have said something, wouldn't he?" I said, wanting him to give me some ray of hope. Pete didn't respond. At this point, I found myself asking and answering my own questions. "I mean, if he wasn't unconscious, he would have had plenty of time to eject—right?"

He didn't respond for a moment and then answered, "Maybe, but knowing Lodge he always said he'd never let himself be taken prisoner by the North Vietnamese. He knew too much."

"What do you mean?" I responded, totally disturbed by this revelation. "You mean, you think he deliberately went down with this plane?"

"Who knows?"

"God, I hope he didn't do that. Pete, you don't think he'd really do that, do you?"

"Angel, do you want another drink?" Pete asked as he motioned to one of the bar waitresses. "Hey Lot, bring me another 'scatch' rocks and another gin'n tonic for Captain Pilato here." Pete always called scotch "scatch."

He stopped answering my questions. Then I started to wonder, *did my incessant probing start to make Pete think what every fighter pilot never wants to think about—that he might have been the one that crashed?*

When I didn't get answers, I gave myself two choices: make stuff up or forget it. Forgetting it wasn't an option. I winced when I thought of someone being trapped inside a flaming aircraft, knowing he was going to crash, and then actually making the decision to go down with the plane. It was unfathomable to me, but then I wasn't a fighter pilot.

The Air Force selected the best men to be pilots and their training was intense. A fighter pilot's survival training instincts are strong. When his jet is hit, his adrenaline kicks in. He assesses the damages. If they're bad, he has a split second to decide to eject. If yes, he grabs the ejection lever between his legs, pulls it up hard as strong g-forces are pushing down against him. The aircraft canopy pops open and snaps off, and out he soars, strapped to his seat, flying through the air like a firecracker. It's that fast.

A person would have to work pretty hard to suppress all that training and those innate survival instincts. Maybe in the 10 seconds before his plane crashed he had time to make a choice. Ten seconds was a long time. I counted, one...two...three...four...five...six...seven...eight...nine...ten. Surely, Bob Lodge must have been unconscious!

I finished my third gin and tonic and thought, *if Roger Locher was alive, he'd be out there all alone in that God forsaken jungle with only some Pillsbury "Space Food Sticks"*[3] *to eat. The Vietnamese swampland was filled with leeches, snakes, and mosquitoes. If he was alive, he wouldn't get much sleep for fear of being captured by blood thirsty commies. If he was injured and they found him, they'd drag him off to the "Hanoi Hilton."*[4] The Hanoi Hilton was what the pilots sardonically called the *Hoa Lo* Prison where the North Vietnamese took captured American servicemen and made them prisoners of war (POWs).

The French built the *Hoa Lo* prison in the 1800s during their occupation of Vietnam. Political dissidents who agitated for independence from France were held there, tortured, and executed. *Hoa Lo,* translates as "fiery furnace" or "hell's hole," which was appropriate because it truly was a hell hole. The North Vietnamese didn't follow any Geneva Convention rules about giving humane treatment to their POWs. They had their own rules. American POWs lived in horrible conditions. They were brutally tortured and put in solitary confinement until the enemy extracted a "confession" from even the most stoic of men. They forced them to state the United States was fighting an illegal war and that they were being treated humanely. Group photos of POWs were sent out for the entire world to see. Sometimes, a willful pilot would be seen in the photo with his hand pointed downward in front of him with his finger in 'the bird' position.

The thought of the ordeal made me sick. I called to the waitress, "Hey, Lot, bring me another gin'n tonic!"

The next day, I asked my secretary Pip to order two more brass nameplates for the Honor Roll plaque in the o-club lobby. I handed her a sheet of paper with their names printed on it. It read:

Major Robert A. Lodge
555th TFS MIA
May 10, 1972

Captain Roger Locher
555th TFS MIA
May 10, 1972

She took it, looked at the names, and said, "Yes, Kapton." She left the office quietly. Nothing more was said. Two days later their names were placed on the Honor Roll plaque. Nobody even noticed. Lodge and Locher were now merely two more casualties of war, with their names on a plaque in the officers' club lobby. Their names weren't the first, and they wouldn't be the last.

¹ The MiG-19 built by Mikoyan-Gurevich Design Bureau in the Soviet Union. It is a second-generation supersonic single-seat, twin-engine jet, comparable to the Air Force's F-100 Super Sabre.

² Charlie was the slang expression for Viet Cong (VC). It stands for the radio alphabet "V" for Victor and "C" for Charlie.

³ Pillsbury Space Sticks were developed in the sixties as a nutritious food snack for the astronauts to take with them on their space missions. They were 44 calories, tubular shaped, came in four flavors, and were wrapped in foil.

⁴ The "Hanoi Hilton" is now partially a museum where the Vietnamese continue to insist that they did not torture any Americans, in spite of numerous accounts, memoirs, and books by POWS to the contrary. In 1999, the Hilton Hotel chain opened a hotel in Ho Chi Minh City (formerly called Hanoi) and was careful to name it "Hilton Hanoi Opera Hotel."

*There can't be good living where there is not good drinking.*
—Benjamin Franklin, American scientist, inventor (1706 - 1790)

# MiG-21 Contest

THE BASE WAS ALIVE with excitement. The fighter pilots were shooting MiGs out of the sky like marksmen picking off clay ducks at a carnival shooting gallery. The restrictive rules of engagement, which forbad pilots from shooting unless they were fired upon first, had been lifted. In three months, our base had racked up 12 out of the 13 Air Force MiG kills[1], and the Navy had done its fair share, too. With this new offensive campaign, maybe, just maybe, we had a chance of winning this war and going home victorious.

Everyone was riding high, and the celebrations were non-stop. Pilots were three deep at the bar, and truck after truck was driven up the steps of the o-club and parked in the lobby. I decided I'd do my part to mark the MiG kills by hosting a contest. It wasn't going to be a drinking contest; we were already good at that, but rather a contest to create a cocktail to immortalize the MiG-21 and our MiG killer pilots.

There were other cocktails named after wartime aircraft and pilots: the Memphis Belle, named after the famous World War II B-17 bomber plane; the B-52, named after the Air Force's very own long-range, strategic Stratofortress; and The Kamikaze, named after the WWII Japanese suicide bombers. I envisioned the MiG-21 cocktail joining the bartender's lexicon worldwide.

Even though two of the MiGs shot down were actually MiG-19s and not MiG-21s, I wasn't going to quibble over the model number. A MiG was a MiG and I wanted the drink named after the Russian's superstar jet, the MiG-21.

I put out the challenge to the fighter squadrons. I think the fighter jocks saw it as one step above a Betty Crocker Bake Off, and so the response wasn't great. Four or five guys agreed to prepare a tasty libation, including Pete Mendellson, who I suspected had gotten the other guys to participate.

On May 17th, the night of the contest, we rolled a portable bar into one of the back party rooms at the o-club and stocked it with all the usual bar liquors plus any ingredients that might be needed to make a nifty cocktail. I could see it all now: the MiG-21 would soon be served in every o-club bar in the Air Force. When the contestants came in, I told them they could use any ingredient they wanted to make their drink, and I'd give them a half hour. I called for a time hack; we synchronized our watches; and I left the room.

When I returned the concoctions were lined up on the table ready to be judged. With a pad and pen in hand, I readied my palette for the challenge.

As I began to sip my way down the row of drinks I thought, *who else is better equipped to judge this contest than someone who has spent every night for the last five years in an o-club bar?*

The guys stood around and chided me, "Come on, Angel, what's taking you so long?" They watched my expressions closely hoping for clues that would give away my preference. After two or three tastes of each drink and a few scribbles on my pad, I selected the winning drink.

"This is it!" I said and pointed to the one in the middle. "I like the taste of this one."

"What? How could you pick that one?" Gerry Volloy said.

"I don't know. I just liked the taste. I guess this one isn't yours, Gerry? Whose is it?"

"It's Mendellson's," the guys piped up.

Pete was grinning from ear to ear. I went over and hugged him. It only took a second before the guys started in, "This whole thing was rigged. She was going to pick his drink no matter what we did. We never had a chance!"

"Wait a minute you guys," I said getting a little defensive. "How could I know which one was Pete's? I wasn't even in the room when you guys prepared the drinks. Christ, it just tasted good."

Pete interjected, "Don't sweat it, Angel. These knuckleheads are just jealous."

Realizing that Pete was backing me up, I said, "You guys are just sore losers. That's what I think. OK, this is it, you guys. The judge's decision is final, and I'm the judge!"

They were still grumbling, but I ignored them, "Pete, never mind these guys. I wanna know, what's in this drink?"

"Well, let's see. I started with some Scotch and ..."

One of his buddies hollered out, "Of course, that's all he drinks anyway."

"OK, zip it, you guys. Let him finish. Go on, Pete, tell us what else is in your outstanding MiG-21."

He continued, "Scotch, a little *Galliano*, and a splash or two of *Cointreau.*"

"Wow, that's it?"

"Yep, that's it. It was sorta taste as you go."

"It's delicious, Pete," I said. "I declare Pete Mendellson, from the 13th Tactical Fighter Squadron, the undisputed winner of Udorn's MiG-21 drink contest. You get free drinks at the bar for a week."

"Shit Hot! All the 'statch' I can drink for a week! Can't beat that," he said as he put his arm around me. I kissed him on the cheek. The guys started to leave. A couple of them were still grumbling that it was a set up.

I said, "Stop whining. The decision of the judge is final."

All of the sudden, as I was walking away, Wayne Frye, a lieutenant colonel from the Triple Nickel and a big bruiser of a guy, came up from behind and picked me up. He started to carry me over to the table, and was preparing to dunk my behind in a huge bowl of ice water that was left over from chilling the beer for the contestants. Frye pulled me tight toward his chest, with one arm under my legs and the other around my waist. Gerry Volloy held my foot and was guiding Frye towards the bowl. My mini dress was scrunched up to my hips exposing my pantyhose. I grimaced and insisted, "Put me down. Damn it! Put me down." They ignored me. So, I raised my voice louder, "Put me down. Damn it!"

Pete said, "Cut the crap you guys. Put her down. Game over."

They were all laughing, and Frye said, "Come on Angel, admit it. You picked your buddy Mendellson to win."

As he moved me closer to the bowl of ice water, I kept insisting, "Damn it! I told you I didn't. He won fair and square. Put me down."

Pete cut in again and said, "Put her down guys. Enough is enough."

Frye stopped one inch short of the bowl and said, "Come on Pete, we're just having a little fun." Frye gave me one more pass over the bowl of ice water before he relented and put me down.

Standing back on my feet, I blurted out, "You wise-asses. I don't know why I put up with you guys."

"Because you flat-ass love us, Angel! That's why," Frye snapped back. "Besides, where you gonna go? You can't get away from us," Frye said still laughing.

I gave him the finger and said, "Boys, the contest is over. Let's adjourn to the bar. The first round is on me."

"Well, that'll work," Volloy said, and off we went.

The next day I made copies of the recipe, illustrated with a sketch of a MiG-21, and sent them off to the Headquarters for the Officers' Clubs at Hickam Air Force Base in Hawaii.

*The MiG-21 Cocktail*

*1 ½ ounces of Johnny Walker Scotch*
*½ ounce Galliano*
*¼ ounce of Cointreau*

*Pour over ice and stir.*

I never received a response. It didn't take off like I thought it would—maybe if we'd had the internet. The only memento I have from the MiG-21 contest is a colorful caricature drawn by the sergeant who did the artwork for our o-club event calendar. It still hangs in a prominent place in my office.

---

[1] MiG kills and models were taken from: Albert F. Simpson, U.S. Air Force Combat Victory Credits, Southeast Asia Historical Research Center, Air University, March 1974.

# MiG-21 Contest

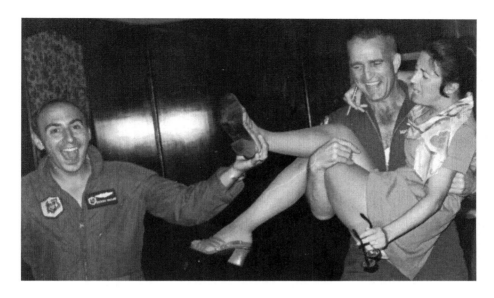

"Sore Losers"
Captain Gerry Volloy and Lieutenant Colonel Wayne Frye
attempt to dunk Captain Pilato

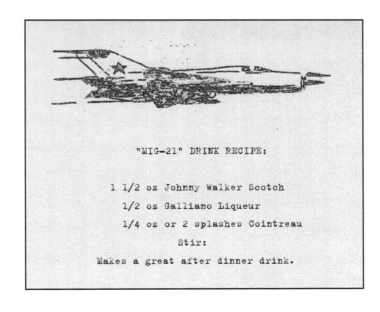

"MIG-21" DRINK RECIPE:


1 1/2 oz Johnny Walker Scotch

1/2 oz Galliano Liqueur

1/4 oz or 2 splashes Cointreau

Stir:

Makes a great after dinner drink.

"Should a gentleman offer a lady a Tiparillo?"

*Our heroes are people and people are flawed. Don't let that taint the thing you love.*
—Randy K. Milholland, American cartoonist (1975 - )
From *Midnight Macabre*

# MiG Killer—Misfit Flyer

AFTER TWO MiG KILLS Captain Fred "Broadway" Olmsted was euphoric. He'd accomplished what he came to SEA to do. He wanted to be part of the action, help win the war, and be an outstanding combat pilot. But nothing ever remains the same, and for every high there's a low. That's how it went for Broadway when he received notification that his mother was seriously ill. He headed back to the States on emergency leave and was scheduled to hop a transport out of Clark Air Base in the Philippines.

While he awaited his flight, he decided to head over to the o-club. He was standing at the bar drinking when some bird colonel tapped him on the shoulder and said, "Are you in the same Air Force I'm in?"

Broadway turned around and responded, "I don't know. What Air Force are you in?"

The colonel, taken aback by the response, barked back at Fred, "Stand at attention, Captain."

"What?" Broadway snapped back. He set his drink down on the bar and readied himself for a confrontation.

In a raised voice the colonel said, "Your hair looks like hell. Go get a haircut in the barbershop downstairs, and make sure you trim that ghastly moustache. And don't come back in this bar until you do. That's an order, Captain." While in the war zone, Fred wore his moustache and his full crop of dark brown hair slightly longer than Air Force regulation permitted, but no one ever cared, until then.

The two men squared off, nose to nose, like two snorting bulls ready to charge. The din in the bar was muted as the crowd waited to see if they'd lock horns. The enraged colonel and the snot-nosed captain exchanged words, but no blows were dealt.

In this case rank won out, and the breast-pounding colonel personally escorted Olmsted downstairs to the barbershop to get him a trim. Much to Olmsted's consternation, he came out looking less like "Broadway" and more like a regular issue captain. The colonel sent his exec officer down to bring Olmsted back to the bar.

The colonel gave him the once over and said, "Now that's more like it, Captain. What d'ya say I buy you a drink?"

Whatever hair Fred had left on his head stood straight up on end. "You couldn't buy me a fuckin' thing." That did it.

The colonel exploded. "I'll have you grounded!" he shouted, "you'll get an Article-15[1] for this." The words "court martial" were even thrown into the mix. MiG killer or not, Broadway was done for. The Air Police were alerted and Olmsted was hauled off to the base brig.

Meanwhile, the colonel called Colonel Gabriel, to notify him that one of his recalcitrant pilots was in the slammer. I'm not sure how Fred got released, but he did. No doubt Colonel Gabriel "encouraged" the colonel to let him go by telling him he was an outstanding combat pilot, a MiG killer, and was on his way home because of his mother's serious illness.

The story circulated through the bar like a comet. Of course, each time the story was retold, it was embellished a little bit more, and with every round of drinks came another round of laughter. We all visualized Broadway's confrontation with the clueless colonel, and numerous toasts were given in his honor, "Here's to Broadway. Hope he kicked that colonel's ass all the way to hell!"

"Here! Here!" The crowd cheered.

A few days later I saw Colonel Gabriel and asked him what was going to happen to Fred. Without missing a beat Colonel Gabriel, in his North Carolina drawl and with an unflinching tone said, "Well Angel, I guess we're just gonna have to take him out and shoot him!"

I looked taken aback. Then I saw his eyes widen and a grin came across his face.

"Don't worry, Angel, we'll take care of Fred."

I was relieved nothing was going to happen to him. I imagined that when

Olmsted returned, Gabriel would probably take him to the bar, buy him a drink, put his arm around his shoulder and say, "Now Fred, next time you'll know better not to be so rambunctious when you're out of the war zone!"

This was our Broadway, true to form, living in the "Danger Zone."

Broadway left Thailand disillusioned by the war, and as he put it, "by the ineptitude and inappropriate meddling of pompous, self-important politicians." He resigned his Air Force commission, but always kept his love for the F-4 Phantom, which he called "the best fighter plane ever built." He made a career as a commercial air pilot and flew for Eastern and American Express for a while. But it would never be like flying those phantoms.

---

[1] An article-15 is a non-judicial punishment that refers to certain limited punishments, which can be awarded for minor disciplinary offenses by a commanding officer.

*The Black Panthers are the greatest threat to the internal security of the United States!*

—J. Edgar Hoover, Director of the FBI (1895 - 1972)

# Black Panther on Base

DURING THE SIXTIES, so many revolutions and movements exploded that it was hard to keep track of them all. The sexual revolution, the feminist movement, and the anti-war movement were just a few. The Blacks, the term African-American would emerge later, ignited their own movement to address the repression and lack of opportunities in their communities by starting a progressive political organization called the Black Panther Party. The Black Panthers were armed and promoted a revolutionary agenda.

Their "Ten Point Plan" articulated such radical ideas as: the desire for power to determine their own destiny, full employment, an end to the robbery by the capitalists in Black and oppressed communities, decent housing and appropriate education, free health care, an immediate end to police brutality and murder, an immediate end to all wars of aggression, trials by a jury of peers, and land, bread, clothing, justice, and peace.[1] With a plan like this, it was understandable why Hoover deemed the Black Panthers as a threat to United States security.

We had several Black Panthers on base. The only one I knew was attached to the 13th Tactical Fighter Squadron, which seemed appropriate because the 13th Squadron was known as the Panther Pack. Their squadron's logo was the head of a black panther with its teeth open, ready to pounce. Coincidentally, this Panther's name was Eldridge, but he wasn't the infamous leader of the Black Panthers, Eldridge Cleaver.[2] That Panther was on the run in Algeria at the time.

When Eldridge arrived at the squadron, he was provided with special housing and even given the particular food he liked. I guess no one wanted any trouble. Eldridge was one of a kind, for sure. The squadron bestowed him with a special assignment, which was to take part in the end of tour (EOT) celebrations. EOTs happened when a pilot completed his last sortie (flight), usually after a year. It meant, after flying numerous combat missions, he hadn't been shot down, killed, or captured and was on his way home alive and well. Eldridge became a showpiece at the EOT celebrations. He'd parade around in front of everyone, and after a while people got used to him being part of the Pack.

One afternoon, a crowd gathered outside the squadron building for a last mission celebration and patiently awaited the pilot's return. The F-4 touched down, the drag chute released, slowing the Mach 2 jet down to a manageable airspeed. The pilot taxied the jet down the runway and back to the squadron pad. His canopy opened, and the ecstatic pilot unclipped his oxygen mask and gave the crowd thumbs up. He climbed down the aircraft ladder, and before he had a chance to wipe the smile off his face, he was tossed into a huge steel barrel full of water. He emerged laughing and drenched, from his neck scarf to his boots. There to greet him were a few of the pilot's favorite o-club waitresses (mostly the cute ones) and a couple of nurses. They rushed up to him all smiles, covered his face with kisses, and draped colorful floral leis around his neck. One of the pilots cracked open the *Cold Duck* and started pouring. The champagne glasses clinked as toasts were given by a host of well-wishers.

In keeping with previous last-flight celebrations, out came the Black Panther escorted by one of the officers. Today, though, he decided not to simply be a showpiece—he was going to be the show. All of a sudden, and without warning, the panther went charging after "Kathy Nurse." He went right for her ankle and took a bite out of it. She let out a blood-curdling scream.

"Get him off of me! Get him off of me!" she yelled. But before they could get Eldridge under control, he'd taken another swipe at her.

Several people went after him and pulled him away.

"Are you all right? Are you all right?" shouted the Squadron Commander as he rushed over to her. "Oh my God! Get the first aid kit and get him the hell away from her!"

"I'm bleeding," she said. She was trembling as two officers lifted her up and put her on the back end of a pickup truck.

This was the first time that Eldridge had gotten out of hand, but what did they expect? He was, in fact, a real black panther, the four legged kind! The squadron had acquired the panther from an Air America pilot who'd gotten him from somewhere in India, the circumstances of which remain somewhat clouded. The squadron kept Eldridge caged up in the squadron building feeding him beefsteaks and who knew what else. Maybe they even threw him an out-of-line navigator or two. Why the panther attacked Kathy was unknown. Maybe he hadn't been fed that day, or maybe he was just sick of being locked up in a cage.

The good news was that Kathy's injuries were only minor. She was more frightened than anything else. All of us who witnessed the event figured that was pretty much the end to Eldridge's tour of duty. Not long after, the squadron decided that maybe this wasn't the place for a panther and arranged for Eldridge to be carted off to the Phoenix zoo, where he enjoyed the remainder of his life. That last mission celebration was one that pilot would never forget, even if a black panther did steal the show.

Note: Read what happened to the black panther at the end of the book in In Their Own Words.

[1] Information on the Black Panthers was summarized from their website: www.blackpanther.org.

[2] Eldridge Cleaver helped found the militant group the Black Panthers in 1966 and became extremely controversial as the group's outspoken Minister of Information and was a spokesman for Black Power. The same year he was wounded in a Panther shootout with Oakland police, Cleaver jumped bail, fled to Algeria and lived in exile there and in Paris. He returned to America in 1975. Paradoxically, in later years, Cleaver renounced his former radical views, became a born-again Christian, embraced conservative political causes and even ran for political office as a Republican. (The Republicans get all the good candidates.) He also struggled with drug addiction and in 1998 died at age 63 from a heart attack.

*Good soldiers never pass up a chance to eat or sleep. They never know how much they'll be called on to do before the next chance.*

—Lois McMaster Bujold, American writer (1949 - )

# All I Want Is a Can of Coors and a Can of SPAM

IT HAD BEEN 21 days since Major Bob Lodge and Captain Roger Locher had been shot down over enemy territory and declared MIA. Meanwhile, it was business as usual. The bombings in North Vietnam persisted at a feverish pace. There were more MIG kills, more celebrations, and more war stories to tell. The pilots gathered around their squadron tables at the o-club banging a dice cup, as they played H-O-R-S-E, and aces wild for the next round of drinks. The Thai go-go girls, in their bikini panties and sequined pasties, danced aimlessly to rock'n roll music blaring from the jukebox. As the pilots smoked, drank, and devoured popcorn, they were consumed with conversations about flying "downtown"—the term they used when they were going to hit targets in Hanoi.

I heard snippets of their conversations as I busied myself around the club. "It's about time they're finally giving us a chance to hit some real targets instead of those goddamn vegetable trucks and water buffalos! We'll show those bastards we can whip their asses."

Even though many of their friends had been killed, no one ever mentioned the impending danger of being hit by a MiG or a SAM. The unspoken mental attitude was—it won't happen to me, and keep those drinks coming.

Nobody had any concern that our bombs were killing civilians as well as military combatants. They weren't real people down there; they were merely targets on a screen and scores to be tallied. Everyone knew "those people" were the enemy and that the enemy weren't "real" people, so it was OK to kill them. Besides, during wartime the commandment "Thou shalt not kill" was suspended.

Captain Clara Schneider, alias "Peppermint Patty," was the only person on base who believed that Roger Locher was still alive. Patty was one of the few women intelligence officers assigned to interpret photos taken by unarmed, low-flying F-4s on reconnaissance missions over North Vietnam.

Patty was smart and thorough, qualities required for an Intel Officer. She spent hours scrupulously reviewing the cockpit voice tapes from the returning pilots' flight recorders and was convinced that she had picked up a beep on one of those tapes. What she heard was a weak but steady beep that lasted about thirty seconds, with no voice transmission. It was transmitted after Lodge and Locher's aircraft had crashed and just before another F-4 had been shot down. Her analysis of the timing of the beep was significant, and it led her to believe that it must be Roger trying to radio for help.[1]

Others interpreted the information differently and suspected the enemy was transmitting the beep through Locher's radio as a trap to draw our planes in for an ambush. She refused to let other people's doubts dissuade her from believing that Locher was still alive and would return. She and Roger were working buddies, and she had developed a crush on him.

One day she came into the officers' club for lunch, and I asked her how she was doing. "OK, I guess," she sighed. "You know, Angel, I believe Roger is still alive, and they're going to find him. Believe me when they do, he'll be okay, and they'll be able to get him out. I just know it."

"I sure hope so, Patty," was my reluctant response. Deep down, I thought, *she was deluding herself.* After 21 days, we hadn't received any word that he had been taken as a prisoner of war. If he did survive the crash, his chances of being alive were getting slimmer and slimmer.

Then one afternoon, Pete Mendellson rushed into my office bursting with enthusiasm and announced, "Angel, they've picked up a radio call signal this morning from Roger Locher's radio. He's alive!"

"What? He's alive! Do you mean it?"

"Yeah, nobody can believe it!" Pete's eyes were lit up, and he was grinning from ear to ear.

My whole body was filled with excitement, but my instincts made me wary about trusting what I just heard.

"What happened? How did they find him? Is he alright?" My mind was coming up with questions faster than I could get them out.

"I don't know all the details yet. All I know is some F-4 pilot from Ubon Air Base[2] returning from a bombing strike over North Vietnam picked up his radio call signal. The strangest thing is that the guy who picked up Roger's radio signal had the same call sign that Roger had on the day he got shot down, 'Oyster!'"

"Jeez, that's freaky. Do they know if Roger is OK? When are they goin' in to get him out?"

"Angel, all I know is that he's still alive. They're gonna try to get him out as soon as they can."

"Try? What do you mean try? You think they might not be able to get him out?"

"Angel, they're going to do the best they can. Christ, he's right on top of Yen Bai, a North Vietnamese Airfield! Not the easiest location for an extraction. They're sending in the SARS (Search and Rescue Squadron) team from NKP[3] with the Jolly Greens[4] and the Sandys[5] to pick him up. If anybody can get him out, they can. Gotta go, Angel. I'll talk to you later. Don't worry, I'll keep you posted," he added as he dashed out the door.

My life at Udorn was like a roller coaster ride. One minute I was in deep despair, and the next I was high with unimaginable hope. But what if they couldn't get him out? What if the North Vietnamese got there before we did? The what ifs were endless, but I could do nothing except wait and hope.

I felt out of control and helpless, like I was driving downhill in a car with no brakes, just hoping for an uphill stretch of road to slow me down. I didn't do much the whole day except hang around the lobby of the o-club telling everybody who came in that they'd picked up Roger's call signal over the radio and that he was alive. But most everyone had already heard the news. I tried to remind myself not to get too excited. Having my hopes dashed now would be worse than dealing with the news the first time.

Then my thoughts turned to Roger. After 21 days, what must Roger be thinking? Had he given up the idea of being rescued? Or had he held on to the hope of getting out of there, like his buddy Peppermint Patty?

I knew Patty must be doing flips. I heard she was over at the wing intelligence office listening to the voice tapes from the flight recorder that had picked up Roger's radio call. She and others were attempting to verify if the voice transmitted over the radio was in fact Roger's. They were convinced it was and that it didn't sound like he was under duress.

A rescue team was put together, but before they could proceed, they needed to verify Roger's identity by asking him questions that only he could answer. Every airman flying combat operations has a list of four questions and answers that are used for just such an incident. One of his questions, "What is your mother's maiden name?" was transmitted over secure lines to the airborne command post and sent on to the flight rescue commander from NKP. Roger answered it correctly. They took extreme precautions because it was possible the enemy might have Roger under duress and that they could be trying to lure the fighters in for an ambush.

The rescue mission proceeded with two Jolly Green Giant helicopters, four A-1 Sandys for some firepower, and two pairs of F-4 Phantoms for fighter escort to patrol the area for incoming MiG attacks.

I was stuck at the o-club, going half-crazy, waiting to hear any news. When Pete came in at dinnertime, he was not smiling, and I knew the news couldn't be good. I could only imagine the worst—Roger must be dead.

"What's going on, Pete," I asked. "Did they get him out or what?" I knew full well what the answer was, but I asked anyway.

"No," he said sadly, shaking his head. "The rescue team tried but was attacked by a SAM and chased off by some patrolling MiGs. They had to abort the mission."

"Oh no!" An overwhelming sense of anguish swept through me. It felt like someone was sitting on my chest. "Now what are they going to do? Are they going to try again tomorrow?" It was now 22 days that he'd been on the ground.

"I sure hope so. They've called General Vogt at 7th Air Force in Saigon to request additional forces to get him out."

"What do you think he'll do? He can't just leave him there on the ground as maggot bait!" I blurted out.

"We'll know tomorrow," Pete said, shrugging his shoulders. He turned and headed for the bar with me following closely beside him. He motioned to the bartender, "Give me a scatch rocks please and a gin'n tonic for Captain Pilato." He proceeded to tell me that the rescue pilots did maintain radio contact with Roger in an effort to keep his spirits up.

"Well, I guess that's something," I said rather disparagingly.

"Yeah, they asked him what he wanted when they picked him up, and Roger told them all he wanted was a can of Coors and a can of SPAM!"[6]

"What?" I said in disbelief, "A can of Coors, yes, but a can of SPAM? God, the jungle has gotten to him! But I guess after you've been out there in that tropical swamp land that long, anything has gotta taste good!"

"Yeah, SPAM. '*Something Posing As Meat*,'" Pete said, shaking his head.

We both smiled at the quip, but the lightness was short-lived. Now we were back to waiting. Roger's fate was in the hands of one general's decision. We ordered another drink to shorten the night. Again my thoughts turned to Roger. How discouraged he must be feeling after this failed rescue attempt. He was probably wondering if they'd risk coming back for him. The night would be longer for him, and he wouldn't have any alcohol for comfort.

The next morning Pete rushed in smiling and giving me two thumbs-up. "The rescue mission is on again! General Vogt gave it the go-ahead!"

"Shit Hot!" I yelped. "Great news! I'm so glad. What a relief!" I hugged Pete exuberantly, and then took a deep breath and said, "God, I hope they can get him out this time."

"Me, too. They're preparing to go in to get him right now."

"How long will it take? Are they bringing him back here?" I inquired nervously.

"Yes, they're bringin' him back to Udorn. It'll probably take a good part of the day, if there isn't a SNAFU."[7]

"OK. Call me as soon as you know."

"I will," he said and headed quickly towards the door. Then I called out to him, "Pete!" As he turned around, I said, "Pete, thanks for letting me know. I love you."

He blushed and with that beguiling smile said, "I love you, too."

The pressure of this decision weighed heavily on General John Vogt who had made a go/no-go decision to continue the rescue. Vogt, a World War II ace, had just pinned on his fourth general's star in April and took command of 7th Air Force at the same time. He had replaced General Lavelle after the congressional investigations over bombing illegal targets. He knew morale was low and that every pilot was right there in the jungle with Roger, wondering what would happen if he was the one who had gone down. He had to weigh the risk of approving an extremely hazardous mission in an attempt to rescue one airman against putting dozens of men and military aircraft in harms way.

Although the SAR motto was "That others may live," and the Airman's Creed was "I will never leave an Airman behind," one had to ask if it was better to sacrifice one life for the overall good? If the rescue was a success, he would be applauded for outstanding leadership; if not, he'd be reprimanded for using faulty judgment. The odds were not in Roger's favor, but Vogt knew he couldn't leave him there. The entire rescue crew understood the risks involved. They were determined to defy the odds and bring Roger and themselves back alive.

Peppermint Patty was down at the Wing Intelligence Office waiting for word of a successful rescue mission. She was anxious, but still managing to maintain a sense of confidence. She had never given up hope that Roger was still alive. She'd always spoke of "when" he'd return instead of "if" he'd return. She prayed for him every day.

Her faith was a hell of a lot stronger than mine. I kept asking myself how God could do this and why had I ever volunteered for this assignment. Of course, God had nothing to do with this mess. Men and governments were the ones who had screwed things up. Now Roger, like all the rest of us, was caught up in the fallout. Hopefully, he wouldn't be another causality.

A massive airpower operation with a total of 119 aircraft was launched the morning of June 2, 1972, and almost equaled that of the May 10th offensive. As a diversionary tactic, F-4s were going to strafe the enemy runway at Yen Bai airfield and render it impossible for the enemy MiGs to take off. Radar-jamming EB-66s were in the air, along the KC-135 refuelers, bombers, and more F-4 escorts. The A-1 Sandys were going in to provide additional cover while Jolly Green Giant helicopters went in with a jungle penetrator to rescue Roger. The penetrator was bright yellow for high visibility, weighed about 22 ½ pounds, and was attached to a cable. It looked like a huge projectile with a three-sided, retractable seat set flush to its shaft. After the penetrator was lowered, the seat could be extended allowing the person to climb on and be pulled up.

The A-1 Sandy Pilot, Captain Ron Smith flew back over to ask Roger one more authenticating question, one developed by Chris Beisner, an Intel Officer and a fellow Kansas Stater, "What is Kite's?"

Roger's immediate response was, "Hell, it's a place to go drink beer!" Everybody at Kansas State knew Kite's was a familiar student hang out.

"Drink beer?" Smith responded.

"Yeah, beer!"

"Well, you sound like the one I want!"

"You're damn right I am," shouted Roger.

That was the proof he needed to confirm that Roger was not being held at gunpoint. The Jolly Greens were cleared to go in.

That day, all I wanted to hear was that one good thing had come out of this senseless war. I wanted to be able to take one brass nameplate off the Honor Roll plaque in the lobby. At about noon, Pip rushed into the dining room and said in an excited voice, "Kapton, Kapton! It's Major Mendellson!" I left my lunch and sprinted into the office. Out of breath I picked up the phone and said, "Pete?"

"They got him, Angel! They got him! They'll be arriving back here soon."

"Thank God!" I said with a deep sigh of relief. Then with slight hesitation I asked, "What about the rescue crew?"

"Yes! Everyone got out safely."

I shouted a loud response, "Shit Hot. I'm so happy."

"You and everybody else." He said, "I'll be over to get you sometime this afternoon when I have a better idea of his ETA."

"Great," I said and started to choke up. "I'll see you then." My heart pounded rapidly, as I tried to grasp the magnitude of the phenomenal feat that had occurred.

When Pete called back I was ready with my camera loaded. I rushed out the door and waited for him. I wasn't wasting one minute. As we headed over to the runway to be part of the welcoming committee, I said, "Pete, I can't believe it. I can't believe they got him out alive and that we didn't lose anybody. Absolutely fantastic! That's all I can say. Thank God! What a nightmare these last two days have been."

"Yeah, you can say that again. Imagine how Roger must have felt!" he replied.

I got a lump in my throat. No, I couldn't fathom how he must have felt being down 23 days in enemy territory alone, hungry, and in constant fear for his life. He must have been devastated when, finally, he saw our planes overhead and made radio contact with them, only to watch them leave. He knew that his location was a hazardous one, even for the most skilled rescue crew. He must have wondered if they'd come back to try again. Even with a strong will, he must have lost hope. Those thoughts paralyzed me, but it was over now. He was on his way back to safety and real food, where his cans of cold Coors and SPAM awaited him.

We parked the truck and raced out onto the runway to meet the aircraft. The incoming A-1s flew a low pass over the airfield. The Jolly Green Giant followed close behind with red smoke billowing out of its sides to signal a victory.

Something good had finally happened, and I was there to witness it. The exhilaration I felt was akin to jumping off a mountain on a zip line. Hundreds of people awaited Roger's return. The noise from the choppers got louder and louder the closer they got to the ground. As the chopper blades wound down, a crewmember opened the sliding door and slowly Roger came and stood at the opening. The crowd started cheering, whistling, clapping, and yelling, "Wayta go, Roger! Shit Hot, Roger! Welcome back!"

His cute, boyish smile beamed through his scruffy beard and the dark circles under his eyes. His worn khaki flight suit hung limp on his gaunt, malnourished body. As he lifted his arm to wave, Marty Cavoto, one of his squadron buddies, popped open a can of Coors and handed it to him. Marty had been saving that bootlegged six-pack of Coors for a special occasion, and he figured this met the criteria. The crowd went wild as he took a slow, savoring sip. "God, it's good to be back," he said with a sigh of relief. Still smiling, he took another swig of Coors and walked through the crowd. Suddenly, the Hospital Commander, Colonel Harmon, came over to break up the celebration. He took the can of Coors out of Roger's hand and said, "Sorry, Roger. You can't have that. You're dehydrated, and it'll mess up your insides." Well, I figured it couldn't have messed up his insides anymore than being on a diet of beetles and berries for 23 days. Guys continued to shake his hand, pat him on the back, and greet him with an abundance of congratulatory cheers.

General Vogt had flown in from Saigon that morning to be there when the mission was completed. He waited at the end of the receiving line with a big smile on his face. He looked relieved, as well as proud of his rescue crew. Vogt had taken a monumental risk, but seeing Roger's smiling face made it clear that it had paid off.

Me? I was crying, but nobody noticed. I had my sunglasses on and everyone else was preoccupied. I tried unsuccessfully to push my way through a wall of tall fighter jocks in their olive drab flight suits. Undeterred, I held my camera up over their heads to get a few good photos of this memorable event.

An ambulance was waiting to take Roger straight to the base hospital. Peppermint Patty was close by and looked ecstatic. As the Flight Surgeon guided Roger into the ambulance, some of the pilots coaxed Patty to get in and go along. She did. Everyone knew how she felt about Roger, and he was about to find out.

Note: Read Roger Locher's own account at the end of the book in In Their Own Words.

[1] Read a full accounting of this incident in *One Day in a Long War*, Jeffrey Ethell and Alfred Price, Random House, 1989, New York, pages 151-164.

[2] Ubon Air Base was one of seven bases in Thailand used to launch air missions over to North Vietnam. It was located in the Ubon Ratchathani province about 300 miles Northeast of Bangkok.

[3] NKP is the acronym for Nakhon Phanom Royal Air Base another base used to fly missions over North Vietnam. It was 360 miles Northeast of Bangkok in the valley of the Mekong River and bordering Laos.

[4] A Jolly Green is an HH-53B twin-turbo shaft heavy-lift helicopter used for long-range rescue. It has a crew of five and two electrically powered 7.62 miniguns.

[5] A Sandy is one of the nicknames for the A1-Skyraider propeller aircraft used as a search and rescue escort and has four 20mm cannons.

[6] SPAM was introduced on July 5, 1937, by Hormel Meats. The name "SPAM" originally meant "Shoulder of Pork and Ham." It was given out to soldiers and those affected by WWII. In the U.K., "SPAM" stood for "Specially Processed American Meats."

[7] SNAFU is the acronym for Situation Normal, All Fucked Up (or for those with delicate ears, all fouled up)!

# Captain Roger Locher's Rescue

"Jolly Green" inbound with rescued pilot
Captain Roger Locher

Captain Roger Locher after 23 days in enemy
territory sipping his Coors

# Captain Roger Locher's End of Tour

Captain Marty Cavato, Captain Sandy Babos, Captain
Roger Locher, Lieutenant Colonel Jim Brunson (Nickel
Squadron Commander), and Major George Nunez.

*It matters if you just don't give up.*

—Steven Hawking, English physicist (1942 - )

# The Debrief

CAPTAIN ROGER LOCHER HAD been rescued from under the noses of the North Vietnamese. Soon after, we learned the dramatic details of his long, 23-day ordeal and the daring and courageous rescue by Captain Dale Stovall's Jolly Green crew.[1] The story was record setting. No one had evaded enemy capture for this long a period of time in the history of the war. Stovall, had commanded his helicopter deep into enemy territory while under hostile fire and would later receive the Air Force Cross, second only to the Medal of Honor. At the time, we didn't know that these actions would garner any accolades. All we knew was that through the skill and courage of all involved one of our boys had made it back alive. For that, we were extremely grateful.

Slowly, bits of information unfolded about Roger's test of wits and his hazardous rescue.[2] While Locher was in the hospital regaining his strength, the intelligence team recorded all the information about his time in enemy territory. Also, Stovall and his crew were extensively debriefed on how they managed a successful rescue operation under such slim odds.

About a week after his rescue, Peppermint Patty, Roger Locher's faith keeper, came into the o-club. It was the first time I'd seen her since Roger stepped out of the Jolly Green helicopter. She was smiling, and she moved like a hundred pound weight had been lifted off her shoulders.

"Hi, Patty, good to see you. Can I buy you a drink?"

"Thanks. Sounds like a good idea."

I motioned to the bartender, then asked, "What'll ya have Patty?"

"I'll have a *chet-chet,*" she said. That was Thai for a 7 and 7 (7-Up and Seagram's 7 Whiskey).

"How's Roger recovering? We're waiting for him to regain his strength. I wanna buy him and the whole o-club a round of drinks to celebrate!"

"I'm sure he'd like that at some point. He's recovering well. Of course, he lost more than thirty pounds, and he's trying to make up for it by eating everything in sight."

"Sounds like his appetite has recovered," I said, smiling.

She described some more details of his recovery and then said, "He's still got welts from those slimy blood-sucking leeches and mosquito bite marks all over him. I swear those vermin ate off half the weight he lost! It's a wonder he didn't get malaria. He keeps saying, 'It's good to be back. It's good to be back.' Believe me, Angel, this whole episode is nothing but a case of faith and stamina on his part."

"Patty, you were right all along. You were convinced he was still alive. I can't imagine what you went through every day wondering what his fate was. Unbelievable! All I can say is, it was absolutely amazing to be rescued alive after 23 days. It's nothing short of a miracle," I said, instinctively falling back on my Catholic upbringing.

"A miracle for sure. I'm still on a virtual high since he returned," Patty said.

"You really have it bad for him, don't you?" I said with a slight grin.

"I guess you can say that," she said as she started to blush. "We've become such special friends while we've been here. I've always been able to talk to him."

"I know what you mean," I replied. "Having someone to lean on over here is so important. I'm really glad he's back safe and sound." Eager to hear more about the ordeal, I steered the topic back to Roger.

"So, Patty, tell me what's he been saying. How did he survive in that God-awful jungle?"

"Well, when their F-4 was hit by the MiG-19, it destroyed their hydraulic system, which left them with no way to recover from the hit. After he ejected and hit the ground, he was in shock for a while but knew he was deep in enemy territory. He immediately tried to radio his position."

"Why didn't anyone pick up his radio signal?" I inquired.

"Remember when I said that I heard a slight beep from what I thought was his radio?"

"Yeah, you thought Roger was trying to radio the others in the flight that he was still alive."

"Well, I was right. Because he was still in shock he tried to send a radio signal, but he'd forgotten to press the voice transmit button," she said, shaking her head. "I just knew I'd heard a faint signal being transmitted."

"Oh, my God, you were so right," I said. I was struck by her shrewd analysis and her persistence in maintaining her position while everyone was telling her it was just "female" wishful thinking.

"He said he had several close calls with the villagers who were out looking for him. After all, how could they miss an eleven ton aircraft crashing into their backyard?"

"Yeah, and if they found him, they'd get a pretty penny for bringing him in," I interjected.

"You got that right. After he recovered from being in shock, he immediately ditched his parachute and scrambled for cover in the thick jungle, about a half-mile away from the aircraft. He heard VC search parties combing the area, shooting off rifles trying to find him. He said he remembered going pheasant hunting in Kansas when he was a kid. They'd have their dog run ahead to scare out the pheasant, and when a pheasant flew up, off went their rifles, and the pheasant was a goner. He said he wasn't going to be the pheasant. He just laid there and stayed as still as he could."

"Wow! Smart thinking," I said, astonished at his ability to think so clearly under the circumstances.

She continued, "One day, some village kids came within thirty feet of him while he was hiding under some rotted jungle foliage. Roger said that if they'd brought a dog along it would've tracked him down in a second. Luckily, the kids were more interested in playing than finding Roger."

"A close call, to say the least," I said, intrigued by everything she told me.

"That wasn't his only close call. Another incident happened with a water buffalo."

"A water buffalo! What happened?"

"One morning Roger came too close to a village and saw people everywhere. He scurried for cover under some thick brush and lay there motionless for hours. Later in the afternoon, a water buffalo was grazing close by. It must have picked up Roger's scent because it ambled right over to his hiding space and started snorting and sniffing. Then the buffalo stepped on a small tree branch covering Roger's ankle. It was all he could do to keep from letting out a groan or moving for fear he'd be discovered. The kids tried to get the water buffalo to move but with no results. Finally, some older kid came running up and kept swatting the buffalo on its hind end until it finally moved, leaving Roger breathing a huge sigh of relief."

"Christ sake, he was really pressing his luck."

"Ya, I'll say. It's probably a good thing that water buffalo couldn't talk!" We both smiled and continued drinking. "The whole thing was frightening, but everyday Roger kept hoping that he'd be rescued. Until the day he heard calls over his radio from another downed pilot who SARS was trying to rescue but couldn't. He thought if they couldn't get that guy out, how were they ever going to get him out?"

"That must have been a pretty dark day for him," I said in a reflective tone.

"Yes," she acknowledged. "He said that was the lowest point of his ordeal, but he still kept hoping."

"Was he able to eat anything while he was on the ground?" I inquired.

Patty continued, "Well, water wasn't a problem. After a rainfall, he'd collect water off the leaves, and at night he'd sneak down to the streams in the area. But food was scarce. He couldn't get to his survival pack after he ejected, and all he had to eat were some of those Pillsbury Space Sticks that were in his flight suit pocket. Those were gone the first day. He ate a few berries and whatever else he thought might be safe. He said there were plenty of squirrels and lizards around, but he decided not to start a fire or shoot off his gun, for fear it would draw attention to his location."

Then Patty finished her drink and said, "I gotta go. I wanna go back over to see Roger again tonight before he goes to sleep."

"Patty, thanks for sharing all of this with me. It's mind-blowing. The whole thing is amazing. He was one lucky guy to get rescued and to have you by his side. Tell Roger we're waiting for him to get over here for some serious drinking and celebrating."

Patty smiled and said, "I will. You can bet he's looking forward to it. See ya."

Roger's recovery went well. He was out of the hospital within a week, and by July, he was ready to head back to the States for pilot training—his reward for being a hero. We never did have that big celebration with him, but one afternoon he came over to the officers' club for lunch. As he was leaving, I stopped him and said, "Wait a minute, Roger. I've got something for you."

I rushed back into my office. I had taken the brass nameplate off the Honor Roll plaque in the lobby, the one that read:

Captain Roger C. Locher

555th TFS MIA

May 10, 1972

I'd had Khun Ack cut a star out of plywood, paint it red, and place Roger's brass nameplate in the center. The red star represented his MIG kill. I'd been waiting for the right time to give it to him. I handed it to him and said, "I thought you might want this." I started to choke up as he looked at it. In a restrained voice he said, "Thanks." That's all that was said. I turned quickly and went back to my office, wiped my eyes, and never saw him again.

A year later, Roger and Peppermint Patty were married. Roger stayed in the Air Force, went to pilot training, and made full colonel. Patty had an equally successful Air Force career with more than 22 years of service. He and Patty have two beautiful daughters. No fanfare was ever made Stateside of this truly heroic man and his brave rescue team.

On September 30, 1977, the remains of Major Bob Lodge were discovered by the North Vietnamese and returned to the U.S. where he was laid to rest in Arlington National Cemetery. Today, hanging in the Pentagon is a collage created by Harley Copic. It illustrates mementos contributed by Lodge's parents of their son's short but brilliant Air Force career.

[1] The 40th Aerospace Rescue and Recovery Squadron crews included: Captain Dale Stovall, Aircraft Commander; Captain Gillespie, Co-pilot; Sergeant Walsh, Fight Engineer; Sergeant Cakebread and Sergeant McQuoid, PJ's pararescue; and Sergeant Welborn, photographer. The other helicopter crew included: Captain Shipman, AC; Captain Zielinski, CP; Sergeant Liles, FE; Sergeant Goodlett & Sergeant Williamson, PJs; and Sergeant Smith, photographer. The four PJ's were indoctrinated as honorary members of the Red River Valley Pilots association, and all received Silver Stars.

[2] Information in this chapter was gathered while at Udorn and from several sources that include: Joseph Bland, "Shot Down in North Vietnam," *The Reader's Digest*, March 1973, page 80-84; Jeffrey Ethell and Alfred Price, *One Day in a Long War*, Random House, New York, 1989; John L. Frisbee, "A Good Thought to Sleep On," *The Air Force Magazine Online*, March 1992, Vol. 75, No. 3.

SECTION FIVE

# Complications

*What is a weed? A weed is a plant whose virtues have not yet been discovered.*
—Ralph Waldo Emerson, American writer (1803 - 1882)

# The Potted Plant

A BEAUTIFUL GARDEN NOW surrounded the commander's newly completed patio. When I looked out my office window, I saw exotic orchids hanging from the patio eaves and gracing the branches of the acacia tree in the center of the yard. A lush green lawn had taken root and the indigenous plants flourished around the inside border of the fence that enclosed the patio.

One afternoon Khun Ack came running into my office. "Kapton, I know nothing. I know nothing," he panted.

"What d'ya mean you know nothing? What's goin' on?" I responded.

"Kapton, Air Pole-lease here. They out in garden. Digging up plants."

"What plants? What are you talking about?" I couldn't imagine what he was talking about, so I looked out the window. Outside, the Air Police (AP) with their K-9 German shepherds were digging up frilly looking plants and stuffing them into bags.

"I know nothing, Kapton," insisted Khun Ack.

As I started to leave my office to investigate, Major George Norwood, the Air Police Chief, appeared in the doorway.

"Angel, I'm sorry to have to tell you this, but your patio grounds have been closed and the entire area is under surveillance."

"For what? Why are your guys destroying my garden?"

"Because it's loaded with marijuana plants, Angel. That's why," he retorted.

"What marijuana plants? Where are they?" I asked with disbelief.

Marijuana was the drug of choice during the sixties and seventies. It was cheap and easily accessible, both on and off-base. People used it to relieve stress, be part of the in-crowd, and escape reality. I never could get the hang of inhaling. I always gagged when I tried to smoke cigarettes. People said I needed more practice, but I figured why work on learning how to inhale when I could get the same effect from legal drugs?

If things got too tense, I could pop a little yellow Valium prescribed by the base physician. One of those brought new meaning to the phrase "chilling out." Of course, alcohol was always available. Besides, getting caught with illegal drugs in the military would result in anything from an Article 15 to getting kicked out.

Chief Norwood continued, "Angel, we got a report from an officer who said he noticed marijuana plants growing all over the place in our backyard."

"Does this mean my backyard is under investigation? Or am I? For Christ sake, George, I don't even know what the stuff looks like."

A few minutes later my boss, Major Bob Anastasio, walked in. I figured the Chief must have called him before he'd dispatched the APs.

"What's goin' on now?" he said, rolling his eyes.

At this point Khun Ack decided to leave the fray. On the way out, he was still mumbling, "I know nothing!"

I shrugged my shoulders.

The Chief quickly chimed in, "Bob, we have a situation here. We got a report about marijuana plants growing over here in the o-club backyard. Seems there's a shitload of it out there, and my guys are pulling it up."

"George, I can't believe that. How did marijuana get out there?" He said, looking at me.

"Damned if I know. I don't even know what the stuff looks like." I reiterated.

Growing up I was always fascinated with nature and had familiarized myself with many of the native plants in New York State, but I never took the time to learn more about the exotic surroundings in Thailand. I was too caught up with my job, the war, drinking, and other activities.

We all went outside to assess the situation. By that time, the efficient airmen had pulled out all the visible marijuana plants and were getting ready to haul them off.

One of airmen saluted the Chief and said, "I think we got it all, Chief."

"Good going. Now, get rid of it," he told them.

"Yes, sir," they said as they left the premises smiling. I suspected that when the other airmen heard about the stash of fresh marijuana there was going to be a big party somewhere.

We surveyed the area to ensure all the plants were gone and to alleviate any fears that a big drug operation was being run out of the o-club's backyard. "Let's get out of this 'joint!'" I said as we all headed back into the club. We laughed and proceeded into the bar to have a drink and theorize about how the plants had mysteriously sprouted up on-site.

The Chief, accustomed to seeing the negative side of things, thought Khun Ack must have had something to do with it. His behavior was, after all, highly suspicious. My boss had no clue. My theory was that wild marijuana seeds had been in the truckloads of dirt we'd hauled in from off-base for the patio garden. I think the reason nothing further came of the bizarre incident had to do with the fact that the Chief was a friend of mine and that I had a reputation for being a straight shooter.

Later that day, I went back outside to assess the damages. As I walked around the yard, I saw one forgotten little marijuana plant on the ground. I picked it up and brought it into my office. I retrieved an empty tin can from the kitchen, filled it with dirt, and planted the only remnant of my drug bust, and I placed it on my office desk in full view. Whenever anyone came into my office, I'd point to it and say grinning, "See my potted plant!"

*I am a woman in process. I'm just trying like everybody else. I try to take every conflict, every experience, and learn from it. Life is never dull.*

—Oprah Winfrey, American television host, producer (1954 - )

# Back By Popular Demand

AFTER SIX MONTHS OF persistent negotiating and cajoling, the general and his boys finally agreed to reverse their ban on strippers at the o-club, provided we follow a few strict rules. The higher-ups were determined to avoid another incident like the one involving the general and the giant birthday cake. I agreed to the terms laid out in the edict, which left no room for misinterpretation. It read like the Ten Commandments:

1. The stripper must keep her bottoms on at all times.
2. The stripper must stay on stage at all times during the performance.
3. There shall be no audience participation with the stripper.
4. There will be no cameras allowed.
5. The club officer must post these rules in plain view for all to read and heed.
6. The club officer will inform the performer(s) of these rules and the consequences if not followed.
7. The club officer and staff are responsible for ensuring that these rules are followed to the letter.
8. Any infractions will be dealt with accordingly.

I smugly flaunted my victory. Now, there'd be no need for the guys to harass me about getting the strippers back into the club.

The first performance was highly publicized. The club newsletter and a poster at the entry to the bar announced "The 'Real Thing' Back By Popular Demand" and listed the new rules. Everyone jammed into the club on Thursday night with great anticipation. I entered the bar with Pete Mendellson and smiled as I looked around at the huge crowd. In fact, I couldn't remember it ever being this packed on a weeknight at 2200 hours.

The room was a sea of olive-drab flight suits, broken only by the bright colors of the pilot's squadron patches, and the miniature red, white, and blue American flags on their left sleeves.

Officers stood three deep along the 30-foot bar engulfed by a low cloud of cigarette smoke, while bartenders scurried back and fourth in an attempt to fill repeated demands for drinks. On stage, a Thai band performed their rendition of the rock 'n roll classic, *Yellow River,* or in this case, *Lellow Liver.* The music was extremely loud, but the volume still failed to mask the slightly offbeat rhythm. No one seemed to notice, though, as the booze and the bravado were in sync. The cash registers rang, "Ka ching, ka ching," and the troops' morale appeared high.

Pete and I pressed through the crowd; it was like trying to exit a New York subway during rush hour. We found our way to the 13th Fighter Squadron table where two seats were saved for their ops officer and his *tealock.* The bar waitresses hurried over to take our orders. We asked for the usual, a double scatch rocks for Pete and a gin'n tonic for me.

The dancer walked on stage, and the crowd immediately started whistling and cheering, "Take it off! Take it all off," before she even got started. The dancer wasn't built like a typical Thai woman. Her large breasts were anatomically out of proportion to the rest of her small-framed body and they spilled over the top of her tightly fitted bikini top. She had long, jet-black hair, succulent lips, and cocoa-brown eyes. She couldn't have been more than 21years old. Although it was hard to tell, the Thais often looked younger than they were.

She started dancing and swaying her hips back and forth, teasing the eager crowd that got more raucous with every sensuous move. The band started playing *The Stripper,* and as the music grew more heated, the crowd grew more frenzied. The dancer responded to the crowd's excitement by thrusting her pelvis to the beat of the music. Her hands slipped under her breasts, pushing them up and almost out of her bikini top. The fighter jocks were transfixed. The rowdy crowd started clapping their hands to the rhythmic movement of her hips and chanted, "Take it off! Take it all off! Show us your tits!"

Still shaking her assets, she turned her back to the audience, slipped off her bikini top and slowly turned to face the anxious crowd. There she was, her voluptuous breasts in full view, waving her bikini top in the air.

The crowd was mesmerized. Even the most virtuous pilot had a hard time resisting the temptation of those magnificently huge breasts. The guys acted like they'd never seen a naked woman before. Of course, it had been a while for most of them.

Then, the dancer swung her top out into the crowd, and everyone scrambled for it like a bunch of frenzied bridesmaids lined up to catch the prized wedding bouquet. A fighter jock in the front row grabbed the flimsy bikini top and proceeded to step up on the stage with the stripper, waving it over his head like a victory pennant.

I turned to Pete and in a startled voice said, "Pete, did you see what he just did?"

"Yeah," he said, laughing.

At first I thought, *maybe he'll just jump off the stage and go back to his seat.* No such luck. The stripper stood in front of the fighter jock, grabbed hold of his hands, and urged him to dance with her. He was flat-ass drunk, and the rambunctious fighter pilots egged him on shouting, "Go to it!" He was six feet tall, and the stripper's bare chest came up to just about his middle. He was in his flight suit and black combat boots. I quickly realized the pilot wasn't one of our guys. He was a TDY jock from Homestead Air Force Base deployed to support the increase bombing raids over North Vietnam.

Then, the worst possible scenario unfolded. The stripper slowly started unzipping the pilot's flight suit, working her way down as the crowd cheered, and the pilot was bumping and grinding his hips to the music.

I turned to Pete, who was fully engrossed, and said, "Pete, this has gotten out of hand."

He hardly heard me, "What?"

The stripper finished unzipping the pilot's flight suit and slowly started to help him slip it down to his ankles. There he was in full view, his flight suit crumpled around his boots, rockin' and rollin' with a huge bulge in his white BVDs.

Shocked, my eyes widened, and my hands flew up to my face as I cringed and groaned out loud, "Oh no! This can't be happening!" The show had deteriorated from the risqué to the ribald, and I couldn't do one thing about it. I felt like I was stuck in the Le Brea Tar Pits. "Oh no, Pete, this is awful! I can't believe this. I've gotta stop this."

"Angel, don't do a thing. If you try to stop this, they'll tar and feather you!" he said in a raised voice.

I realized Pete was right. Reasoning with a crazed mob was impossible. Everyone was wild with excitement and encouraging the combo to continue. The onstage duo and the crowd were feeding off each other. They had become one.

Then, out of the corner of me eye, I saw Colonel Smith, the Wing Commander. The first week strippers are allowed back in the club, and it turns into a free-for-all. I again tugged at Pete's sleeve. "I've gotta stop this. Look who just walked it to the bar, the Wing Commander. This has gone too far."

I sat there trying to be invisible and fantasized about disappearing through a trap door in the floor. I realized I was in trouble, especially now that the Wing Commander witnessed the whole sordid event. I thought, *if they hadn't made the restrictions so stringent this wouldn't have been so bad.* In fact, it might have been hysterically funny, but I wasn't laughing. There was a time in my life when I fretted about going to hell, now I was more worried about catching hell.

I wondered what went wrong. I had briefed the band and had the translator tell the stripper the rules. Clearly something had been lost in the translation. I was going to have a lot of explaining to do. Finally, two guys from the pilot's squadron dragged the reluctant pilot off the stage. The crowd booed and hissed as the drunken pilot staggered off. A shit-eating grin covered his face as he waved his prized bikini top high in the air. His buddies tried in vain to get his flight suit pulled back up, but he kept trying to get back on stage.

Finally, the music ended. The stripper gave a bouncy bow and exited stage left. The band took a break, and the crowd began to unwind. Everyone was laughing and carrying on while they recounted what had just transpired. At last, I freed myself from the chair and made my way through the crowd toward the back room. As I pushed through the crowd, I ignored a couple of comments from the pilot who yelled, "Good goin' Angel. Hell of a show!"

Pete rushed after me shouting, "Where are you going? What are you gonna do?"

"I'm gonna fire her, that's what I'm gonna do!"

Pete was startled, "What? Why are you gonna do that?"

"Damn it! She knew the rules. It's her ass or mine."

I walked into the back room where the stripper was puffing on what looked like a cigarette. Her eyes were glazed over and her body glimmered with sweat. Without skipping a beat I said, "You're fired. Fired. Do you understand? You're fired!" I said in a very loud voice. "You knew the rules. You knew you weren't supposed to have anybody get up on stage with you, and worse yet, take his clothes off!"

I'm sure the perplexed stripper didn't understand half of what I was saying, but she understood my raised voice and the angry look on my face. She kept repeating, "So-o sorry, so-o sorry, Kapton." She wrapped her robe tightly around herself and recoiled as I just kept spewing out words like an erupting volcano. Deep down, I knew it wasn't really her fault. She'd given the audience what she thought they wanted, and she'd done one hell of a job. Her performance had ignited the crowd.

Pete followed along after me and appeared in the doorway as my outburst trailed off.

"Angel, come on. Settle down. Let it go." He took my arm, and we started to leave the club.

"Did you really fire her?" he asked, with a mixture of disbelief and amusement.

"Yes, of course I did. What did you expect me do? She blew it, and those drunken idiots that call themselves officers made damn fools out of themselves and me!"

Pete tried in vain to reassure me, "Angel, it wasn't your fault. There wasn't anything you could've done to stop it."

Ignoring his efforts to console me, I continued, "Pete, did you see the Wing Commander? Colonel Smith saw the whole thing."

"Hell, Angel, don't worry about it. The Old Man looked like he was enjoying it."

Even though it was midnight, I decided I better call Colonel Ellsworth. I knew it would be better for the Base Commander to hear about it from me rather than be surprised tomorrow morning at the Wing Commander's stand-up briefing. He answered the phone and sounded like I had awakened him.

"Colonel Ellsworth, sir, this is Angel. Sorry to bother you at this late hour, sir, but I thought you ought to know what happened tonight at the club."

"That's OK. What is it?" he responded, his voice still groggy.

I quickly described the entire episode. Then I told him, "And so, I fired her."

After a long pause, the colonel repeated, "You fired her?"

"Yes, sir."

Then he hesitated and asked, "Was she the one with the big…ah, the big…ah…"

"Yes, sir."

"You fired her?" he repeated, now fully awake.

Exhausted from the evening, I said, "I didn't think there was anything else I could do, Colonel. The general made the rules pretty explicit."

"Well, I guess you're right. There really wasn't much you could do. Thanks for letting me know. I'll see you tomorrow."

Pete and I left the club, and as we walked back to his trailer he said, "What did the Base Commander have to say about all of this?"

"He was glad I let him know, but he seemed to be more concerned about losing the stripper with the big bazooms."

Pete laughed, shook his head, and said, "It figures, that old letcher."

"Why did they set up those restrictions? It's a war zone. Who the hell gives a damn, and why should I be the one to enforce these dumb rules anyway?" Pete put his arm around me as I started to cry.

"Oh, Angel, come on, you're making too much out of this. Everyone thought the show was great. The gal gave them what she thought they wanted."

"But, I had to fire her," I said as I wiped my eyes and nose. "What else could I have done? I just didn't know what else I could do. God, I'll never hear the end of this."

Pete continued to hold me and said, "You're right about that, Angel."

We went into his trailer and went to bed. He hugged me and made love to me in an effort to make the night go away. It seemed like it took me forever to get to sleep. I kept replaying the night's events over and over again. What had all this come to? I wasn't running an officers' club. I was running a strip joint with call girls for waitresses and a bunch of lascivious drunks for customers. "War is hell," that's what the guys kept saying. Or was it an excuse to raise hell?

By the next morning, everyone had heard what happened and knew that I'd fired the stripper with the big bazooms. They couldn't believe I'd fired her, and they kept riding me about it. "How could you, Angel? She was the best thing we ever had. You'll never find another one like her," they said as they held their hands out in front of them to indicate the enormity of her breasts. Somehow, the very harassment I had tried to avoid had escalated out of proportion. Of course, I strongly defended my position, but to no avail. If I hadn't fired her, I would have caught hell from the top. Now that I'd fired her, I was catching hell from the troops. There was no winning.

At the time, I never asked myself why I needed to get the strippers back in the club in the first place. Why hadn't I seen the ban on strippers as a blessing in disguise? The general had done me a favor by banning the strippers. He did for me what I wouldn't have been able to do for myself. He didn't care what the guys thought of him. He thought the whole thing was lewd and wasn't afraid to say so. As a woman, I would have been harassed beyond belief if I'd tried to stop the strippers.

I had rationalized the whole thing. It's wartime. People do strange things. The guys needed to have some fun. You can't be too hard on them. A stripper was no big deal. All I had to do was turn my head in the other direction and say it was part of my job. Things that were unacceptable someplace else were alright here. Or were they?

I think I wanted to get the strippers back because I wanted them to think I could get the general and his boys to change their minds. I wanted to show them I had some power. Bottom line, I wanted to be one of them. I wanted to be liked. Lastly, I didn't want to be seen as a prude. I'd give them what they wanted no matter what the cost—to me, to them, or to the Thai women. I guess I had become one of them. I didn't know what I stood for anymore. I thought I was being more liberal and less uptight, but maybe I was just becoming more immoral.

Six years after I returned to the States, I was on reserve duty at Andrews Air Force Base in Washington, DC. While waiting to have dinner at the officers' club, I noticed another officer in line. "Do you wanna share a table?" I asked, "We'll probably get seated faster."

"Sure, sounds like a good idea," he replied.

During dinner our conversation led to what we'd done during the war. I told him I'd run the o-club at Udorn Air Base in Thailand. His face flashed with recognition, and he said, "You're the one who fired the stripper with the big bazooms!" He started laughing, "We heard about the incident at Hickham Air Force Base in Hawaii. I can't believe I've finally met the living legend!" I started laughing and retold the entire incident in full-living color.

Fourteen years later, at an Air Force Open Mess Conference, I was telling someone that I'd been stationed at Udorn Air Base during 1971-1972. The guy asked me if I'd been there when the pilot had gotten up on stage and taken off his fight suit and danced with a nude stripper. He proceeded to tell me that his Base Commander at Maxwell Air Force Base had called in all of his Squadron Commanders and briefed them on the incident. He told them that he wanted assurances that nothing like that would happen on his base. Shocked, I replied, "They heard about this in Alabama?" Then I proceeded to tell him the story and cleared up a few of the details. No, the pilot hadn't taken off all his clothes; and yes, the stripper still had on her bottoms. It seems like she lost another article of clothing with each retelling of the story. I thought it best to set the record straight. After all those years, I was finally able to see the incident for what it was—a funny one.

*Two legged creatures we are supposed to love as we love ourselves. The fourlegged, also, can come to seem pretty important. But six legs are too many from the human standpoint.*

—Joseph W Krutch, American writer, naturalist (1893 - 1970)

# Late Night Intruder

ON THE TOP STEP of my BOQ, it was waiting for me. I'd never seen anything this big except maybe under a glass case in a museum. A huge black beetle, about three inches long and two inches wide with a wingspan of about four inches, was blocking the entry into my room. During the rice-harvesting season in Thailand, these beetles, called rice bugs, were around in droves, feasting on the rice crop much like locusts devour wheat. The big difference between a locust and a rice bug was that Westerners didn't find the locust appetizing.

The Thais found the rice bugs, with their bellies full of rice, to be an epicurean delicacy. Some Thais made a business of catching them and selling them at their food stands in town. For just a few *baht* you could buy a deliciously crispy, fried rice bug. At night, the rice bugs were attracted to the large floodlights on base. I could hear the "zizzing" sounds from the fluttering of their wings. I'd hurry past the lights hoping that one wouldn't land on my head.

Now I was face-to-face with one as it just lay there, daring me to pass by. I outweighed this creature by 120 pounds. I could've just walked around it, but I didn't. I wasn't about to try to kill it—too messy. Instead, I thought about how I was going to remove it without touching it. Then, out of the corner of my eye, I saw General Searles' Thai security guard with a rifle over his shoulder, pacing back and forth around the perimeter of the general's hootch. I hurried back down the stairs, walked up the road, and greeted the guard, *"Sawadee krup."*

*"Sawadee kah,"* he responded bowing slightly, hands folded in prayer position.

I knew he'd surely enjoy the rice bug more than I would, but how was I going to explain to him that there was a rice bug on my step? It became a game of charades.

I searched for the word for food and started pantomiming. "You want food, hum, *gin khaao.*"

The guard smiled and nodded his head as he tried to grasp my translation.

I continued, "Bug. Rice bug. Big. Rice bug." I made my hands into the shape of the bug and cupped my fingers to my mouth and said, "Eat. *Gin.*" He continued to nod. I wasn't sure if he understood me or was just being polite, so I continued.

"Rice bug. Up there," I said, pointing to my BOQ building. He continued to nod and smile. I continued to repeat myself, my voice getting louder, which often happens when a foreigner tries to be understood. Finally, I motioned for him to follow me. He left his post, and we hiked over to my BOQ. When we got to the top of the stairs, I hoped the bug would still be there. If it wasn't, the guard might think I had something else in mind. Luckily, it was.

When the Thai guard saw it, his eyes lit up as he scooped the large rice bug into his hand. With his rifle still over his shoulder, he carried off his treasure smiling and said, *"Kop kun kah."*

*"Kop kun krup.* Thank you," I replied with my hands folded in the prayer position.

We both got what we wanted. I entered my room with a sigh of relief, knowing that the rice bug's life would serve a higher purpose than me banging it to death with the heel of my shoe. And a happy Thai was going to have a delightful midnight snack.

*He who has a mind to do mischief will always find a pretense.*
—Publilius Syrus, Roman writer (1ˢᵗ century B.C.)

# Out of Control Card Game

THE PIERCING SOUND OF the phone ringing late at night startled me out of a sound sleep. I jumped down from my top bunk and grabbed the receiver.

"Captain Pilato speaking," I said still half asleep.

"Hello, Capt'n Pilato. This is Sergeant Williams."

"Yeah," I said, squinting to see what time it was. The clock read 0200.

"Capt'n, sorry to bother you, but there's been an accident at the club," he said.

"Oh good grief! What's happened now?"

"One of the bartenders got hit with some flying glass, and a piece landed in his eye."

"Oh my God! Who was it?"

"Vit."

"That's the new kid?" Vit was a new hire and the brother of Dom, one of our cashiers. He'd only been there a couple of weeks, and I'm sure the chance to work on an American Air Force base at the officers' club where he could make *maak maak baht* was a dream come true. Bartenders earned 20 cents per hour, and that combined with nickel, dime, and even quarter tips was a considerable amount of money by Thai standards.

"How bad's he hurt?"

"Don't know yet, Capt'n. A couple of the waitresses took him over to the base emergency room. He was bleeding pretty badly when he left here."

"How did it happen, Williams?"

"Not quite sure of all the particulars, ma'am. The waitresses came in and—"

"Never mind," I interrupted. "I'm on my way over. You can fill me in when I get there. Meanwhile, shut down the bar and tell everyone to leave."

"Capt'n, you mean close the bar entirely?"

"Yeah, you heard me," I snapped.

"Where are they gonna get a drink?"

"I couldn't care less. Just shut it down. I've had it with all their shenanigans."

I hung up the phone, threw on some clothes, and quickly headed over to the club. My mind was racing. *These pilots' childish games and cowboy behaviors hadn't resulted in hurting one of them, but a 21-year-old kid. I only hoped that it wasn't too serious. Hadn't the head bartender instructed him on what to do when the crowd got drunk and out of hand? I guess that was a moot point now.*

I came through the swinging doors and stopped at the bar entrance to survey the damage. The place reeked of spilled beer and stale smoke. The mirror behind the bar was shattered, and the floor was covered in broken glass. Broken and toppled bar glasses were strewn about; chairs and tables were in disarray; and a few shit-faced guys were being held up by the bar, still shooting craps. The place looked worse than on a normal bad night.

Sergeant Williams was in the process of telling the last of the pilots to leave. I heard one of them start to argue with him, "What d'ya mean, you're shutting this place down? Who says?"

"Captain Pilato, the club officer, gave me orders to close the place down, sir. There's been an accident, and for safety reasons we're closing the bar."

"I don't see any accident. Tell that club officer I wanna see him," the plastered officer insisted.

"Sorry, sir, the captain's not here right now, and I don't think you wanna mess with this club officer. The captain can get meaner than a tiger that hasn't been fed in a week. Besides, the Air Police are on their way over here, and you don't wanna end up in the morning blotter report do you, sir? Why, if the Old Man sees your name on the blotter, you'll be as good as grounded."

Drunk or not, these guys understood what being grounded meant—no flying. "This place is supposed to be open 24 hours a day. You can't shut it down," the pilot grumbled, as he started to walk toward the door.

As I approached Sergeant Williams, I could see the officer was not buying it. "I wanna see the club officer. Where is he? This is my club. I'm a dues-paying member. Damn it! And I want a drink."

"Good evening, Sergeant Williams."

"Good evening, ma'am. I was just asking the major here to vacate the club. Seems he doesn't wanna leave. He wants to talk to the club officer," he said and raised his eyebrows.

"Oh, he does, does he?"

I turned to the major and said, "Pardon me, Major, I understand you wanna talk to the club officer."

"Yeah, I do. Who the hell are you?" he barked.

I stood erect, my feet firmly planted, and my arms crossed in front of me. I focused my intense Italian eyes squarely on his and responded curtly, "I'm the club officer, Major. What was it you wanted?" I held my ground, but my stomach was doing somersaults.

He leaned in toward me. His breath reeked so badly of alcohol that if I'd struck a match, it could have lit the air on fire. "Listen here, little girl," he said as he puffed up his chest and stood up to his full height. "It's my club. I'm a dues-paying member. You can't shut the club down."

I stiffened my stance and said, "I just did, Major. You heard the sergeant. I suggest you leave now and avoid any further incident," I said and pointed toward the front door.

"Oh yeah? Who's gonna make me?" he taunted me like a schoolboy looking for a fight.

"Capt'n, let me handle this guy," Sergeant Williams interjected. "No need for you to mess with him. The Air Police will be here any minute."

"Thanks, but I'll handle him."

The major just stood there, with one hand holding onto his beer bottle, and the other pointing at my face as he insisted that he wasn't leaving. Suddenly, I snapped. I grabbed him by the collar of his flight suit and pushed him out through the front swinging doors. His body, pliable from the liquor, responded like a marionette. Out he went onto the porch yelling, "You haven't heard the last of this!"

With a gleeful smile, I waved good-bye and hollered back, "Good night, Major."

Sergeant Williams shook his head and smiled, "Good goin', Capt'n."

I turned to him, relaxed my stance, let out a deep sigh, and said, "Thanks. You know, I think I'm getting the hang of this! Come into my office and finish giving me a full report on what happened here tonight." As

I walked into my office I thought, *this time maybe being a woman had given me an advantage.*

"OK, Sergeant Williams, give me a blow by blow of the incident. Start from the beginning."

"Well, Capt'n, I was in the dining room when it happened. Kat, the bar waitress, came running in hollering for me to come quick. There was a fight in the bar and Vit, the bartender, was hurt. Best I can piece together is a group of the pilots were drinking and playing cards. Kat said they started arguing. Then suddenly they picked up some big pilot and threw him over the bar. He hit the mirror shattering it into a million pieces and took a bunch of the glasses with him."

"Yeah, I saw that," I said.

He continued, "I don't think Vit ever saw it coming. It all happened so fast. He was cornered at the end of the bar, and that's when the piece of flying glass must have hit him in the eye."

"Are you sure it was his eye?" I pressed.

"Yes, Capt'n, I saw his eye. By the time I got there the damage was already done. His hand was over his eye, and blood was coming down his face and neck. He was moaning and pretty shook up. I put some ice in a napkin and put it over his eye."

"Oh, God, how awful—the poor kid," I said as I winced and put my hand over my own eye. "Who was involved in the brawl?"

"I don't know, Capt'n. Mostly TDY guys, maybe. I was too preoccupied with taking care of Vit at the time. By then, they'd all scattered. When I asked around, nobody was sure who'd done what," he recalled.

"It figures," I said. "They're not gonna rat anybody out. I'll have to question the other bartenders tomorrow. Right now, I'm going over to the base hospital to see how Vit's doing. I'll see you tomorrow night, Sarge. Thanks for taking care of Vit. It ought to be quiet the rest of this shift."

"Right. I'll get the bar cleaned up before I go off shift, Capt'n."

"Thanks."

By the time I arrived at the base hospital, Vit's sister, Dom, and Captain Fred "Broadway" Olmsted were waiting for the doctor to finish assessing Vit's condition. When Dom saw me, she rushed over and said, "Oh, Kapton, Vit hurt bad. His eye bad, Kapton. Officers who do this 'number 10.' Vit eye bad," she said and started crying.

Fred put his arm around her and said, "Dom, come on now, Vit's gonna be all right." He had her sit down, and his presence seemed to reassure her.

Fred, our MiG killer, had also learned how to speak Thai, which he practiced on the o-club waitresses. It became a mutual admiration society. They fawned all over him, and he got extra good service, food, coffee, and plenty of smiles in return. His charm and wit captured the attention of Dom. Her personality was typical of most Thai woman: sweet, shy, pleasant, and accommodating. Broadway would come up to the cashier's window and say something to her in Thai, make his transaction, and leave her smiling. Dom was easy on the eyes, spoke mediocre English, and became captivated by Broadway's charisma. He convinced her to date him, and soon she became his *tealock*. They were inseparable. Fred wouldn't turn out to be like the other guys who left their *tealocks* with only tears and a *tealock* bracelet. After his tour, Broadway would come back to Thailand, and bring Dom back to the States to marry her.

I bent down to Dom, put my hand on her knee and said, "Dom, I'm so sorry about what happened to your brother. He's going to be OK, Dom. I just know it."

Dom wiped the tears from her eyes and said, "Kapton, officers do bad to Vit. Not right. Not right."

"I know, Dom. They're number 10. I'll take care of it. Don't you worry. I promise I'll get whoever did this to Vit," I said.

I stood up and turned to Fred Olmsted and said, "Well Fred, how bad do you think it is?"

"Hell, I don't know. This waiting is killin' me," he replied.

Just then the doctor walked out through the white hospital doors. "It doesn't look too good," he announced. "I'm afraid his eye is in pretty bad shape. He needs eye surgery, and we can't do it here."

"Why not? What d'ya mean you can't do it here?" Fred blurted out. "Surely there must be something you can do for him."

"We don't have an eye surgeon here," the doctor said. "And even if we did regulations prohibit us from treating foreign nationals on base. There's an eye surgeon at the Adventist Mission Hospital in Bangkok. If you can get him there, they might be able to help."

Dom picked up on the conversation and said, "Vit eye, he go blind?"

"It's gonna be OK, Dom. We're gonna work it out," Fred said, as he tried to comfort her. He turned to the doctor and said, "We can get him on the MEDEVAC plane to Bangkok first thing in the morning that leaves in a couple of hours," he said, checking his watch.

The doctor interrupted, "Sorry, Fred. He can't get on the Air Force MEDEVAC. He's Thai. It's only for Air Force personnel."

"Jesus Christ, doc, I don't give a damn about the regulations! This kid isn't gonna lose his eye," said Fred.

"Well, I've done all I can," the doctor said. "I'm sorry." He started to walk away.

"Wait a minute, doc. You've gotta help us. There's gotta be a way around the regs," Fred persisted. "What if I flew on the MEDEVAC with him?"

"I'm Sorry, Fred. I'm afraid you'll have to take him commercial air," the doctor replied.

"I can't believe the U.S. Government won't help this kid. After all, it was U.S. military personnel that put the glass in his eye in the first place," Fred retorted.

Fred turned to me and said, "I can't believe this. Christ, if I could throw him in the back seat of the F-4, I would. These guys are assholes. I guess I'll have to take him on commercial air. Damn it, I'm not gonna let him lose his eye. Not if I can help it."

I interrupted, "Fred, there's a flight that leaves for Bangkok at 0900. I take it when I go down there for procurement meetings."

"That's two hours later than the MEDEVAC flight," he said. "But, I guess, if that's the only way to get him there, that's what I'll hafta do."

I put my hand on Fred's shoulder and said, "Thanks, Fred. I know that Vit will be in good hands with you there. I sure hope he doesn't lose his eye because some drunken pilots lost a stupid card game. If he does, there's gonna be hell to pay. Call me from Bangkok, and let me know what happens. OK?" I scribbled my o-club phone number on a scrap of paper and handed it to Fred.

"OK, I'll call you." He put Vit and Dom in the front seat of the squadron truck and drove off to Base Operations to wait for the commercial aircraft to arrive.

I walked back to my room. It was going on 0500. I was totally exhausted from the whole episode. I thought, *this is the last straw for these guys. I didn't know what I could do. All I knew was I wanted to slap 'em silly. Maybe, it would knock some sense into them.* I was too tired to think about it any more. It would have to wait until morning. I went back to my Q and was asleep before my head hit the pillow.

*If it will feed nothing else, it will feed my revenge.*
—William Shakespeare, English writer (1564 - 1616)
From *The Merchant of Venice*

# Getting Even

I SHOWED UP AT the club just before noon. I was still exhausted and angry over last night's incident, which had needlessly injured Vit. Pip and Sergeant Doc Holliday, my NCO in charge, greeted me. Holliday was called "Doc" after the legendary Doc Holliday, popularized in the Wyatt Earp television series. He'd been here three years and kept getting his tour extended. Thailand had grown on him. He cross-trained into the club management field a few years before and took care of the club like it was a prized car. He was the number two guy in the club and ran the operation by the book. He shot first and asked questions later.

"I heard what happened to Vit last night," Doc said. "I read the log book and talked with Sergeant Williams just before he left early this morning. Those boys made quite a mess."

"Yeah, I'll say. Christ, can you believe it? Those SOBs did one of their John Wayne routines, and now this kid could lose his eye. Have we heard from Captain Olmsted yet?" I asked, pacing the floor.

"No, ma'am." Pip and Doc both replied in unison. "All we know, Kapton," said Pip, "is that Kapton Olmsted and Vit got on the commercial C-47 that left at 9 o'clock."

I ate some lunch, and then at about 1400 I got a call from Fred.

"Hey, Angel, I'm checking in. The news isn't good. Vit's eye was too far-gone. They couldn't save it. The force of the glass penetrated his lens too far and ruptured it beyond repair. He'll be blind in that eye."

"Damn it! I was hoping for the best. Fred, it was really good of you to take care of Vit. Thank you."

"Hell, somebody had to do it. The poor kid was so scared. We're coming back to Udorn on the last plane out. See you some time tomorrow. I'm exhausted and gotta fly tomorrow morning at 0500."

"Thanks again, Fred. Hope you can get some sleep. I'll see you when you get back," I said and hung up.

I called Doc Holliday and Pip into my office and gave them the news. "I'm very sorry. I hate to have to tell you this, but they couldn't save Vit's eye. He's going to be blind in that eye." I told Pip to bring in the other supervisors, and I'd tell them.

They gathered in the outer office, and I explained what happened while Pip translated. The supervisors excitedly exchanged words among themselves. I could only imagine what they were saying. *This is what we have to put up with to earn a living around here. I bet they never find the jerk who did it.*

Then Pip asked, "Kapton, they want to know if you know who did this to Vit, and what will happen to them?"

"I don't know yet. I'm working on it. When I find out, I'll let everyone know. Whoever was responsible for this will be dealt with accordingly," I said in a determined tone. If I found out who did this, I wanted him to get, at the very least, an Article 15. After they left, I turned to Doc and said, "You know, Doc, their shenanigans are no longer cute—they're acting like hoodlums." He kept nodding his head as I continued to expound. "Well, maybe that's a little strong, but they certainly weren't acting like officers and gentlemen. We're dealing with a bunch of out of control three-year-olds." I walked back into my office with Doc trailing behind me.

Doc continued, "You got that right, Capt'n. You know, if these boys keep acting like three-year-olds, maybe you ought to treat 'em like three-year-olds."

"What d'ya mean? You can't tell these guys anything. Hell, I've tried. It's like pissing in the wind," I fired back.

"What I mean Capt'n is, if they're acting like kids, treat 'em like kids. Moms don't let little kids drink out of glass cups. They let 'em use plastic cups," Doc said with a mischievous grin. It seemed that he'd been cogitating on the idea and was looking to see what kind of a response he'd get.

As he was talking, his idea was resonating with me. "You're right, Doc. I got it. Find out how many cases of those eight ounce plastic cups we have on hand in the warehouse."

"Matter of fact, Capt'n, I checked our inventory this morning. We've got about 22 cases. At 500 per case that makes 11,000 cups, plus what we've got in the party room closet."

"How many drinks do you figure we serve around here a day, Doc?" I mused.

"Well, let's see," Holliday lifted up his clipboard and glanced at his figures, "About 1,000 to 2,000 or thereabouts."

"What does that give us?" I asked, too tired to do the math.

"That's about a week's worth," he said, looking at his clipboard again.

"Great!" I said with conviction. "Take all the glasses off every bar in the club and replace them all with plastic ones. Put a notice at the entrance to the main bar that until further notice we're using plastic cups."

"Right, Capt'n. No problem. Can do easy," he said as he hurried out the door with a look of satisfaction on his face. About halfway out, he turned around and said, "I'll call the NCO club and other clubs at U-Tapao, NKP, Korat, and Ubon and see if they have any plastic cups they can spare. We could have them here in a day or so."

"Good. Go get 'em, I said. I'll call procurement in Bangkok to see how long it'll take to get some more in here from the States. And Doc, if anyone asks why the plastic cups, tell 'em when they grow up I'll give 'em back real glasses."

That afternoon, when the main bar reopened for happy hour at 1630, all the glasses on the bar had been replaced with plastic ones. I killed time until about 1930, when I figured there'd be a crowd in the bar. I walked in, ordered a gin and tonic, and waited for the inevitable.

"Hey Angel, what's with the plastic cups? What happened to the glasses?" asked one of the pilots.

"Well, here's the deal," I said, "last night some guys tried to John Wayne this place. They threw some drunken pilot over the bar, shattered the mirror, and a piece of flying glass landed in the bartender's eye. Now the kid's blind in one eye. So, I figure when you guys start behaving like adults, and I find out who's responsible for this incident, I'll consider putting the glasses back on the bar. Frankly, as far as I'm concerned, you guys can drink out of plastic cups for the rest of my tour."

"Come on, Angel," one of the guys insisted. "It was an accident.

Nobody's to blame. It wasn't intentional. The kid was in the wrong place at the wrong time."

"Yeah, yeah, the wrong place at the wrong time. Why don't you try telling that to him?" I snapped back.

I attempted, unsuccessfully, to find out who was responsible. I tried to get the Wing Commander to take some action, but McHale and Gabriel, my allies, were gone, and no one was interested. The war they were fighting was much more important than my personal vendetta. I even took the glasses out of the full colonels' private dining room in an effort to get their attention. Annoyed by my stubbornness, Colonel Smith, the Wing Commander, who had replaced Gabriel said, "Angel, you've made your point, now give us our glasses back. Forget it, it was an accident. There are more important things to be addressed."

After two weeks of me trying to punish them with plastic cups, we ran out. I was forced to put the glasses back in the bar. All I heard after the glasses were back was, "It's about time." It was business as usual. Nobody cared and no one, except Vit, would remember the incident. But I would.

When researching this book I caught up with "Broadway" in Tennessee and found out that Major Dean White was the one who had been thrown over the bar, as I had suspected. Who threw him is still a mystery. Broadway hadn't told me at the time because he and Dean were in the same squadron.

*I think we all wish we could erase some dark times in our lives. But all of life's experiences, bad and good, make you who you are. Erasing any of life's experiences would be a great mistake.*

—Luis Miguel, Mexican musician (1970 - )

## It Must Have Been the Shrimp

I FLEW TO BANGKOK for the monthly procurement meeting and decided to take the train back to Udorn to see the countryside. It took eight hours, and even though I purchased a first class ticket, it was hard to point to anything on the train that resembled first class. I sat upright in a hard back seat, which made it difficult to take a little catnap, let alone get comfortable. The sound of the steel wheels rolling over the metal tracks kept pace with the back and forth swaying of the train: click-clat, click-clat, click-clat. The aroma of Thai food mixed with cigarette smoke filled the air, and the car was crowded with Thais squatting in circles, eating, and talking in their singsong language. Outside of Bangkok, it was rare to see a *falong* and even rarer to see a woman *falong* riding on a train by herself, which explained the longer than usual stares I kept getting.

The train passed mile after mile of water-flooded rice fields filled with green shoots popping through the water. Women with their long skirts were bending over to harvest the rice as water buffalo grazed in the lush fields. It all looked like a travel postcard. At twilight, the glow of the oil lamps could be seen hanging from the open-sided houses on stilts.

My stomach felt queasy. I figured it was either the motion sickness from the train ride or something I ate at dinner last night. Because it persisted, I started thinking it was the shrimp. Seafood was always a prime candidate for food poisoning. I hoped it was only a mild case, because I hated being sick. Whatever it was, I'd be glad to get back to Udorn where I could catch some Zs in my own bed.

Bob Barnett was there to pick me up. I was glad to see him. I gave him a kiss and a quick hug. "Hi, Angel, how's it goin'? How was the procurement meeting?" he asked.

"The meeting was as exasperating as ever. Every time I go down there, they add one more regulation to tie the club manager's hands. It's totally fucked. A couple of guys get some kickback money off some entertainment contracts from hiring rock 'n roll bands, so now all the entertainment contracts have to go through procurement. I guess those guys can get the kickbacks! I'll tell ya, I'll be really glad when I'm out this bureaucratic nightmare."

"Yeah, they make everybody pay for a few guys' screw ups," he replied. "The train trip must have been something else. You look a little pale."

"I'll say. I felt like I was on a teeter-totter and the smell was enough to gag me. I feel a little nauseous. I think it was the train ride or something I ate. I just wanna get some Zs. I didn't get much on the train. You can drop me off at the Q."

When I got back to my room, I didn't feel much better. I went to the bathroom and threw up. I figured I might feel better if I got what was ailing me out of my system, but it didn't seem to help. I climbed up onto my top bunk, laid flat on my back, and fell asleep. When I woke up a few hours later, I went over to the club and got some club soda to try to settle my stomach. I did a little work and then met Bob for dinner. I didn't eat much and told Bob I wanted to turn in early. I was still tired. He walked me back to my room and said, "Hey, I'm worried about you. You're never sick."

"Thanks, Bob. I'll probably feel better in the morning."

The next morning, I jumped down out of my bunk and rushed into the bathroom without even checking to see if it was occupied. I put my head over the toilet bowl and threw up until there was nothing left in my stomach. I felt hot and clammy.

Then, an absolutely frightening thought flashed into my head. *Oh my God, this might not be food poisoning—it might be morning sickness.* How could I be pregnant? My system had shut down a few months after I arrived, and I hadn't had a period for eight months. How could I get pregnant if I wasn't having any periods? I convinced myself I was probably jumping to conclusions. Nevertheless, the frightening thought persisted. What if I was pregnant? What would I do? What would Bob think about it? We could get married. It wouldn't matter if the baby came early. My mom would say, "The second baby comes in nine months; the first one comes anytime after the wedding."

When I saw Bob that day, I thought it best to tell him my suspicion and see what his reaction was. "Bob, I don't think I'm sick from something I ate."

"Oh, what d'ya think it is?" he said.

"I don't wanna alarm you, but I think I might be pregnant."

With a tone of disbelief he said, "What? How d'ya know?"

"I don't know for sure, but if it was something I ate, it would have been out of my system by now. I'm going over to the base hospital this afternoon, and then I'll know for sure."

"Let's not overreact. Let's wait'n see what the doctor says." That was all he said.

That afternoon I showed up at the hospital intake desk, and the sergeant asked, "Afternoon, Capt'n, what can we do for ya today?"

"I think I have a case of food poisoning," I told him. The last thing I was going to say was that I was there because I suspected I was pregnant. I didn't want that rumor spreading around base.

When I got in to see the doctor, I got right to the point. "Doc, I don't think this is food poisoning. I've been sick to my stomach, throwing up in the morning, and I feel nauseous. I think I might be pregnant."

"You think so? When was your last period?

"Eight months ago."

"Eight months ago!" he said, a little shocked.

"Yeah, that's what I said. How can a woman get pregnant if she hasn't had a period for eight months?"

"Well, it can happen."

"That's good to know now!"

He handed me a plastic cup and said, "Angel, tomorrow morning when you get up, take a midstream urine sample and bring it in. We'll run a test ASAP."

"Please don't put my name on the sample. I need this to be confidential. If I'm pregnant, I don't want it blabbed all over base," I said sternly.

He said, "Don't worry, I'll handle it."

"Thanks, Doc." I left feeling that I could trust him.

The next morning I was sick again, and I knew I must be right. The test would only confirm my worst fears. I dutifully collected my urine sample and carried it over to the base hospital. The doc said to come back over in the afternoon. I went back to his office and sat there fidgeting and thumbing through an outdated *Stars and Stripes* newspaper. I knew what the results of the test were as soon as the doctor opened the door.

"Well?" I said. "What's the verdict?"

He said in a sober voice, "You were right. You're pregnant."

My heart sank, and my throat started to tighten up. "You know, Doc, this is one of those times I wish I wasn't. I guess I assumed if I wasn't having any periods, I didn't need to worry about using precautions. I guess it's too late now." The doc did a pelvic exam and assessed that I was about six weeks pregnant.

"What do you want to do?" he asked with an empathic look.

"I guess I'll have to get back to you. I wanna talk with my boyfriend and see what he thinks about all of this. I'm getting out of the Air Force in a few months and could have the baby, but I don't want a shotgun wedding. I want the kid to have a willing mother and father," I said with the emphasis on the willing.

I left his office, and my thoughts rambled. *What is Bob going to say? We were getting serious, and maybe it would all work out. We could get married. We loved each other. It would be OK. He likes kids, but then again maybe he wouldn't go for this at all. Maybe he'd want me to have an abortion.* I didn't want to think the worst. I decided to wait and see what he would say when I told him.

I met Bob for dinner. I was scared to tell him the news, but I was still hopeful he'd suggest getting married and keeping the baby. But something down deep told me that wasn't what he was going to say.

"Hi, Bob."

"Hi, Angel. Well, what did the doc say?"

"He confirmed it. I'm pregnant," I said with a dreaded look on my face.

"Gosh!" He said. He looked like he'd been hit in the stomach with a football. I've never understood why a guy acts so surprised when a woman tells him she's pregnant. He acts like he wasn't there when it happened. Bob remained quiet as I started to come up with suggestions about what we could do.

"Bob, I know the timing is a little off, but we could get married now while we're still in Thailand, or we could wait until we get back to the States. Either way, we have to decide something really soon. I don't wanna wait too long. The doctor thought I was about six weeks along, and after 12 weeks it'll be too late." I was talking like marriage was inevitable, and it was only a matter of deciding when.

Then it hit me. *He's not upset because the timing is off, he's not thinking of marriage at all. Oh my God!* As that thought raced through my mind, I started to lead the conversation in another direction. "Bob, I can tell by the look on your face that you're not thrilled about this. Well, neither am I. All I can say is, I want this baby. But I can't force you into anything. For me, I can handle having a baby in less than nine months after marriage, but I don't want the shame of having a kid out of wedlock, or the emotional ordeal of giving it up for adoption. Besides, Bob, there's one thing I know for sure, and that is a kid needs to have a mother and a father."

Finally, he said, "Yeah, right. I understand. I just wasn't ready for this."

Then, I gave him an ultimatum. "Bob, this decision rests with you. If you don't want me or the baby, you have to tell me right away, because the only other alternative is an abortion." I hated even uttering the word, but a decision had to be made soon.

Up to this point, I'd been doing most of the talking, and I wasn't sure where he was coming from. Of course, it's hard to know what someone is thinking when you're doing all the talking. It's even more difficult when the person's responses are vague and noncommittal. I realized the conversation was going nowhere. We hadn't come to any decision, and I just kept rehashing the options. Finally, I said, "Bob, why don't you think about it. You know where I stand on all of this. I want this baby."

He said, "Yeah, I need some time to think about it. I really hadn't planned on this. I'm not sure what to do."

"OK, but we can't wait too long," I repeated, "Time is of the essence."

He said, "Yeah, I understand. How long do you need?"

I wanted to say, *Five minutes you idiot,* but instead I said, "Ah…um…how about Thursday? That's in two days."

He said, "OK. I'll get back to you then," almost like he was following up on a sales call.

"OK, Bob. Until then, I think it's best if we don't see each other. You need to come to this decision on your own."

"Angel, just one thing. I even hate to ask you this, but are you sure?"

"What d'ya mean, am I sure? I told you what the doctor said."

"I mean…" he hesitated.

Then I grasped what he was getting at. "Bob, if you're implying that you think the baby isn't yours, you're dead wrong. You know that you're the only person I've been sleeping with for months. Besides, Pete Mendellson had a vasectomy."

His implication was quite a blow, but I guess I deserved it. I suppose every guy wants to think he's the only one. He knew of my involvement with Pete. But once I presumed my relationship with Bob was serious, I abandoned that affair and decided to be faithful to him. Now, I'd have to wait and see what fate brought me, and fate's name was Bob.

*Being unready and ill equipped is what you have to expect in life. It is the universal predicament. It is your lot as a human being to lack what it takes. Circumstances are seldom right. You never have the capacities, the strength, the wisdom, the virtue you ought to have. You must always do with less than you need in a situation vastly different from what you would have chosen.*

—Charlton Ogburn, Jr., American writer (1911 - 1998)

# A Predicament

WITH THE THURSDAY DEADLINE closing in, I anxiously awaited Bob's decision. I was too preoccupied to do much of anything. My morning sickness continued and was an ever-present reminder of the mess I'd gotten into. I hadn't told anyone else about my situation, but I felt the need to talk with someone. Counseling services on base were nonexistent, and even if they were, you'd be tagged as a mental case for using them. If you wanted to be consoled, you went to the bar. The only person I felt I could confide in was Pete Mendellson. Over the past few months I tried to distance myself from Pete because I wanted to solidify my relationship with Bob, a single man who was going to be my ticket to respectability.

I still loved Pete, but he'd never be mine. He knew I wanted to see Bob exclusively, and while he didn't approve of him, he also knew what I wanted and respected my wishes. I wasn't sure how Pete would react to my news, but I considered him my best friend, someone who had looked out for me after McHale had left. I was waiting for him when he came into the club one night.

"Hi, Pete, can I join you for dinner?" I asked.

His eyes lit up and he said, "Sure!" We hadn't been seeing much of each other, only at a few squadron events.

In an anxious tone I said, "I need to talk with you."

"OK," he said. "What's up?"

"I don't wanna eat here. Let's go to the Royal Thai where we can talk."

"OK. No problem. Let's go," he replied.

After we ordered our food, I just sat there searching for the words to begin.

"Angel, what's the matter?" he said. "You're not your usual talkative self."

I started to choke up. He looked at me and put his hand on mine. "Angel, what's wrong?"

"Pete, I don't know how to say this." I hesitated for a moment before continuing and then I said. "I'm pregnant."

He tightened his grip on my hand and said, "God, I had an idea that was it."

"How did you know?" I asked.

"By the look on your face. You look terrible. What does Bob think about this?"

"I'm not sure. He's thinking it over. I put the decision in his hands," I said, looking down at the table.

"That prick! What does he have to think about? Why doesn't he just marry you, for God's sake? That son of a bitchin' weasel."

"Pete, I know how you feel about Bob, but I can't and won't force him. I've seen it ruin too many marriages. I don't want him hanging it over my head every time we have a fight in our marriage and saying, 'Well, I would've never married you if you hadn't been pregnant.' No, Pete, I don't want that."

"Angel, it's not totally your fault. After all, numb-nuts was there when it happened."

"Don't worry, Pete. It will all work out. I didn't mean to burden you with this, but I needed to talk with someone. You were the only one I knew I could trust."

After dinner we walked back to the BOQ, and Pete kept his arm wrapped around me the entire time. I hadn't eaten much, and I felt mentally and physically nauseated. When we got to the top of the stairs, he gave me a tight embrace, and I started crying. He held me until my sobs subsided. "Angel, if you need me, I'm here," he said.

As he turned and started to walk down the stairs, he looked back at me. His perpetual smile was gone, and in its place was sadness. "Pete, thank you. I love you," I said through my tears.

"I love you, too, Angel."

On Thursday morning, Bob called me at the office and asked if we could go downtown for dinner.

"OK," I said.

"I'll pick you up at 1830." I could tell he'd already made his decision by the tone of his voice.

I imagined how it would play out. He'd take me to dinner, and when we got there he'd give me some bullshit story about how he wasn't ready to be a father. I didn't want to go to dinner, but I decided to hear what he had to say. I was hoping I was wrong. I felt like I was in court waiting for the jury's verdict. *Will the defendant please rise? Has the jury reached a verdict? Yes, we have, Your Honor. We the jury find the defendant, Captain Pilato, guilty as charged on all counts: sex outside the holy bonds of matrimony, loving sex too much, getting pregnant, being desperate for love, and most of all, not using her brains.* The judge would thank the jury and sentence me straight to hell.

Catholic school taught me that sex and sin are synonymous, and sins of the flesh are the worst kind. They are so serious that I wouldn't even warrant a stopover in purgatory. At least, if I were sentenced to purgatory, I'd have the hope of getting out someday. Of course, I'd have to solicit friends and family to pray for me. That's if I had any friends who thought enough of me to do that. In my case that might be difficult. I imagined they'd all be pointing their fingers at me and yelling, "Sinner! Screw up! You stupid, stupid girl!"

No, I was on my way straight to hell, but I felt like I was already in hell. By virtue of my actions, or rather by my lack of virtue, I'd created my own hell. How much easier it would have been to follow the rules I'd been taught as a youth. If I had, I wouldn't be in this mess. I guess I deserved the consequences.

I decided to turn my thoughts to a better scenario. Maybe Bob didn't have his mind made up after all. Maybe, just maybe, he had decided we should get married and keep the baby. That's what I wanted.

When he came to pick me up he greeted me with, "Hi, Angel, how's it goin'?"

*How's it goin'?* I thought, *I'm a wreck and he asks 'How's it goin'?'*

"OK. How are you?" I asked. At that point, I immediately knew. He didn't have to take me to dinner to break the news. Why bother to even step one foot out the door? I just wanted him to tell me and forget the damn dinner. I was sick to my stomach anyway.

We arrived at the restaurant, sat down at our table, and Bob said exactly what I knew he'd say. "Angel, I've given this a lot of thought…"

*OK, get out the violins.*

"…and I know how much you wanna have this baby…"

*No, you don't. You'll never know.*

"…but I'm just not ready to be a father yet…"

*Of course not, you're still a child yourself—just like Tim and Pete said.*

"…I just can't do this. I'm sorry."

*Yeah right. Sorry, my ass—that's a nice afterthought. He isn't the one who'll have to go through the abortion.*

Although I'd suspected what he was going to say, the finality of his words hit me hard. I listened a little longer, and when I'd had enough of his excuses, I shot back at him like a poison dart.

"I knew you'd say this. I guess I didn't expect anything else from you." I got up and started to walk out of the restaurant. I wanted to get as far away from him as possible.

"Hey, wait a minute. Wait a minute," he called as he dropped some money on the table and came after me. "Why are you so angry? You said you wanted to leave it up to me."

"Yes, I know that's what I said. I gave you a choice, but you made the wrong one."

When I said I wanted to give him a choice, I was trying to be fair. I didn't want to be a burden on him. By doing that, I was denying everything I ever wanted and hoped for: love, marriage, and motherhood. Instead, what I'd ended up with was a total mess that I'd have to clean up on my own. He wouldn't have to deal with it at all. He'd rather play football!

Why did he think he could just walk away? Didn't he realize that if you slept with someone you'd have to take some responsibility for your actions? I surmised that he'd slept with me because it was fun, because it was convenient, and because screwing around with me was better than getting involved with a Thai. But ultimately, it was because I'd let him. I'd learn an expression much later that is, "Did you ever realize that when you were having problems in your life, you were always there?"

What I didn't realize was that underneath all my anger was a deep sense of resentment and sadness. I had wanted to hear the words every woman imagines she'll hear when she announces she's pregnant. "Darling, I'm so happy for us. I love you so much." I suppose that idea came from some fanciful Doris Day movie, but my movie wasn't going to win any Academy Award. It was turning out more like a B-rated horror film.

He took me back to my BOQ room and tried to say something. I didn't let him. All I wanted to hear from him was that he loved me, that everything was going to be all right, and that he wanted this baby, too. Instead I slammed the door in his face and yelled, "Fuck you!"

There I was, alone in my dark room flat-out scared. My anger at Bob blinded me to where the real anger lay—with myself. I didn't want to see that because I'd have to take responsibility for my part in this mess. It was easier to direct my anger outward.

Still, I wasn't going to make this easy on him. Why should I? I was hurting, and I wanted him to hurt, too. It appeared that we'd been moving down the path toward a long-term committed relationship, but he was just playing me. In retrospect, I guess I should have figured that out before I'd slept with him.

The next morning I went back to the base hospital to see the doctor.

"Well Doc," I said with a distressed look on my face. "I talked to my boyfriend, and he doesn't want the baby. He said it wasn't the right time, maybe later after he gets out of the Air Force."

"What do you wanna do?" he said.

"It doesn't matter now. I can't raise this kid on my own without a father, and I can't force him to marry me. The only thing left to do is to terminate this pregnancy." I started crying as the enormity of the decision hit.

Then the Doc handed me a tissue and threw in a SNAFU along with it. "I'm sorry, but you can't have an abortion at this hospital."

"What d'ya mean?" I said as I blew my nose and continued to cry.

"Abortions are illegal in Thailand, which means we can't do it here," he said.

"When did this happen? Don't military bases in foreign countries operate under U.S. laws? And abortion is legal in the U.S. now.[1] Besides, I know another WAF who had an abortion here a few months ago."

"Angel," he interrupted, "there's one other reason. The hospital commander is a Catholic, and he doesn't believe in abortion."

"I get it. He's imposing his belief system and using the Thai law as a shield. That son of a bitch." I started to panic. "What am I gonna do, Doc?"

"If you want an abortion, you'll have to go to the Philippines,"[2] he explained.

"What? This is crazy! This is getting way too complicated. Everyone is gonna know I'm pregnant. What am I gonna tell people when they ask me why I'm going to the Philippines? They'll put two and two together!"

"You can tell them that you're going to have an operation and that we don't have the facilities to do here," he suggested.

"Right! I could say that, but all they'd have to do is take one look at me and know it was a bald face lie. They're all gonna know I'm pregnant."

"Angel, they won't know unless you tell them. Let 'em think what they want."

I left feeling worse than ever. Why was this becoming so complicated? I guess I was being punished. All this red tape was supposed to make it harder for a woman to have an abortion. It gave her time to think and maybe she'd change her mind.

All these complicating factors only added to my suffering, but I guess that's the price a woman has to pay for sleeping around. I didn't want to have an abortion. I don't think any woman does. But it's a decision that only a woman can make. She can discuss it with her impregnator, her doctor, or her spiritual adviser. But in the end, it's still her choice. She's the one who'll be ultimately responsible for raising the child.

Must the woman bear the sole punishment for a mistake two people made, while the man gets off Scot-free? In the past, society made the man suffer by forcing him to marry the woman. Now, no one was forcing anyone to do anything. The new values of the sixties and seventies had freed men more than ever before. All a man had to say now was, "I think you ought to get an abortion," and the woman was "free" to do it. No fuss, no bother.

This new found sexual freedom had done nothing for women. And yes, they could now fool around like the guys, but if a woman got pregnant, the burden fell on her. The man, for the most part, was off the hook. The best a woman could hope for was that he might help pay for the abortion. It was a small price to pay for playing around and abdicating responsibility.

I guess Mother was right when she said, "Angelica, keep your dress down. Remember, all a man has to do is pull his pants up and walk away." And walk away he did.

[1] In 1973 Roe v. Wade, 410 U.S. 113, the Court held that the Constitution protects a woman's decision whether or not to terminate pregnancy and that a State may not unduly burden the exercise of that fundamental right by regulations that prohibit or substantially limit access to the means of effectuating that decision.

[2] In 1978, Congress included language in the Department of Defense (DOD) appropriations bill prohibiting DOD funding of abortions except in cases of life endangerment, rape, incest, or severe health consequences.

*In the end, you'll know which people really love you. They're the ones who see you for who you are and, no matter what, always find a way to be at your side.*

—Randy K. Milholland, American cartoonist (1975 - )
From *Something Positive Comic*


## A Plea


WITH MY FATE SEALED, I had to make arrangements to get to Clark Air Base in the Philippines. Before I could leave Thailand, I needed written travel orders to board a military aircraft. In the military, travelling without orders made your status AWOL or Absent Without Leave. This meant I had to go to my boss, Captain Mike Anthony, who had replaced Major Anastasio, to get permission for him to execute the orders. He wanted to know why it was necessary to go to Clark Air Base, and so I fed him the story.

"Well, Mike I have a tumor that needs to be removed, and our base hospital doesn't have the facilities to do it," I explained.

"Gosh, I'm sorry to hear that. Are you feeling alright?" he asked.

"I'm feeling OK. Thanks for asking."

"When do you need to leave?"

"I'd like to leave as soon as possible," I said with a sense of urgency.

"It's too bad you have to go all the way to Clark for the operation. It must be pretty serious if our base can't operate on it."

"Yes, well, it's in the uterus. The doctors here can't handle it." I said and hoped that if I mentioned a female body part, it would shut him up. It did.

"I'll put in the orders today and walk it over to personnel. I'll ask them to expedite it," he said. Captain Anthony was also Bob Barnett's boss, and I surmised he probably already knew I was pregnant, but he still went along with the charade.

Every day I battled morning sickness, and I felt fatigued and disconnected. It would take 10 days for personnel to process the orders—so much for expediting. I waited and waited, still hoping that Bob might change his mind about the baby and agree to marry me. It soon became clear he wasn't going to change his mind, and I wasn't going to coerce him. As each day dragged on, I felt like I was being held prisoner, not only on base, but also by my own thoughts.

I didn't want anything to do with Bob. I called Pete and asked him if we could go to dinner again, and he agreed. Once we were seated and the waiter took our dinner order, I began recounting my conversation with Bob. "Bob said he doesn't wanna have the baby now, maybe later, after he gets out of the Air Force in a year."

Pete looked crushed, "Did you tell that asshole that the baby wasn't gonna wait that long for him to grow up!"

"I'm so angry, Pete. I really thought he would come around. Maybe he's right. Maybe this isn't the right time to have this baby."

"Angel, it's never the right time to have a baby, but you're pregnant now."

I began to feel nauseous, and before I could even get up from the table, I started to throw up. Pete smiled and said, "Oh no! Wait a minute, Angel. I'll get you some saltine crackers." I got up from the table and started to clean up the mess. A waitress scurried over, "Oh, Kapton. You sick! So sorry, Kapton."

"No problem. I'll be fine," I said as I walked out of the dining room.

Pete came with the saltines and said, "Come on, Angel, this meal is too hard on you." I munched the saltines as we walked back to his trailer arm in arm. We sat down on his steps.

"Angel, I don't want you to go through with this."

"What d'ya mean, Pete?"

He seemed to be having a difficult time getting the words out. "Angel, this isn't right. You shouldn't have to do this. I know you want this baby. I don't want you to go through with this abortion."

"What? Please, Pete, this is hard enough on me without you saying this," I said and started to choke up.

"Angel, I know—I know. What I wanna say is, I will pay for it."

"Pay for what? Pete, what are you getting at?"

"Angel, I'll pay for you to raise this baby. I know how much this means to you. I don't want you to do this."

I started to tremble and cry, and my body ached all over. I couldn't believe what I was hearing him say. "You mean you're willing to pay to raise a child that isn't yours just because you know how badly I want a child?"

He said without hesitation, "Yes, Angel. I've thought a lot about this. I even thought maybe the baby could be mine."

"Oh, sweetie, you had a vasectomy three months ago." I said, a little perplexed.

"I know, Angel, but sometimes those swimmers can still get through. I even went over to the clinic to check my sperm count, but I'm still shooting blanks."

"Oh, Pete," I said and I touched his hand. "That's the kindest thing you could've ever said to me. That's why I love you so much."

"Angel, I mean it. I want you to think about it—I mean really think about it. You've got time to change your mind. I wanna pay for raising this kid."

"Pete, you've been drinking too much Scotch. You're not thinking straight. You're going home to your wife and family. Why would you ever wanna be stuck paying to raise another kid that wasn't even yours?" I was talking him out of it for his own good.

"Angel, I haven't had any Scotch tonight!"

"Pete, you don't wanna do this. When you get back to the States, you'll come to your senses and be sorry you ever volunteered for this assignment."

"Angel, listen to me. I wanna do this," he insisted in a sincere voice.

"Pete, you are being too generous. I can't let you do this to yourself." I said and started to cry.

"I'm not doin' anything I can't handle. Besides, what about you, Angel?"

"I'll be OK," I said in between sobs. "I don't wanna raise a baby without a father. I love you for offering to do this, but it wouldn't work, Pete. You're such a good soul. I wish you weren't married."

"Angel, I know you won't believe this." He hesitated as he weighed his words, "Angel, if I didn't have the kids, I've thought about what I would do. I'd...I'd..."

I interrupted, "But you do, Pete. I would never expect you to do anything else. That's what makes you a decent, honorable man."

"You're probably right, Angel. I guess I couldn't leave."

"Pete, I wouldn't want you to. You love them, and that's what makes me love you."

Pete's genuine concern for me was unparalleled. How someone could give his total, nonjudgmental support without wanting anything in return escaped me. Maybe that was one of the qualities necessary for love to be present in a relationship. The more he was there for me, the more I fantasized about him being single. What if? What if? But what ifs weren't reality.

The cold hard facts were that he was very much married, with young kids, and he was going home in a couple of days. There was another factor in play here. If he were single, he probably would never consider me the "marrying type." The marrying type is a woman who inspires thoughts of purity, stability, family, hearth, and home. Someone you want to take home to meet the family. She's the Margaret Anderson type, the mom from the TV series *Father Knows Best*. She's the kind of woman the officers' wives feel comfortable with. The kind you meet at church. Men like her because they're in control. That's what the marrying type of woman provides for him: a feeling of being in control. That's why he marries that type of woman and stays married to her. No, if Pete were foot-loose and fancy-free, he wouldn't want me. I just didn't fit that description.

*Gone - flitted away,*
*Taken the stars from the night and the sun*
*From the day!*
*Gone, and a cloud in my heart.*

—Alfred Tennyson, English poet (1809 - 1892)

# Another Good-Bye

ONLY A FEW DAYS remained before Pete left for the States and before my fateful flight to the Philippines. The sun was shining every day in Thailand, but I felt like I was living under a dark cloud. In those last days, Pete remained silent. He didn't discuss his offer to pay for the baby again. I knew he was concerned for me. It was written in his eyes and in his compassionate smile, which made my decision even harder. I knew that unless Bob changed his mind, which appeared unlikely, there was no turning back.

I began to prepare for Pete's departure. I went to his last mission flight, snapped pictures of him getting dunked in the squadron water barrel, and smiled as everyone toasted him a fond farewell. I placed the celebratory floral leis around his neck and kissed him as the crowd whistled. His *sawadee* party was in two days. My beautiful black cocktail dress was a little snug around my midriff. Pete, with his captivating smile and sparkling blue eyes, picked me up for the party and said, "Angel, you look beautiful tonight."

I hugged him and said, "Thanks Pete."

Pete never left my side the entire evening. At the dinner table, he either had his arm around me or held my hand under the table. When the time came for his farewell, one of the officers got up in front of the room and read a tribute:

"To Major Pete Mendellson, OPS officer extraordinaire. This citation is to accompany the award of 'King of the Truck Stop.' Whereas; Major Mendellson has distinguished himself by his loyal and dedicated service to ANGEL'S TRUCK STOP during the period of July 1971 to July 1972. During this period Major Mendellson was the single most ardent supporter of the truck stop bar and popcorn machine. Through uncanny skill and persistence, Major Mendellson has been able to drink his fair ration of 'scatch' (as he calls it) while butter was dripping from his elbows. Pete, as the older guys call him, has on occasion been able to have popcorn delivered to his table when no one else in the club could get any. It has been suspected that he may have an *in* with the club management. Major Mendellson has also been noted to be a frequent guest at the truck stop annex, which for you new guys is located on the 3rd floor of the BOQ Building 199 in the Northeast corner. It sometimes rains buckets of water in that area when there is no rain anywhere else. The outstanding accomplishments of Major Mendellson reflect greatly upon himself and the 13th Tactical Fighter Squadron."

During the roast, everyone was laughing and Pete and I were blushing. After the party, we walked back to Pete's hootch.

"Angel, I feel absolutely terrible about not being here when you get back. I'm worried about you having to go through this all by yourself," he said as he gripped my hands. "That Barnett is an absolute, total fuck up! I'd like to beat some sense into him."

"It's OK, Pete. I'll be OK." I found myself consoling him even while he was trying to console me.

"I love you, Angel."

"Pete, you're making it difficult for me to say good-bye. I love you, too." Tears started streaming down my cheeks. He leaned over and kissed them off one by one.

"Angel, my flight for the States leaves out of Bangkok on Friday. Fly down with me and see me off. You need to get away for a while. Besides, I wanna be with you for as long as I can."

"Pete, I don't know if I can skip out of here without people realizing I'm AWOL." Even as I was saying this, the idea was taking shape in my mind. The thought of getting away was very appealing.

"It's only for a one night," Pete rationalized. "No one'll miss you for that short a time. We can fly down in the morning, and you fly right back the following afternoon. I'll get the ticket for you."

"What if Bob finds out?" I queried. "So much for me being faithful to him."

"Angel, what do you care what he thinks? He hasn't given you any reason to be faithful. He doesn't give a damn about you. If he did, he wouldn't be letting you go through this ordeal by yourself. He'd at least be goin' to the Philippines with ya."

"I'll have to think about it, Pete. I guess, if there's a chance that Bob and I could ever get together, after all this mess, I probably shouldn't go. But I do wanna see you off, and God knows I'm gonna miss you—you've been my rock. No one has cared about me as much as you have."

"Angel, you're not still thinkin' you've got a chance with that loser—are you? Forget him. You deserve better. Please come with me to Bangkok."

"OK," I said, "I'll think about it." We stopped talking and went to bed. He hugged and kissed me, and I welcomed each kiss. Our passion overwhelmed us as we both realized this could be our last time together.

I kept thinking about Pete's invitation. When he called me the next day, I said, "Pete, I've decided to go to Bangkok with you."

"Great! I bought your ticket this morning," he replied. I guess we both knew I'd say yes.

I said, "I've talked to Pip, and she agreed to cover for me, in case my boss or Bob Barnett comes looking for me."

Pete said, "Great, it'll all work out, Angel.

Then I thought, *if Barnett suspected that I was going to Bangkok with Pete he'd be angry. But why? Would that mean he cared, or was it merely his male ego being hurt? Did he really want me, but just not now? I was conflicted because he allowed me to hope that marriage and children were in the future. Could I ever have a future with him? Without a solid promise from Bob, I decided to go with Pete to Bangkok. He was the one who'd been there for me through this whole ordeal, and I wanted to see him off.*

While in Bangkok, Pete asked me one more time to think over my decision. I put my hand to his lips. I didn't want to hear it again. All I could do was cry. He was going back home to a wife and kids who were eager for his return. On his long flight back to the States, he'd have time to shed his skin and grow a new one before he embraced them.

As for me, I was going back to Udorn, and soon I'd be getting on a plane for the Philippines. Two losses were coming right on top of each other, and all perspective was lost in the chaos. The last words Pete said to me before he stepped foot onto the plane were, "I love you, Angel." All the words I'd ever longed to hear a man say, unfortunately, had come from the wrong man.

*I have come to understand that life is composed of a series of coincidences. How you react to these—how we exercise what some refer to as free will is everything. The choices we make within the boundaries of the twists of fate determine who we are.*

—John Perkins, American writer (1945 - )
From *Confessions Of An Economic Hit Man*

## No Turning Back

It was the day before I was to leave for the Philippines, and I was still hoping Bob would have a change of heart. But time was running out. Instead he remained steadfast to his position and kept his distance. He didn't want to be confronted by my anger. Besides, I saw any attempt on his part to console me as phony. It wasn't his body that was going through physical and emotional changes. He never saw me before I left.

A dreaded trip always seems to take forever, and my trip by military transport to Clark Air Base was wearisome and long. An Air Force Blue Bird bus shuttled me over to the base hospital where I was assigned a room. I unpacked the few toiletries I'd brought, undressed, and slipped into one of those dreadful green hospital gowns. I sat upright in bed and looked around the sterile room. The ward was quiet except for occasional noises from the nurses' station.

Suddenly, the silence was broken with a cheery, "Hi, Angel, how's it goin'? It's good to see ya!" In the doorway stood Margaret Chisholm, a nurse who'd been stationed at Udorn.

"Margaret! Hi! What a surprise. How are ya? It's good to see you, too," I said. For a brief instant I forgot why I was there. I was just happy to see a friendly face. She walked over to my bed, and we exchanged warm hugs. My delight was quickly stifled when I realized she might discover why I was at the hospital.

Then she said, "I was talking to one of the nurses, and she said a woman officer from Udorn was here. When I found out it was you, I thought I'd come by to say hi."

"That was so kind of you," I replied.

Margaret, an Air Force captain, was a tall and rather homespun type of woman. When she was at Udorn, she never spent her free time carousing with the fighter pilots. Instead, she occupied her time by visiting a local Thai orphanage that was run by an elderly Italian missionary nun named Sister Antonio. Margaret had taken me there to visit the children, and I'd even brought Bob Barnett with me on one occasion.

Sister Antonio, with help from a few Thai women, operated the overcrowded orphanage. I watched Sister as she went from crib to crib picking up the crying babies. She rocked each little bundle while saying in Thai, "I love you, and God loves you, too." She handed me a baby and said, "Holda him. Holda him. They all needa so mucha love."

The babies all seemed to cry in unison when she entered the nursery, almost like they sensed Sister's presence. They seemed to know that if they howled louder and longer she might come and hold them. As she picked up the crying babies, her warm, loving spirit seemed to fill each little heart, if only for a few moments.

Margaret had fallen in love with the children and was moved to adopt two Thai girls that were six and seven years old. One of the girls had a deformed leg, which made it very difficult for her to walk. Margaret told me, "Angel, I think this is my way of doing something good to make up for this horrible war." I saw her as noble and saintly. She was a person who would certainly enter heaven, at the head of the line. I, on the other hand, was on an express train to hell.

Some people saw Margaret's choice to adopt differently. When I went on and on to Tim McHale about how wonderful I thought she was for doing this, he just said, "Angel, her life is over. No man will ever marry her with those two kids." That surprised me. I couldn't imagine that adopting two girls would make Margaret appear unattractive.

Then she asked the dreaded question, "What brings you here, Angel?"

There was no way I was going to tell this selfless, saint of a woman why I was here. She'd be appalled and realize what kind of a woman I was. I couldn't compare to a woman who had the guts to raise two orphans on her own. So, I blurted out the same lie I'd told everyone else who had asked me why I was going to Clark Air Base, "I've got a small tumor that couldn't be operated on at Udorn."

"I hope it's nothing serious," she said.

"No, they told me it wasn't anything to be concerned about, just minor surgery. But I wanted to get it taken care of before I left the Air Force and still had medical benefits. At any rate, I'm stuck here until Thursday."

"Well, I'm glad you're getting it taken care of," she said.

She appeared to believe me, and as a nurse assigned to the pediatric ward, she wouldn't have any reason to look at my chart. Of course, she could have already read my chart, but thankfully she seemed to accept my explanation. If I'd told her the truth, I would have been reduced to tears and forced to confront the tragic reality of the situation. Avoiding reality was the only option I seemed to have. I turned my attention back to Margaret.

"How are those two sweet girls of yours?" I asked.

"They're doing just great," she said, beaming. "Seeing that your surgery isn't until Thursday, would you like to come over to our house and see them?"

"Absolutely, I'd love to see those two little cuties. It'd be a welcome diversion from being alone in this hospital room and doing nothing." It was exasperating to have to wait two days for a 30-minute procedure. I was convinced that the delay was a plot to exacerbate my already heightened anxiety.

"OK, I get off duty in a half hour, and I'll be back to pick you up," she said, smiling.

I got dressed and waited for Margaret to come back to take me to her house on base. As we opened the door to the screened-in porch, her two girls appeared clad in cute little dresses with their ebony hair in braids. The girls rushed to welcome Margaret with outstretched arms, and she greeted them with hugs and kisses. I wondered if all the hugs withheld in those tender early years at the orphanage could ever be replenished. It might seem like it would leave their cup half empty, but from the looks on their young faces there seemed to be enough love to go around.

The girls seemed to be thriving under Margaret's tutelage and nurturing. Their transformation from two little Thai girls into two little Americans was readily apparent. In a matter of a few months, they had gone from only speaking Thai to saying, "OK, Mom," "sure," "yeah," and "you wanna play?" They were like little sponges soaking up every morsel of information from their new world. Seeing how their new identities had developed was like watching a butterfly emerge from its chrysalis.

Janie, the one whose leg was badly deformed from birth, had already had two operations since arriving at Clark, and her smiling face showed no discomfort. She was a brave, little seven-year-old. She wore a leg brace and used crutches, but over time and after numerous operations and physical therapy, it was predicted she'd be able to walk with only a slight limp. The care she was getting was a far cry from the Thai orphanage.

Later that night, when I returned to the hospital, my room seemed even more like a prison cell. It started to rain, and Margaret had said a monsoon was on the way. As sheets of rain pelted against the window, my claustrophobic feelings intensified. Pacing back and forth, I reflected on my evening with Margaret and her children. I looked at her as strong and brave. She took on an enormous commitment as a single mom with only her optimism and faith in God to sustain her. I saw the task as totally overwhelming, but I admired her strength and stamina. Now that I was alone with time to reflect on my decision, I began to think, *maybe I could muster up the courage to have the baby alone, like Margaret had done. But then again, she had adopted the children. She wasn't having an illegitimate baby. I just couldn't face the shame of being an unwed mother, and for me, marriage and children went together.*

I decided to call Bob and try to convince him to change his mind. Maybe he'd finally see that having this baby was the right thing to do. I asked the orderly where a phone was, and he directed me down the hall. I hurried to make the call.

I picked up the phone and said, "Operator, this is Captain Pilato. I need to make a phone call. Please connect me to Udorn Air Base, in Thailand. It's an emergency."

"Captain, I'll do the best I can," the airman replied. "But the monsoon has downed a lot of the lines, and the ones that are left are for priority usage." I whispered to myself, "Dear God, please let me get my call through." The airman tried unsuccessfully for the next few hours. I even tried again the next day, but to no avail. It seemed a man and a monsoon had sealed my fate.

When the dreaded Thursday morning arrived, the nurse came in to take my vitals. She rubbed the top of my left hand with a cotton ball soaked in alcohol and searched for a good vein. She handed me a small pill and said, "Take this. It'll relax you." Within a few minutes, I started to feel groggy.

Two young, energetic male orderlies entered the room, leaned over my bed and said, "Are you ready to go for a ride?" Their floral surgical caps brought a touch of lightness to the dark moment.

With a reluctant smile I said, "Sure." They moved my limp body to the transport stretcher. "Your colorful caps sure look great," I said in a woozy voice.

"We hafta do something to liven up this place," one of them said.

As they rolled me down the hall, all I saw was the hospital's bright white ceiling, broken only by an occasional fluorescent light fixture. The orderlies joked along the way to the operating room, amusing each other and me. They parked the stretcher outside the operating room and said, "You'll be going into the operating room in just a few minutes ma'am."

"Thanks for the ride. Please tell the doctor I wanna see him," I asked.

"Will do, ma'am."

A few moments later the doctor appeared. He was Asian-American and seemed to be plagued with the lack of emotion that stereotyped his culture. He was the same doctor who'd come to my room the day before to discuss my procedure. His lack of bedside manner immediately turned me off. When he had asked me, in a condescending tone, "What are you going to do to prevent this from happening again?" It took every ounce of restraint to subdue my impulse to say, *"Doctor, I plan on never fucking again in this lifetime!"* Instead, I said nothing. He strongly suggested that I consider some birth control options, like an IUD.[1] I was filled with guilt and shame as I told him I'd think it over.

Now, lying on the stretcher I realized that not taking precautionary measures would be irresponsible. When the doctor came out, I told him, "I've decided I want you to insert an IUD."

Curtly and without any expression, he said, "Very well then, I think that would be for the best. I'm going to insert an IUD called the Dalkon Shield.[2] It will ensure you against any future mistakes."

Resigned to my fate, my only response was, "OK."

They rolled me into the operating room, and the nurse connected the sodium pentothal tube into the slowly dripping tube of saline solution with practiced ease and skill. It took effect almost instantly. Going under with sodium pentothal was what I imagined dying would be like. It made me think that maybe, if I were lucky, I wouldn't wake up from this operation. Instinctively, I began a silent act of contrition. Maybe I could sneak into heaven like the thief on the cross. "Oh, my God, I'm heartily sorry for…"

[1] An IUD (Intrauterine Device) is a small object that is inserted through the cervix and placed in the uterus to prevent pregnancy. A small string hangs down from the IUD into the upper part of the vagina. The IUD is not noticeable during intercourse. IUDs can last 1 to 10 years. It works by changing the lining of the uterus and fallopian tubes, affecting the movements of eggs and sperm so that fertilization does not occur.

[2] The IUD called a Dalkon Shield is a small, flat, crab-shaped, plastic device with fins projecting out from the sides. In 1974 A. H. Robbins pulled the shield off the market due to faulty design. It was proven that the designer, Dr. Hugh Davis, knew about the defects when he sold it to A.H. Robins. The defective IUD caused 235,000 injuries and 20 deaths. These stats are from the Encyclopedia of Birth Control, Marian Rengel. For more read *At Any Cost: Corporate Greed, Women and the Dalkon Shield,* Morton Mintz, New York, Pantheon, 1985.

*Let no one who loves be unhappy... even love unreturned has its rainbow.*
—James Matthew Barrie, Scottish writer (1860 - 1937)


# Bunk Bed Baby

WHEN I RETURNED FROM the Philippines, I tried to settle back into my routine at Udorn, but the dismal circumstances I'd gotten myself into weighed heavily on my mind. While I counted the days I had left in this den of iniquity, my roommate Anna was in the throes of a love affair with a TDY fighter jock named Matthew "Andy" Anderson. Their affair had been going on for some time, and I often found myself trying to sleep while the two of them made love in the bottom bunk. This had happened one time when Bob and I were in the top bunk. We'd pretended to be asleep while Andy and Anna were below. We could barely resist the urge to applaud once their muffled sounds of passion had subsided. Andy would slip out of the room in the morning, as the dawn light peeked though the faded curtains. These were the love patterns of a war zone. I imagine it was on one of those nights that Heather was conceived.

Anna, a rural town girl from Montana, was sweet, shy, and vulnerable. She vowed never to get involved with a married man. She was aware of what could happen to a woman if she were taken in by the likes of a "silver-tongued devil," as we sometimes called men like him. No, she'd seen others succumb, and she knew better than to fall into that trap.

But Andy was different; he was "separated" from his wife. It had been three years now, and his divorce was imminent. He claimed it was going to be final three weeks after he got back to the States. At first, she was reluctant to believe him and held back her heart. But he was relentless. Anna even inquired about Andy's character from his squadron buddies, who all affirmed that he was a "good guy." They confirmed that Andy was just having a hard time at home, and Anna was exactly what he needed. Of course, their endorsement was parallel to, "honor among thieves."

"Anna," he told her, "I don't know who's hurt you in the past, but I'm not gonna hurt you. I'm a man you can trust. Faith and trust is what it's all about, Anna." His persistent, seductive words began to sound more and more believable.

"Anna, what do I have to do to prove how much I care for you? I love you." His words rolled off his tongue with the ease of an expert salesman.

His declarations led her to believe they could have a future together. He poured out his tales of woe. Things weren't going well at home; they hadn't been for a long time; and his wife had deceived him by sleeping with his brother. Hearing how he'd been deceived and mistreated led Anna to think that his wife was despicable. Who would stay with such a woman? It was good that he was finally going to leave her.

He deserved better, Anna thought, someone who would be loyal and loving. He only stayed with his wife for the children's sake, and when the divorce was final, he'd be able to be with a woman who understood him—someone like Anna. How noble he'd been. Of course, there was the wonderful sex. "Anna, sex with you makes me feel like a real man, like I can conquer the world!" he claimed.

It all sounded believable, and Anna started to let down her guard and trust him. Before long, she was head over heels for Andy. And why wouldn't she be? He epitomized all the dashing traits of a fighter pilot. He was extremely attentive to Anna, of course he could be, what else did he have to do in SEA but fly, drink, and mess around.

Andy's squadron had already returned to the States when Anna found out she was pregnant. When he left Thailand, he'd assured her that as soon as he got back to the States, he'd write her. But no letter ever came. She wasn't too concerned because she'd be back in the States soon, and she'd tell him then. It would all work out.

Anna and I talked about her choice to have the baby. "Anna, are you sure you wanna do this?" I asked. "Is he really getting a divorce? He's got two little kids. Do you think he wants another one?"

"His divorce is gonna be final soon, and I know he'll be happy about the baby," she said with conviction. I wanted this to work out for her. Just because it hadn't for me, didn't mean there couldn't be a Hollywood ending for her.

"Anna, what are you gonna do in the meantime? Are you sure you wanna wait to tell Andy? Isn't there any way to get in touch with him now?"

"I don't wanna write him a letter," she replied. "I wanna tell him in person." She was convinced of his loyalty and his character.

"Do you wanna have this baby without knowing for sure if Andy is gonna come through for you?" I was concerned for her and afraid that he wouldn't keep his word.

"I can't have an abortion," Anna said. "I couldn't go through that. Besides Angel, no matter what he thinks of me, I love the Andy I knew in Thailand, and this is his baby." Her mind was made up.

My concern was that even if the Air Force signed a waiver allowing her to continue to serve, she'd be raising the baby on her own. The Armed Services' policy concerning pregnancy had always been controversial. It was President Truman who issued an executive order that gave the services permission to summarily discharge a woman if she became pregnant, gave birth to a child, became a parent by adoption, or had a minor child or stepchild at home at least 30 days a year. The military took it as an ironclad mandate. Regulations were written, and military women who became pregnant, whether or not they were married, were forced to resign and given an honorable discharge.[1]

Thankfully, a few tenacious women decided to challenge this policy and brought their cases to the courts. Captain Susan Struck, a 26-year-old nurse who had gotten pregnant while in Vietnam, decided to challenge the Air Force's policy. When Captain Struck's commanding officer found out she was pregnant, he ordered her back to McChord Air Force Base in Tacoma, Washington. She was told that if she had an abortion, she could retain her commission. If not, they were prepared to discharge her for "moral and administrative reasons." The moral part was a pregnant woman would set a poor example to the other women in the military. If they let her stay in the Air Force, it would imply that they condoned such behavior. Captain Struck was Catholic and had no intention of aborting the baby. She planned to have the baby and give it up for adoption, and she refused to leave quietly.

With the backing of the American Civil Liberties Union (ACLU), Captain Struck brought her case to the courts claiming the Air Force was unduly discriminating against her and was violating her due process rights under the 5th Amendment, which is part of the Bill of Rights, and protects against abuse of government authority in a legal procedure. The lower court ruled in favor of upholding the Air Force's policy. Struck's attorneys kept filing stays against the Air Force to stop her discharge. Meanwhile, the baby couldn't wait for the Air Force to settle the dispute, and Struck ended up being the first military woman to have a baby while on active duty.

The Air Force was still determined to discharge her. Her case, the legal stays, and her appeal brought a wave of media attention about the military's discriminatory policy for discharging pregnant women. What made this case more inflammatory was Captain Struck was not married, and wasn't sure who the father was. Either that, or she wasn't telling. It became a media circus and made for titillating gossip.

Not all military women supported Stuck. Some turned on "one of their own" and agreed with their male counterparts. They said things like: "You wouldn't want to see a pregnant woman marching in a parade;" "Women want to be home raising a family, not having a career;" and "A pregnant woman would hinder the mission of the Air Force." My assessment was, if the unofficial Air Force's mission was to "Fly, Fight, and Fuck," then Struck had already proven she could accomplish the last "F."

I believed women ought to be able to stay in the Air Force if they got pregnant, or at least be given a choice. I must confess I was a little embarrassed by the situation. She was unmarried, didn't know the father's identity, wasn't keeping the baby, and was leading the charge against this Air Force policy. The media attention made it seem as if all Air Force women were promiscuous. Now the public would judge all of us as one. Ideally, it would have been better if a married woman had challenged this policy, but the media wouldn't have found that as sensational. But perhaps, a married woman would never have felt the need to challenge the policy. Keeping her job might not have seemed as critical if she had a husband to provide for her and the child.

The case was on its way to the Supreme Court, and the Air Force was confidant that it could win. The Solicitor General was concerned with the constitutional repercussions, so he called off the dogs and gave Struck a waiver allowing her to remain in the Air Force.

In March 1971, the Air Force announced a new policy.[2] It would provide waivers for women who became pregnant or became a parent by adoption. They also changed their recruiting policy to allow women with children to enter the Air Force. I guess you could say that this Captain "Struck" a blow for freedom. All the military women who came after her should be grateful for her courage to stand up against a formidable opponent—the entire United States Air Force.

Anna had the baby, but Andy's divorce wasn't final yet, some SNAFU with the paperwork, and he still hadn't told his wife about Anna. When baby Heather was eight months old, Anna came to visit me in Florida where Andy was stationed. He was going to see the baby for the first time and Anna still hoped Andy would come through for her and Heather. He said he'd send her child support and pay for Heather's college education, but he never did. His superficial charm, his ability to manipulate, his pathological lying, his self-centeredness, and his lack of remorse typified the classic traits of a sociopath. Anyone would find it hard to detect these traits, let alone a sweet gal from Montana.

After that visit, I lost touch with Anna for a long while. Later, when we reconnected, I found out she never married. She'd stayed in the Air Force, made full colonel, and was a Maintenance Squadron Commander for fighter jets. Her competence as a commander was evident every time an IG inspection team hit the base. Her squadron was always written up as exemplary, which was no small feat for any commander, let alone a woman commander. When her chance to be promoted to Deputy Commander of Maintenance (DCM) came up, she was denied the promotion. No reason was given. The Air Force was now savvy enough not to admit they didn't want a woman DCM, but she figured it was because she couldn't stand up at the urinals. Later, someone handling colonel promotions confirmed her suspicions—off the record. Although her performance reviews were among the best presented to the promotion board, it was determined that no woman could ever be a DCM in a major wing.

Anna retired from the Air Force. Heather became a physician's assistant, got married, and had a sweet girl of her own. I reconnected with Anna and went to visit them. When Heather, now 35 years old, walked in the door, I was taken aback. I was looking at the spitting image of Andy. Later, I mentioned this to Anna and she said, "Yeah, I can never get away from him. Every time I look at her, I see Andy."

[1] Executive Order 10240 signed by President Harry S. Truman in 1951.

[2] Information on this topic was gathered from *Women in the Military: An Unfinished Revolution,* Major General Jeanne Holm USAF (Ret.), Presidio Press, 1986, pages 289 - 303.

*Take my word for it, the silliest woman can manage a clever man, but it needs a very clever woman to manage a fool.*

—Joseph Rudyard Kipling, English writer (1865 - 1936)

## Taking One for the Team

THE ARRIVAL OF THE new Base Commander at Udorn brought a continual barrage of inquiries concerning the club, which made Colonel Ellsworth a royal pain. As the Thai waitresses would say, "He number ten."

He was the second Base Commander in eight months. Along with a new Wing Commander and two more Vice Commanders, it seemed like everyone knew how to run the club better than I did. By this time, I knew the drill. Never mind that I'd been there nine months, had run other clubs for four years, and the club was in the black. I was a woman, which made me suspect. So, I began things with Colonel Ellsworth like I did with every new commander, by reiterating my background and qualifications for managing the club. After a period of observation most of them would relax once they realized that the club was running smoothly, but not Colonel Ellsworth.

As the Base Commander, Colonel Ellsworth was entitled to ask me anything to get up to speed on what was happening at his club, but his questions were incessant. That, and the fact that he hung around the club constantly, made it seem like he was on a surveillance operation. The members weren't complaining, and the financial statement, the most visible indicator of a well-run club, was in the black. So, what was his problem? That's what Sergeant Bradshaw wondered.

"What gives, Capt'n?" he complained to me one afternoon. "I answer this guy's questions, and then he comes right back again with some more insignificant crap or some other nitpicking complaint."

"He'll get over it, Brad." I assured him.

"Capt'n, I think Colonel Ellsworth is after something more than a tender steak, if you get my drift!" he said as he raised his eyebrows.

I looked at him and said, "If that's what he's looking for then I'm afraid he won't get any here. I'm just sorry you have to bear the brunt of all this."

I continued to tell Brad some more bits of information. "You know Brad, he even tried to get me to set him up with Lot, the bar waitress."

Brad chuckled. "That won't work. She's already taken."

"Did you know he's got his wife stayin' in a hotel in Bangkok?" I added.

"Is that a fact? Well, wouldn't ya know it? All the other guys are here unaccompanied, and he's got a little comforter in a hotel an hour away. Boy, he's something, and he's still after some tail! That takes the cake," he said, shaking his head.

"Yeah, and I'm not gonna be his pimp or his fill-in," I said with a disgruntled look on my face.

"Good luck, Capt'n. I tell ya, this guy is on a mission!" he said as he left my office.

Bradshaw was right. Ellsworth asked me to come to his office to answer some more questions about the club. When I reported to his office, I realized that it wasn't the club he was after. He looked at me in a way that made me feel like he was mentally undressing me, and his tone of voice indicated another agenda.

Pretty soon he started talking about my great legs and asking me if I wanted to come over to his hootch to have a drink. I tried to ignore him and change the subject, but he was relentless. After five years in the Air Force, I knew when a fastball was coming. I was careful not to give him any encouragement, but that only made him more aggressive. He was in his late 40s, tall, dark, and not unattractive, but his looks were lost on me. The more I ignored him, the more he tried to get my attention. Why is it that ignoring a man seems to make him more aggressive and saying "no" is interpreted as meaning "yes?"

This went on for awhile until finally I told Sergeant Bradshaw, "I've had it, Brad. I'm gonna do whatever it takes to put a stop to Ellsworth's continual assaults on all of us."

"What are you gonna do, Capt'n?"

"Well, we know what he wants."

"Oh no! You're not gonna do that, are you, Capt'n?"

I looked at him, shrugged my shoulders, and said nothing.

That night, while I was on duty, there was one extra item on my agenda—the Base Commander. Like the lunar tide washing debris onto the shore, in he strolled.

"Good evening, Colonel Ellsworth. How are you this evening, sir?" I said in an unaccustomedly charming voice.

"Good enough. How's our Angel tonight?" he said with a leer.

"Couldn't be better, sir," was my chipper response. I looked him in the eye and gave him an ever-so-slightly coquettish smile.

My plan was a relatively simple one, and it was one only a woman could execute. After the good colonel finished his dinner I was waiting for him. He moseyed over to me.

"How was your dinner, sir?" I asked. "Hope you enjoyed it. Can I buy you a drink, Colonel?"

"That would be mighty nice of you, Angel," he replied, looking self-assured.

We talked awhile about who knows what. I smiled and appeared interested. I knew he'd throw out the ball sooner or later, and sure enough he did.

"Well, Angel, if you ever need someone to talk to, you know I'm always available for you. You know where my hootch is, don't you?"

This time, instead of letting the ball whiz by, I caught it. "Why thank you, Colonel Ellsworth, that's very kind of you—good to know," I said with a coy smile.

"Well it's getting late Angel, I guess I'll be going," he said. There was no doubt what he had on his mind.

"It's been good talking with you, Colonel. Thanks again for offering to be available for me, sir. Who knows, it might be sooner than you think."

He left the club smiling. I waited until I had a few gin and tonics under my belt, and then just before the bewitching hour of midnight, I marched over to his hootch carrying a tall drink. Before I got there, I poured the drink all over my head and tossed the glass. I knocked on the door repeatedly until he opened it.

"Good evening, sir. You said if I ever needed you…well, here I am."

"Come in. Good grief. What happened to you?" he said with a startled look on his face.

"Well, sir, those jocks were at it again. After you left, a bunch of them came in and started goofing around. I got in the middle of it, and the drinks went flying everywhere, and now I'm drenched to the bone."

"Here, let me get you one of my shirts and get you out of those wet clothes." He went to his closet, got me a shirt, and said, "Here you go. Get changed, and I'll fix you a drink. It's a gin'n tonic, isn't it?"

"Yes, sir, that's it. Thanks," I said as I headed for his bathroom. "I'll be right out." I freshened up, took off my clothes, and slipped into his shirt. I took a deep breath and walked back to the living room.

"I feel much better. Thanks for the shirt." The shirt came to just above my hips. He handed me the drink, and I sat down right next to him on the couch. Already lightheaded, I took a few small sips while he started to move his hand up my leg. I didn't resist him. Instead, I set my drink down and told myself I was doing this for the "good of the order." We adjourned to his bedroom and did the deed. A couple of hours later, I headed back to my room and took a hot shower.

The next morning when Sergeant Bradshaw came in I said, "Brad, I don't think Colonel Ellsworth will be bothering us anymore."

"He won't? How's that, Capt'n? I saw you talking to him last night at the bar. Did you get him straightened out?"

"Well, I guess you can say that," I said as I shrugged and tightened my face—half grinning and half not.

"Oh no! You didn't, Capt'n?" he said and grimaced.

"Brad, I took one for the team last night, and that's all I'm gonna say about it."

He turned around and left my office shaking his head. Then almost immediately he returned with a quizzical look on his face. "Capt'n, I'm sorry, but I just have to ask one thing. How was the old coot?"

"Well, for an old guy, I guess he was OK." We both laughed. Brad went back to his office, and I continued with the duties at hand. After that, Colonel Ellsworth was as sweet as could be. I never went back to his hootch, although I let him think I might. Sometimes, a girl has to do what a girl can do.

*The best way to deal with bureaucrats is with stealth and sudden violence.*
—Butros Butros-Ghali, Egyptian UN Secretary General (1922 - )

# Dead End Investigation

I WAS IN MY office working on a budget report when Sergeant Bradshaw came in and said, "Capt'n, there's a guy in the accounts receivable office who's lookin' through our files."

"What? Who is he, and what's he lookin' for?"

"He didn't say."

"Where's he from?"

"I'm not sure. I think he's from the OSI."

"The OSI! What the hell are they up to? Brad, go find out who this guy is, and what the hell he's doing here. If he won't tell you, throw his ass out of the club. Plain and simple!" I couldn't imagine why the Office of Special Investigations (OSI) was snooping through our files. But then, they were always trying to dig up something and somebody.

"OK, Capt'n. That's all I needed to know." He headed straight back to the accounts receivable office, confident that if there were any repercussions, he wouldn't catch the flack, I would.

A few minutes later he returned with a smug look on his face. "Capt'n, I asked the guy what he was doing here and told him that if he didn't tell me I had orders to throw him out."

"OK, OK, so what gives?" I demanded.

"He's from the OSI, just like I figured, and he's lookin' at your expense account for illegal charges."

"What? Illegal charges?" I replied in a voice two octaves higher.

"Yes, Capt'n. That's what he said."

"Well, what does he expect to find?"

"Don't know," he shrugged, "but that's what he said."

"Did he say who authorized this? Was it coming from the OSI or the Base Commander?"

"He didn't say, Capt'n, but my bet is that the Base Commander probably had something to do with it, or at least he has to know about it."

"That spineless jellyfish! Or should I say, that bastard."

"Well, I think that about sums it up, Capt'n," he said, grinning. "What are ya gonna do?"

"I'll tell you what I'm gonna do. I'm gonna call that S.O.B. Ellsworth right now, and trust me, there won't be much left of the dear colonel when I get through with him."

"Capt'n, do you really think you ought to do that?" Bradshaw said as he tried his best to keep me from my own impetuousness.

"Brad, I'm getting short, and frankly, I don't care. I've had enough of this bullshit. I'm leaving soon, and I might as well take a few of 'em with me. As the jocks would say, 'no guts, no glory.'"

"Then go get him, Capt'n," he said as he raised his arm in a power to the people sign.

I picked up the receiver, composed myself, and dialed the Base Commander's office.

An airman answered, "Base Commander's office. Airman Richards speaking."

In a voice as restrained as possible I said, "This is Captain Pilato. Is Colonel Ellsworth in? I need to speak to him. It's important."

"Just a minute, Captain, I'll see if he is available."

My heartbeat hastened like an anxious hunter waiting for the right time to fire.

Finally, the airman came back on the phone and said, "He'll be right with you, Captain." Of course the dear darling wanted to talk with me. After our little escapade, he probably assumed I was panting for him. In a calm and deliberate voice, not wanting him to suspect what was about to hit him, I said, "Good morning, Colonel. How are you?"

"Fine, Angel. How's my favorite club officer?"

"How am I? Well, Colonel, I'll skip the niceties and get right to the point. Would you mind telling me why the OSI is in my club investigating my expense account?"

His silence permeated through the phone as he realized this was not a social call. He seemed to be searching for the right words to respond. "I don't know why they're there," he said, somewhat taken aback.

I wasn't sure, but I suspected he had to know the status of all ongoing OSI investigations, so I said, "What d'ya mean, you don't know? Aren't you the one who approves all the investigations before they proceed? You mean no one briefed you on this?" Either way, I had put him in a corner. If he really didn't know, he'd look like a dummy. If he did know, he'd have to admit I'd caught him in a lie.

Still somewhat hesitant he said, "Well, they just told me about it this morning."

"Oh! What did they tell you? What are they looking for?"

"Angel, they wanna make sure you aren't charging unauthorized meals on your club officer's expense account."

To get the full significance of this, it's necessary to understand how the club officer's expense account system worked. The Air Force clubs were different from most civilian membership clubs, which allow their managers to eat meals at the club as part of their compensation package. As an officer, I was required to become a member of the club, pay monthly dues, and pay for any services I received at the club, just like any other member. Being the manager brought no special privileges.

Regulations allowed every club manager to have an expense account with a monthly allotment of $100. However, it couldn't be used to buy club members or employees drinks, meals, or thank you gifts, and it couldn't be used to purchase liquor from the class VI store. Because of these restrictions, most club managers hardly used their expense accounts. The only items that could be charged on the expense account were meals eaten on duty after regular duty hours. For example, if the base's hours of operation were from 0730 to 1630, and a club manager was in the club at 1800 supervising a special club function, he could charge his dinner on his expense account.

Since we were in a war zone, the club operated 24 hours a day, seven days a week, and I was on call all the time. A case could be made that the regular hours of operation might be considered vague, making it hard to determine when I was off or on duty. I proceeded to explain this dilemma to the colonel.

"Yes, sir, I've charged some of my meals on the expense account because at any time I could be on duty, and I figured it wasn't any big deal. Besides,

Colonel, if you wanted to know about my expense account charges, why didn't you just ask me?" I said in a frustrated tone.

I couldn't believe that after our little interlude he didn't have the common decency to ask me directly. But I guess for him this OSI probe wasn't anything personal—it was strictly business.

Then I said, "Sir, if you don't want me to charge my meals on the expense account, I won't. I'll just go in the kitchen and taste test the food. But we've told the employees not to eat on the job. So, do you want me to be a bad example? Or would it be better for me to occasionally charge some of my meals to my expense account? Look, Colonel, I'm getting short. If you want to investigate me at this late date, I don't much care. You haven't got a case, and if I have to get a lawyer, I will."

Maybe he saw the ridiculousness of the whole thing, or he'd had enough of my verbal battering. In any case he said, "OK, OK, Angel, I'll call off the dogs."

"Thank you, sir," I said curtly and slammed down the receiver. Sergeant Bradshaw, who I was sure heard every word, quickly came back into the office and said, "Well, Capt'n, I'm waiting for the official word. Do I get to toss this OSI bum out of the club?"

Feeling rather self-righteous I said, "Tell him to get his damn, nosy ass out of my club. If he's got any questions, tell him to go see Ellsworth."

Smiling, he gave me two thumbs up and said, "My pleasure, Capt'n. Consider it done."

I was exhausted from the whole encounter. My audacious behavior with the Base Commander stemmed from the fact that if I had not been getting out of the Air Force within a month, my actions could have been considered insubordination. However, at this point I'm sure the Base Commander didn't think that holding my feet to the fire was worth his time or effort. That's why it seemed strange that I was being investigated. What did they expect to find, and what could they possibly do to me at this late date?

In reality, these investigations stemmed from the "dirty dozen," a group of overseas club managers who were caught skimming money off of slot machines and getting kickbacks from entertainers and other vendors. After that fiasco, many regulations, including the use of an expense account, were tightened to the point that you couldn't sneeze and grab a tissue without approval.

Stealing and fraud weren't new. Whenever money is involved, there are always opportunities for greed to rear its ugly head, and in Southeast Asia, the opportunities were rampant. Also, because personnel were only assigned for a year, infractions were harder to trace. Unfortunately, the avarice of some made it unbearable for the rest of us. Incidents like those perpetrated by the dirty dozen gave the OSI a motive to suspect any officer or noncommissioned officer who ran a club of being a crook. The OSI, paranoid specie that it was, couldn't imagine anyone being honest.

The actions of the dirty dozen were outright stealing. I always considered myself totally honest, but maybe the fear of being court martialed and disgraced wasn't worth taking a chance. Charging my meals and stretching the on-duty, off-duty rule was about as risky as I got. Besides, how much could I eat for $100?

SECTION SIX

# Returning Home

*All the changes are more or less tinged with melancholy, for what we are leaving behind is part of ourselves.*

—Amelia E. Barr, American-English writer (1831 - 1919)

# Ten Days and a Wake Up

SERGEANT BRADSHAW CAME INTO my office and said, "Capt'n, how many days left."

I responded with, "It's 12 days and a wake up." I was getting short, and the time seemed to be going in slow motion.

"Capt'n, you're definitely FIGMO."[1]

"You got that right. It can't be soon enough." My body was there, but my spirit was gone. The people who had meant anything to me had left. I saw no reason to interact with any of the new officers that arrived.

A few weeks before, Bob Barnett had departed for his new assignment in Florida. He tried his best to make amends, but my anger was too intense. One day, in a fit of rage I yelled out, "You're a bastard. I guess I was good enough to fuck, but not to marry!" Instead of letting our relationship die a natural death, I presumed that if I ranted long enough, I could change his mind and make him want to marry me. He said over and over again, "Angel, I am sorry. I never meant for this to happen. When we get back to the States, things'll be different. I've got a year left in the Air Force, and then we can work it out and have kids."

I didn't realize that he never loved me. He merely wanted to stop being the target of my rage. Even after being strongly advised by Tim and Pete that Bob wasn't the right person for me, I still thought I could get what I wanted from him. Persistence always seemed to work in my professional life, and I assumed it could work in my personal relationships. I was too naïve to understand that you can't make anything happen when only one person wants to make it happen. I was trying to justify one mistake by making another one.

The end of my tour was near, and all I was focused on was getting out without any more incidents. During the last few months, I managed to get the Base Commander off our backs, have an OSI investigation dismissed, and dispel any suspicion that I knew how marijuana plants had gotten into the o-club's backyard.

Now, just when I was about to slide into home base, the club accounting staff called a foul. They told me there was a $2,000 inventory shortage. How was this possible? The staff redid the inventories and reworked all the figures, working late into the night to no avail. It was impossible that we could have lost money considering our large membership and our extended hours of operation.

The accounting staff kept saying, "Sorry, Kapton, we not find inventory error." Since the inventory discrepancy couldn't be resolved, a write-off was imminent. The fact that my financial statement was going to show a loss during my last month was devastating. When that statement hit headquarters, it would be another indicator that a woman couldn't adequately run an officers' club in a war zone. Even though every month prior had shown a profit, the only thing they'd remember was the last financial statement.

I couldn't understand how it had happened, but my suspicions were that it might be my Thai staff's way of paying me back for insulting one of their own. The Thais were very polite and very accommodating. They'd never tell you to go to hell or argue with you. This inventory debacle could have been a surreptitious way for them to even the score.

The incident that may have triggered their little vendetta had happened a few months ago. I received a tip from the OSI that Pren, our head cashier, and Mr. Ling, the Chinese merchant, were in cahoots to abscond with the o-club's daily cash deposit. It seemed a little strange that Mr. Ling, who drove a Mercedes and seemed pretty flush, would want to steal a few hundred bucks from the o-club. Also, I couldn't imagine that Pren, who was considered well paid by Thai standards, would put his job in jeopardy. Even though there seemed to be no apparent motives, I decided not to take a chance. Because previously, a German employee, who had always been reliable, had stolen $1,200 from the daily deposit, and because theft was rampant on the military bases in Southeast Asia, I decided maybe the tip was credible.

On the day Pren and Mr. Ling were supposed to run off with the cash, the Air Police (AP) surrounded the o-club, guns in hand. They looked ready to try out what they'd learned in Air Police training school. Pren started out the front door of the club, and the APs arrested him with the cash still in hand and on the way to make the deposit. Mr. Ling was nowhere in sight. All Pren could say as the Air Police handcuffed him and took him off to be interrogated was, "Kapton, Kapton, what are they doing? I not trying to steal anything!" In the end, there was no proof that he was actually going to steal the money; he'd hardly left the building. The whole fiasco ended up being a huge loss of face for Pren, and an even bigger embarrassment for me.

I never knew whether Pren was going to steal the money or whether it was a set-up. Even though I tried to explain my actions to the Thai staff, it was fruitless. Pren came back to work and things seemed to return to normal. I couldn't speak Thai, so who knew what they were saying? I don't think Pren and the others ever fully forgave me. It appeared I'd been the brunt of a bad joke, like someone had stolen my clothes on the beach after going skinny-dipping.

In the meantime, the Combat Support Group threw a going away party for all the officers who were preparing to leave. Everyone received a brass mug engraved with, "IN FOND APPRECIATION OF A JOB WELL DONE—SAWADEE." Each of us stood up to say a few words of farewell. I welcomed the opportunity and launched into my swan song, "In a few days I'll be leaving on a jet plane headed back to the States. I couldn't be happier. No amount of money could get me to stay another minute. This assignment was, no doubt, the worst assignment I've ever had, and to think I volunteered for it! I resigned my commission shortly after I got here because the restrictive regulations made running an officers' club a nightmare. Club managers have been expected to operate with their hands tied behind their backs. As for my replacement, God help him, he'll be here in a month. The other day someone asked me 'who was going to run the club until he got here' and my response was, 'I don't know—probably everybody!' Maybe returning to civilian life will be saner, but that remains to be seen. Best of luck to all of you who are leaving. It's been a pleasure serving with you, and my condolences to all of you who are left!" I didn't know until after I left the *sawadee* party and walked through the dining room, that the club's PA system was on broadcast mode, and everyone in the club was privy to my little farewell speech.

Despite all that had gone on, Pip organized a going away party for me off-base. A small group of employees, including my boss, Captain Mike Anthony, and my roommate, Anna, showed up to wish me well. They presented me with a beautiful gold bracelet and showered me with floral leis. I was touched by their gesture.

The next day the movers came to pack up a few treasures I was bringing back to the States: a load of celadon china that I purchased in Chiang Mai, some hand-carved teak furniture, and some woven wicker objects. The one treasure I wasn't taking home I'd left in the Philippines. All my belongings weighed more than the 66 pounds of luggage I'd arrived with, and the Base Commander was kind enough to sign a waiver allowing it to be shipped back at the government's expense. The Air Force would store it for six months, and then I'd have to decide where I wanted it shipped.

On my final "wake up," I went over to the officers' club, ate breakfast alone, and paid cash for my last meal. Shortly before I was ready to leave, I received a phone call from Colonel Ellsworth, "Angel, I'd like to see you off today. I'll be over to pick you up at 0930."

"Oh, that's very nice of you, sir, but that won't be necessary. Sergeant Bradshaw can take me in the o-club pickup."

"No, I wanna take you to the airport and see you off," he insisted.

I realized he wasn't going to take "no" for an answer. In the military you don't set boundaries. They are set for you.

"OK, Colonel," I said, "then I'll see you at 0930, sir." To my surprise, he arrived with a bouquet of red roses fit for a beauty queen. He handed them to me and smiled.

I said, "Why, thank you, Colonel. That's so thoughtful of you."

He said, "You deserve it."

I wasn't sure if the roses were amends for the OSI debacle, a thank you for the one-night-stand, or simply a kind good-bye gesture. Who knows, maybe he was taking me to the airport to make sure I got on the plane. I said good-bye to some of the staff, and we proceeded out the front door where the colonel's blue staff car was waiting to take me to the airport.

About a dozen people came to the airport to see me off. They put flower leis around my neck, just like they did the day I arrived. I took the leis and the roses on the plane with me along with all the memories from the past 11 months. I sat down next to one of the fighter pilots from the 13th Squadron who was being reassigned to States. As the plane lifted off, I started sobbing. It was like a levee had broken. I turned to him and said, "I don't know why I'm crying. I hated this place."

"It's just good to be leaving. That's reason enough," he replied.

_____

[1] FIGMO is a military slang term that means forget it or f--k it; I have my orders to leave this assignment or go to my next assignment.

Captain Pilato's *Sawadee* party
saying good-bye to friends

*This is how the world ends; not with a bang but with a whimper.*
—T.S. Eliot, American poet (1888 - 1965)

## No Parades

"HELLO, THIS IS THE operator in Anchorage, Alaska. Will you accept a collect call from Angelica Pilato?"

As soon as the plane landed at Elmendorf Air Force Base, I made a beeline for a pay phone to call home. I was eager to hear a familiar voice on the other end of the line.

"Alaska?" My dad responded somewhat startled.

"Yes, sir, Alaska. Will you accept a collect call from Angelica Pilato?" she repeated. I listened on the other end of the line and wondered if he was going to accept the charges.

Still a little perplexed he said, "Is it Angelica?"

"Yes, sir, Angelica Pilato. Will you accept the charges?" she said again in a rasied voice.

Finally, he said, "Yes, I will."

"Go ahead, ma'am, your party is on the line."

"Hi, Dad. It's me," I said, relieved that he finally agreed to accept the charges.

"I know it's me," was his corny reply. "You're calling from Alaska? God, that ought to cost me a mint."

"Dad, you told me to call you as soon as I got back in the States. That's what I'm doing," I said, somewhat exasperated.

"Yes, I know I said that, but you're in Alaska."

"Dad, I hate to break it to ya, but Alaska is part of the United States." I couldn't believe we were having this conversation after a year of not being able to communicate except through tapes, a few letters, and one fragmented phone call on Easter Sunday.

"Well, I know that," he said as if I had insulted his intelligence. "But Alaska isn't really part of the States. It's up there near Canada."

"Dad, do you want me to pay for this call when I get back to Rochester," I said and started to get a little annoyed.

"No, no, Doll, I'll pay." Realizing that he needed to change the subject he asked, "How are ya, Doll? I can't wait to see you. It's been a long time."

"I can't tell you how glad I am to be back in the States, Dad. I can't wait to see you and everybody else, too." As I spoke my voice started to crack.

"It'll be wonderful to have ya back here where you belong. When are you gonna get here?"

"I'm gonna fly out of here to Travis Air Force Base in San Francisco where I'll process out of the Air Force. I'll see a few friends while I'm there, and then I'll fly down to L.A. to see Aunt Angie, Cousin Eleanor, Marianne, her husband, and that three-year-old nephew of mine. Then I'm gonna go to Uncle Freddie's dealership. I'm gonna buy a car and drive across the country. I think it'll take me about two to three weeks to get to Rochester. I'll probably be there sometime around the end of September. I'll call ya along the way."

"OK, Doll. I'm looking forward to having you home. Make sure Uncle Freddie gives you a good deal on your car. Do you want me to call him?"

"No, it's OK. Don't worry. I'll work a deal with him. I gotta go now—I gotta get back on the plane. Besides, this call is gonna cost you an arm 'n a leg!" I chuckled.

"Yeah, I know, but you're worth it."

"Bye, Dad. I love you," I said, choking up again. "See you soon. Gotta go."

"OK, Doll, see you soon." His voice sounded like it was starting to crack a little, too.

"See ya, Dad." I hung up the phone and rushed back to the aircraft. I made sure to dry my eyes before I reached my seat.

My homecoming was uneventful, but at least I was alive and free, unlike many of the guys I'd been stationed with who were killed or taken POW. The sobering realities of this futile war hit me hard. My disillusionment with war would stay with me for a lifetime. In the beginning, I'd hoped to be part of a celebrated war, like the "Good War" that my uncles were a part of. Everybody loved those WWII guys, and they were all heroes. I wanted something I could be proud of, but all I felt was shame and bitter resentment.

Why couldn't it have turned out that the good ole' U.S. of A. won? Maybe we weren't the good guys. All of us were caught up in the "John Wayne Effect." A good-looking, tough-talking, gun-toting guy with only the best of intentions comes into town, wins everybody over, kills the bad guys, and gets the girl. Everyone cheers him on, and all ends well. It was a formula that sounded doable, but that only happened in mythical, Hollywood movies.

The fighter pilots often said, "We're gonna go in there and John Wayne that place." Well, the only place they John Wayned was my officers' club with their drunken bar room fights, clong sweeps, and carrier landings on beer soaked tables.

After being in that macho, military environment, some of that "John Wayne Effect" had rubbed off on me. I'd become one of them. You can't walk in the mud without getting your shoes dirty. Now, I'd need to channel my competitive, combative energy somewhere else, where it would be less damaging to others and to myself. But could I? The "John Wayne Effect" was easy to get caught up in and very intoxicating.

When the troops returned from the Vietnam War, there were no cheering crowds, no ticker-tape parades, no high school bands playing John Phillip Sousa music, and no kids waving tiny American flags to welcome us home. The U.S. and its people turned their backs on their veterans. They had confused the war with the warrior. We were viewed with disdain and were publicly scorned for serving our country. We were instructed not to wear our uniforms in public for fear that someone would attack or harass us.

My uniform was neatly packed in my suitcase. I was sneaking back into the States and didn't need to mention to anyone where I'd been. I was going to be low-profile and stay out of the fray. I was merely a 29-year-old woman traveling across the country, returning from somewhere, on my way to nowhere. I desperately wanted to get on with my life and get back to normal, whatever that was. I wanted to forget the whole year and everything that had happened to my friends, my country, and me. But I never would. The experience had left an indelible mark on me. The glories of war had eluded me, if there can be any glories from war. All that was in front of me was a long drive home to Rochester, New York, to be greeted by my widowed dad who'd be glad to have his little doll back home. Now, maybe he'd have someone around to cook for him. After all, wasn't that what a good Italian girl was supposed to do?

Shortly after I got back to Rochester, I reconnected with Bob and talked him into marrying me. It was a beautiful wedding at my parish church. It had all come together like I wanted. Unfortunately, I found out he'd been sleeping with a girl from his office before and after our wedding. He said that he never really wanted to marry me. When I asked him why he had, he said, "The ball had just started rolling, and he couldn't stop it." He told me that the girl he was involved with was the first girl he ever wanted to have his baby, which put me into a deep depression. The marriage ended after six months. It took two years and $150 paid to the Diocese of Orlando, Florida to get the marriage annulled. The grounds were that he never wanted to marry me or have children.

*Tomorrow is the most important thing in life. Comes into us at midnight very clean. It's perfect when it arrives and it puts itself in our hands. It hopes we've learned something from yesterday.*

—John Wayne, American actor (1907 - 1979)

## Sawadee

IT SEEMED STRANGE TO be going to see them now, in this way. I was in Washington, D.C. for a conference, and I figured it was time. My hotel was close to the Metro station, and I could get there quickly. The smell of autumn was in the air, and the sun felt warm on my face as I walked toward the train. A gentle breeze rustled through the trees, and the leaves shimmered with a beautiful blend of rustic oranges, ruddy reds, and brilliant yellows.

I spotted an outdoor flower stand and stopped to purchase a small bouquet of flowers. I asked the flower vendor for a bunch of red carnations.

"Sure, anything else?" He asked.

"No thanks. That'll be all."

He added a few pieces of baby's breath and some fern, and wrapped the bouquet in green floral paper.

"That'll be four dollars and fifty cents."

I handed him a five and said, "Keep the change."

The Metro entrance was just up ahead. I looked at my watch. Hopefully, it would be on time, and I wouldn't have to wait. As I stepped onto the steep escalator that led down to the Metro platform, a strange feeling came over me. It wasn't just the feeling of being in an unfamiliar place; it was a hollow feeling that grabbed at my insides. It was the same feeling I'd get when anticipating the unexpected, a feeling of uneasiness, like when my commander or boss called and said, "I'd like to see you in my office."

The Metro came into the station right on schedule. The doors slid open, and I got on and quickly found a seat next to a window. Opposite me was a pleasant-looking, middle-aged man. He looked up as I sat down and said, "Someone's gonna be happy to get those flowers!"

I looked at him with a smile and quietly said, "Yes." Then I turned away, not wanting to engage in idle chitchat. I found myself thinking I'd been rude for not engaging him in conversation and revealing the real reason for the flowers. Why I felt the need to tell a perfect stranger what the flowers were for annoyed me. He didn't need to know. Besides, I just wanted to be by myself.

The Metro made several stops, and I kept looking up for my exit. Then I saw it. Next stop—Arlington National Cemetery. My whole body tensed up as the Metro slowed to a stop. I moved slowly through the open doors and walked up the long flight of stairs leading back into the daylight. It seemed like a long way down Memorial Drive to the cemetery. It was a walk I was dreading. I was here to see some of the guys who had been stationed with me at Udorn and hadn't made it home. The few who had touched my life.

It was only a few months ago that I had been on reserve duty talking with my boss from Andrews Air Force Base. We discussed what he wanted me to accomplish during my two weeks on active duty. Then, at the end of the conversation, he said, "Gosh Angel, I was sorry to hear about General McHale. I know he was a good friend of yours while you where in SEA."

"What d'ya mean? What happened to him?" I said, somewhat startled.

"You mean you haven't heard?"

"No, I didn't. What happened?" I said, not prepared for what he said next.

"He was killed in a plane crash a week or two ago," he said in a somber tone.

"I can't believe it. How did it happen? Where was he? Who was flying the plane?" I asked in rapid-fire mode.

"He was on his way to give a talk at some military general's meeting, and the plane overshot the runway and crashed into flames. They're not sure who was flying the plane, or the Air Force isn't tellin', but everyone on board was killed."

"Oh my God, how awful. I can't believe it. He was such a great guy. I just can't believe he's gone."

"Yes." he said. "It's a tragedy for his family and the Air Force. They had him slated for a bright future."

"The Air Force has lost a true leader. It won't be the same without him. Thanks for letting me know," I said and started to choke up.

I had quickly escaped into the ladies room, hid in one of the stalls, and quietly cried my eyes out. I was glad no one came in to interrupt my private time. I thought, *why did this have to happen to him? Another good man had been taken from us!*

Finally, I reached the cemetery where brass eagles loomed over the wrought iron gates that marked its entrance. As I walked over the threshold, I said to myself, *why am I putting myself through this?* My eyes welled up as I tried to hold back the tears. I don't know why I was worried about crying. People wouldn't think it was odd if they saw me crying. After all, I was at a cemetery.

Before I reached the visitor's information center, I pulled myself together enough to ask the woman at the desk, "Can you direct me to these burial sites?" I said as I gathered my composure and handed her a sheet of folded paper with the names written on it: Captain Leo Thomas, Major Robert Lodge, and General McHale.

She got out a map and began looking up the locations of the gravesites. As she found each one, she marked it with a red X. She connected the "Xs" on the map. She gave me the map with instructions to the first gravesite. "The closest one is in Section 30. Go down Eisenhower Drive, past the memorial gate, continue down Schley Drive, and turn left on Curtis Walk."

I proceeded to Leo's gravesite. When I saw his name on the tombstone, I cried as I reflected on how young Leo had been and how his son had never gotten to know his dad. I felt a sharp, stabbing pain in my chest. My whole body was filled with an overwhelming sense of grief and loss. Memories of that year in SEA flooded through me like it was yesterday. The events and actions from that time had filled me with so much anger, but mostly I felt a deep sadness. All these men had been lost in the prime of their lives; my government had deceived me; and my religious faith no longer sustained me. My idealism was shattered, and the life I had imagined, with a family and children, had never materialized. All that remained was a sense of emptiness and remorse.

I laid some flowers on his grave, saluted, and sobbed uncontrollably. An endless stream of tears poured out all my pain and sadness. I couldn't stop—I didn't even try. When I got to the last grave, it hit me. Where was I to go from here? I had come to say farewell to Leo, Tim, and all the others, but more importantly, I needed to say good-bye to all my regrets and to the person I'd been then. I put the last of the flowers on the grave, saluted, and said, *"Sawadee."* It was time to say good-bye.

# Epilogue

WHAT HAPPENED AFTER THE First Edition? Since the release of the first edition of this book, new information has come to light that I wanted to include in the second edition. One question that was answered was where on earth did the Roger Locher's can of Coors come from? I discovered that Marty Cavato had produced a can from his bootlegged stash. This fact was too good to leave out, so I added it to the chapter "All I Want Is a Can of Coors and a Can of SPAM." I don't think Roger ever got his can of SPAM.

I reconnected with "Peppermint Patty" who was invaluable in clearing up several items. She also shared with me what she went through when Roger was on his 23 days involuntary "camping trip" in North Vietnam. She said, "I was a country music fan, and I had some Tammy Wynette albums, one of which included the song *Bring Him Safely Home to Me*. Every day I played it very loudly and sang along at top volume! I always joked that either God heard my prayer, (how could He NOT!) and felt sorry for me, or He heard me and brought Roger back to shut me up!" I think, maybe God liked hearing country music too, or it wouldn't have taken 23 days to rescue Roger.

She had such faith that Roger was alive that about a week or more after Roger had been missing, she went into the Laredo (Fast FAC) room where their lockers were. She saw one of the other pilots clearing out Roger's locker. She demanded to know what he was doing, and he said, "I'm cleaning out Roger's locker, because he's not coming back." Her response was visceral. "You leave his stuff right where it is because Roger IS coming back." She must have put the fear of God in him because he left leaving everything intact. It's best not to mess with a woman on a mission with conviction. And she was right.

Patty said that every year on May 10th, the day Roger got shot down, she prepares a special meal for him, and on June 2nd, they celebrate the day he was rescued, by drinking whatever beer they have on hand.

For years I had told people that the fighter pilots had driven their Jeep up the stairs of the o-club, when in fact they had "carried it up the stairs." Thanks again to Marty Cavato, Joe Kittinger, and others for clearing up that fact. A question was raised about the date that the Jeep first arrived in the lobby of the o-club. Was it February 21st or March 1st? After 40 years, memories are not what they used to be. Some said one date, some said the other, and some didn't remember. So I decided to leave it the way I remembered it. Either way, the credit still goes to the outstanding efforts of the Triple Nickel squadron.

The Triple Nickel's First Sergeant, Gerald Roy, told me every time the pilots shot down a MiG and celebrated at the o-club, he'd come over the next morning and settle up the bill for the broken glasses. He thought it best to deal with my sergeant instead of me because he'd heard I didn't like the pilots using the club for target practice.

I decided that it was important to add all the MiG Killers during my time at Udorn, highlighted in Appendix A. Unfortunately, I don't have all their photos, but thanks to Marty Cavato, I included several wonderful photos from his collection. Also, for quite awhile, I had been working on a list of all the POWs, MIAs, and KIAs from Udorn during my timeframe but was unable to figure out how to create an accurate list from a list of 200 plus names. With the help of Woody Cox, we figured out the 14th TRF downed crews. Several Triple Nickel and Panther Pack pilots confirmed the accuracy of my list, which is Appendix B.

The book also generated so many people who told me about family members who served, were injured, or killed in the Vietnam. John Bouchard shared that his brother David has been missing since 1968. He's still hopeful that his bother's remains will be returned from Laos in 2012. Others told me of their struggle with the decision to terminate a pregnancy or their disappointments with love lost. All these conversations touched me at a deep level.

The most extraordinary thing that happened was when I received an e-mail, through my website, from the Leo Tarlton Thomas III, the son of Leo Thomas, now 40 years old, who was seven months old when his dad was KIA. His e-mail asked if I knew his dad and could he buy a copy of my book. The inquiry was so unexpected, it brought tears to my eyes. I could not imagine how he had found out about my book.

I e-mailed him immediately and said, "Yes, of course, I knew your dad, and he's in my book." I told him he didn't have to buy a book; I'd send him one as a gift. That exchange was followed by a warm phone conversation. As to how he found out my website, he said, "It was Memorial Day weekend, and I'd been surfing the web looking for information about my dad and stumbled upon it." He mentioned that he couldn't repeat the steps he took to get to my website, but he figured it was meant to be.

He turned out to be such a fine young man, thanks to his mom who made every effort to keep his dad's memory alive for him. Tarlton, as he liked to be called, is married with two children. He told me that he'd had an opportunity to go the Air Force Academy, like his dad, but when asked why he opted not to, he said, "I want to see my kids grow up."

After our conversation, I called Joe Kittinger, the Triple Nickel Squadron Commander at the time Leo was KIA. We discussed several things that I had not been aware of at the time of Leo's tragic accident, some of which are included in the chapter "Fast Friends." Joe also sung Leo's praises, as we all did. He told me to give "the kid" his phone number and if he wanted to call him, he could. Roger Locher heard that I had connected with Leo's son and sent an e-mail with more information about Leo's flight, which he asked me forward to Tarlton. It seems that Roger was the Weapons Systems Officer (backseater) in the F-4 with Major Roger Carroll, who was Leo's wingman on the day Leo got shot down.

Connecting all these individuals with Tarlton has hopefully shined some light on his dad's life and filled a space that has been empty for so long. This has been one of the most rewarding outcomes from writing this book. Serendipitously, I had been hunting for a photo of Leo for years, and thanks to Tarlton, a wonderful photo of his dad is included in this edition.

Many friendships have been revisited, and stories retold, which has proved to be very rewarding. Several Udorn veterans expressed interest in contributing to a collection of stories. Who knows that might be next.

# In Their Own Words

# The Man Who Spent 23 Days in Enemy Territory

Email from Colonel Roger Locher

Dear Angel,

I finally got around to reading your book, the first edition, and only have the following two cents to add.

The day I got shot down, Bob did fire on the second MiG we were behind. We were too close to fire a missile at the MiG for the missile to arm up properly, and I guess Bob thought he could intimidate the MiG driver to bail out. He fired an AIM-7 almost simultaneously as we were hit because I heard the "whoosh" as it left the aircraft. I forgot to confirm with John Markle about this sequence last June when we were in Denver at Steve Eaves' funeral. Since everything happened all at once, I don't know if he fired before we took a hit or while we were getting hit. But the MiG fired a missile and got away. The MiG-21 pilot probably bought the MiG-19 pilot a round at the bar.

I did not make an external radio transmission from the time we were hit until I bailed out. I think the words you are using were probably from my accounting of inter-cockpit communication with Bob before I bailed out or maybe from Ethell's book. What you have about someone seeing the aftermath of the crash was true, probably from Steve Eaves' debriefing. They were under attack, getting out of town, and really did not have the time to watch our aircraft from the time we were hit to impact. Probably, it was some wishful thinking on their part that maybe someone got out of the aircraft even if they never saw it. Maybe you remember a 13th TFS crew getting shot down by a SAM in the February-March '72 timeframe. Returning crewmembers said they took a direct hit; aircraft blew up; and they most likely died. Two weeks later, Capt. Edwin Hawley, the backseater, was on the front cover of either Time or Life magazine, bandaged up and in Hanoi. In the article, the North Viet Namese were saying what good people they were by saving his life and giving him medical treatment.

What Patty told you about hearing my beeper six minutes after I was shot down and six minutes before Harris/Wilkerson were shot down is correct. That's the only time I used my radio that day. I was already evading and just wanted to say, "This is me. I'm on the ground, and I'm OK." I had turned on the beeper for about five seconds and thought I'd transmitted voice also. About a week later, I had the nagging suspicion that maybe I didn't go over to voice. I didn't, which was maybe a good thing. I kept on my mission of getting the hell out of there instead of camping out talking on the radio.

Some parting tidbits: When I was thinking of food while on my camping trip, I would have given $38 for a big plate of Udorn O-Club fried rice. $38 was the cash I had on me. I usually ate fried rice for breakfast at your club before I went to work.

I remember you giving back my MIA brass nameplate. Thank you very much!

Special thanks for getting me linked up with Tarlton Thomas. I'm still working on getting some information to him for his family's archives. If it weren't for your efforts, I would have never known about Leo's son.

Thank you for getting a bunch of us old warriors talking about details of the period. We need to share our histories before we roll into the nursing home. I guess then we can make up any story we want!

And thank you for being a great O-Club manager; it was the best O-Club I've ever been a member of!

I'm out of "facts." Remember to keep on trusting, but always "verify" the "facts" they give you.

Cheers,

Roger Locher

Author notes: I'm so appreciative of Roger's and Patty's input on several levels. They both gave me some other corrections that are included in this edition.

I was interested in finding the magazine that Captain Hawley was in and found it in the April 7, 1972 issue of LIFE. It was sad to see his photo as a POW because I remember his smiling face at the o-club bar.

# News on Eldridge the "black panther"

Combined information from: Roger Locher, Patty Locher, Marty Cavato, Harry Jones, The Phoenix Zoo, and "Eldridge - The Story of Friendship," written by Captain Dana Drenkowski for the Zoo in 1994

For the record, Eldridge was not really a panther, but rather a leopard. That's what Harry Jones, Director of Marketing, Research, and Evaluation at The Phoenix Zoo reported. The 13th Tactical Fighter Squadron called it a panther because they were the Panther Pack.

When the leopard was acquired by the 13th TFS, they held a "name the mascot" contest at the o-club. Supposedly, Dave Harris, a Triple Nickel GIB (back seater), won the contest. He compared the panther to Eldridge Cleaver, the Black Panther leader. The 13th TFS crowd was incensed that someone from another squadron won the contest. Roger Locher said he wasn't sure what the prize was, but the o-club no doubt made out on some bar sales.

In 1973, as the war was winding down, the 13th decided to find Eldridge a new home. They investigated several zoos and selected The Phoenix Zoo. It took several enterprising squadron members using several creative methods to get Eldridge to Phoenix. The Air Police offered up a sentry dog travelling kennel. Contacts within the Military Airlift Command (MAC) agreed to fly him to Hawaii. American Airlines volunteered to ship him to Los Angeles. And finally, a car rental company donated a truck to drive him the last leg of the journey to his new home.

Over the years, several of the pilots visited the zoo to check in on Eldridge. Jim Bell, one of the Triple Nickel pilots, reported that Eldridge was in the large cat habitat with some other cats getting use to his environment and appeared to be enjoying his surroundings, lying lazily in the sun. When Jim yelled, "Eldridge!" Eldridge perked up, ran to where Jim was, put his claws on the fencing, and looked over at Jim! The visitors seemed a little surprised. They had no idea of Eldridge's infamous and illustrious past.

Eldridge lived a pleasant life with his companions, fathered six offspring, and passed away at the age of 25 in 1994. Three of Eldridge's offsprings survived; two males and a female were sent to the Jackson Zoo, Memphis Zoo, and the International Exchange.

See a photo of 13th TFS's black "panther" at http://en.wikipedia.org/wiki/13th_Fighter_Squadron.

# O-Club used for Bomb Shelter

Information from Captain Marty Cavato

Marty Cavato and Frank Scoggins were playing foosball in the back bar at the o-club when a red alert came on the base TV station announcing that the base was under attack. Frank turned to Marty and asked, "Whatta ya think we should do?"

Marty said, "They're either trying to blow up the airplanes or the officers' hootchs. The o-club bar is probably the safest place to be."

So they both decided to sleep under the pool table in the back bar. They were awakened by Colonel Coleman Baker, the Director of Operations, who had come in with the early morning air crews to eat breakfast around dawn.

Later, when Cavato and Scoggins went back to the squadron they discovered Marty was right—a sapper had tried to blow up the F-4s. A sapper was someone who infiltrated a base and tried to blow up strategic assets. They are the loose equivalent of today's suicide bombers. The sapper had strapped a bomb around his waist. When he refused the order of the Air Police to halt, he was shot, and he fell into the drainage ditch by an aircraft revetment next to the Triple Nickel building. When he landed on the ground, his explosive detonated.

The squadron's night duty officer had found shelter inside a closet. He had his pistol drawn the whole time after the sapper tried to come into the building. Some of the guys watched one of the base docs picking up what was left of the sapper. Marty still has a memento from the event—a piece of metal from the attacker's bomb.

# Appendix A

## MiG Killers Statistics[1]
### 432nd Tactical Reconnaissance Wing
### Udorn Air Base
### February 1, 1971 to September 30, 1972

| DATE | AIRCRAFT COMMANDER | WEAPONS SYSTEMS OFFICER | SQUADRON |
|------|--------------------|-------------------------|----------|
| Feb. 21 | Maj. Robert A. Lodge | 1Lt. Roger C. Locher | 555th TFS |
| Mar. 1 | Lt.C. Joseph W. Kittinger Jr. | 1Lt. Leigh A. Hodgdon | 555th TFS |
| Mar. 30 | Cpt. Fredrick S. Olmsted Jr. | Cpt. Gerald R. Volloy | 13th TFS |
| Apr. 16 | Maj. Edward D. Cherry | Cpt. Jeffrey S. Feinstein | 13th TFS |
| Apr. 16 | Cpt. James C. Null | Cpt. Michael D. Vahue | 523rd TFS |
| Apr. 16 | Cpt. Fredrick S. Olmsted Jr. | Cpt. Stuart W. Maas | 13th TFS |
| May 8 | Maj. Barton P. Crews | Cpt. Keith W. Jones Jr. | 13th TFS |
| May 8 | Maj. Robert A. Lodge | Cpt. Roger C. Locher | 555th TFS |
| May 10 | Cpt. Richard S. Ritchie | Cpt. Charles B. DeBellevue | 555th TFS |
| May 10 | Maj. Robert A. Lodge | Cpt. Roger C. Locher | 555th TFS |
| May 10 | 1Lt. John D. Markle | Cpt. Stephen D. Eaves | 555th TFS |
| May 12 | Lt.C. Wayne T. Frye | Lt.C. James P. Cooney | 555th TFS |
| May 31 | Cpt. Bruce G. Leonard Jr. | Cpt. Jeffrey S. Feinstein | 13th TFS |
| May 31 | Cpt. Richard S. Ritchie | Cpt. Lawrence H. Pettit "Doc" | 555th TFS |
| June 2 | Maj. Philip W. Handley | 1Lt. John J. Smallwood | 58th TFS |
| July 8 | (2) Cpt. Richard S. Ritchie | Cpt. Charles B. DeBellevue | 555th TFS |
| July 29 | Lt.C. Carl G. Baily | Cpt. Jeffrey S. Feinstein | 13th TFS |
| Aug. 12 | Cpt. Lawrence G. Richard (USMC) | Lt. Cdr. Michael J. Ettel (USN) | 58th TFS |
| Aug. 28 | Cpt. Richard S. Ritchie | Cpt. Charles B. DeBellevue | 555th TFS |
| Sept. 9 | Cpt. Calvin B "Bryan" Tibbett | 1Lt. William "Bud" Hargrove | 555th TFS |
| Sept. 9 | (2) Cpt. John A. Madden Jr. | Cpt. Charles B. DeBellevue | 555th TFS |
| Sept. 16 | Cpt. Calvin B "Bryan" Tibbett | 1Lt. William "Bud" Hargrove | 555th TFS |

From July 10, 1965 to January 7, 1973 the Air Force recorded 137 MiG kills. The 432nd TRW is credited with 35 MiG kills.

[1] MiG Killer statistics taken from *U.S. Air Force Combat Victory Credits Southeast Asia,* Albert F. Simpson, Historical Research Center, Air University, March 1974.

# Appendix B

**POW-MIA-KIAs**

432nd Tactical Reconnaissance Wing, Udorn Air Base

September 1, 1971 to September 1, 1972

| DATE OF LOSS | NAME | STATUS | DATE RETURNED *REMAINS RETURNED | UNIT |
|---|---|---|---|---|
| Sept. 10, 1971 | Cpt. Jason (Lee) Cornwell III | MIA/KIA | *Aug. 1, 1994 | 555th TFS |
| Sept. 10, 1971 | Cpt. Andrew Ivan Jr. | MIA/KIA | *Aug. 1, 1994 | 13th TFS |
| Oct. 1, 1971 | Cpt. James V. Newendorp | KIA | *Oct. 1, 1971 | 14th TRS |
| Dec. 3, 1971 | Cpt. Charles P. Russell | Killed | Dec. 3, 1971 | Det.1 56th Sp. Ops. |
| Dec. 18,1971 | Maj. Leland L. Hildebrand | POW | Mar. 28, 1973 | 13th TFS |
| Dec. 18,1971 | 1Lt. Kenneth R. Wells | POW | Mar. 28, 1973 | 13th TFS |
| Dec. 18, 1971 | Maj. Kenneth Johnson | POW | Mar. 14, 1973 | 555th TFS |
| Dec. 18, 1971 | 1Lt. Samuel R. Vaughan | POW | Mar. 14, 1973 | 555th TFS |
| Dec. 19, 1971 | 1Lt. Daniel R. Poynor | KIA | *June 3, 1994 | 523rd TFS |
| Dec. 19, 1971 | Cpt. Leo T. Thomas | KIA | *June 3, 1994 | 555th TFS |
| Feb. 1, 1972 | Cpt. Paul G. Bast | Killed | Runway Accident | 13th TFS |
| Feb. 17, 1972 | Maj. Robert H. Irwin | MIA/KIA | *Nov. 1, 1989 | 13th TFS |
| Feb. 17, 1972 | Cpt. Edwin A. Hawley | POW | Feb. 14, 1973 | 13th TFS |
| Apr. 20, 1972 | Major Edward K. Elias | POW | Sept. 15, 1972 | 14th TRS |
| May 10, 1972 | Cpt. Dennis E. Wilkinson | MIA/KIA | *Aug. 1, 1978 | 13th TFS |
| May 10, 1972 | Cpt. Jeffery L. Harris | MIA/KIA | *May 29, 1997 | 13th TFS |
| May 10, 1972 | Maj. Robert A. Lodge | KIA | *Sept. 30, 1977 | 555th TFS |

# Appendix B (cont.)

| DATE OF LOSS | NAME | STATUS | DATE RETURNED *REMAINS RETURNED | UNIT |
|---|---|---|---|---|
| May 11, 1972 | Lt.Col. Joseph W. Kittinger Jr. | POW | Mar. 28, 1973 | 555th TFS |
| May 11, 1972 | 1Lt. William J. Reich | POW | Mar. 28, 1973 | 555th TFS |
| May 20, 1972 | Cpt. James W. Williams | POW | Mar. 28, 1973 | 555th TFS |
| June 6, 1972 | Lt.Col. James A. Fowler | MIA/KIA | Remains not returned | 523rd TFS |
| June 6, 1972 | Cpt. John W. Seuell | MIA/KIA | Remains not returned | 523rd TFS |
| June 13, 1972 | 1Lt. Gregg O. Hanson | POW | Mar. 28, 1973 | 555th TFS |
| June 13, 1972 | 1Lt. Richard J. Fulton | POW | Mar. 28, 1973 | 555th TFS |
| June 27, 1972 | Col. Farrell J. Sullivan | MIA/KIA | *June 3, 1983 | 523rd TFS |
| June 27, 1972 | Cpt. Richard L. Francis | POW | Mar. 28, 1973 | 523rd TFS |
| July 3, 1972 | Cpt. Marion (Tony) Marshall | POW | Mar. 29, 1973 | 13th TRS |
| July 3, 1972 | Maj. Stephen H. Cuthbert | MIA/KIA | *Dec. 20, 1990 | 523rd TFS |
| Aug. 13, 1972 | 1Lt. Francis W. Townsend | MIA/KIA | *Dec. 2, 2002 | 14th TRS |
| Aug. 13, 1972 | Cpt. William A. Gauntt | POW | Mar. 27, 1973 | 14th TRS |
| Aug. 19, 1972 | Cpt. Roger E. Behnfeldt | MIA/KIA | *Sept. 24, 1987 | 14th TRS |
| Aug. 19, 1972 | Maj. Tamotsu Shingaki | POW | Mar. 29, 1973 | 14th TRS |

Note: Every effort was made to include all the men that were at Udorn during this time period. My apologies if any are missing or incorrect. Information compiled from www.pownetwork.org/ and www.virtualwall.org/ and 432nd Tactical Reconnaissance Wing quarterly history reports and Udorn Veterans.

# PERMISSIONS

Made in the USA
Charleston, SC
17 October 2011